HISTORY'S GREATEST WARS

THE EPIC CONFLICTS THAT SHAPED THE MODERN WORLD

JOSEPH CUMMINS

AUTHOR OF *WHY SOME WARS NEVER END*

CRESTLINE

This edition published in 2013 by
CRESTLINE
a division of BOOK SALES, INC.
276 Fifth Avenue Suite 206
New York, New York 10001
USA

This edition published by arrangement with Fair Winds Press.

Text © 2008, 2009 Joseph Cummins

This edition first published in the USA in 2011 by
Fair Winds Press, a member of
Quayside Publishing Group
100 Cummings Center
Suite 406-L
Beverly, MA 01915-6101
www.fairwindspress.com

10 9 8 7 6 5 4 3 2 1

ISBN: 978-0-7858-3053-5

Library of Congress Cataloging-in-Publication Data available

Cover design by Peter Long

Printed and bound in China

CONTENTS

INTRODUCTION

All the wars included in this book are thunderous affairs, wars that Mars himself would be proud of. None of your three-day wonders or saber-rattling standoffs, but wars with meat to their bones, wars that took the world by the throat and shook it. Starting with the Greco-Roman Wars and moving on to the Soviet-Afghan War, each one of these twenty-five *History's Greatest Wars* has been of extraordinary importance in making the world the place we find it today, for better and for worse. There is a reason for a book like *History's Greatest Wars*—it's to remind us that we are born of fire and blood, shaped more by conflict than peace. War is rarely a surprise, only a shock.

The Greek victory against the Persians in the Greco-Roman War helped Greek culture and literature—that all-important sense of the individuality and imperishability of the human spirit—survive. The Punic Wars between Rome and Carthage, as savage as they were, gave those of us who live in the western world our civilization, law, money, and language. The Muslim conquests of the first millennium spread the message of Allah across what is now the modern Middle East and into North Africa and Spain, and the Crusades and the Spanish Reconquista fought to reclaim this lost territory (of both flesh and spirit) in the name of Christ, thus setting up violent religious dichotomies that exist to this day.

Bloody civil wars shaped France, the United States, China, and Russia, unleashing new forces. Some of these forces (the abolition of slavery and the overthrow of oppressive *ancien régimes*) were positive, while others (the advent of totalitarianism in the Soviet Union and Mao's China) were massively negative.

Covering twenty-five wars in a relatively short 300 pages means that one must focus on what is essential. Each chapter of this book covers a single war, and provides a quick overview, the detailed story of the most essential battle of the war, the biography of the most influential figure (or figures) of the conflict, and two or three short articles that cover diverse aspects of the conflict, from military innovations (which, in the Punic Wars, meant a fiendish little shipboard spike known as the corvus) to a description of one aspect of any particular war—in the World War One chapter, for instance, "Life in the Suicide Ditch" gives a précis on living in the trenches of the Western Front.

Aside from giving both an overview and more detailed depiction of each of these important, world-changing wars, what I have tried to do is bring clarity to my descriptions of both strategy and combat. The English word *war* comes to us from the Old

English *werre* (and the Old French *guerre*). Both descend from the Old German *werran*, meaning "worse," but there is also another Old German root variant, *verwirren*, which means "to bring into confusion."

Wars are confusing affairs. Any authentic description of combat captures this—the blast of gunfire (or deluge of spears); the screams of the wounded and dying; the sudden rushes and pell-mell retreats. Battles change, quite literally, one's perception of the world. When the young Goethe bravely and foolishly wandered through the midst of the pivotal Battle of Valmy during the French Revolutionary Wars, he saw the earth and sky colored by what he later described as "a blood-red tint." The conceit of a romantic German poet? Yet sixty some years later, a Union soldier at the Battle of Antietam during the U.S. Civil War noticed the same phenomena under a hail of bullets and artillery fire—the landscape turning red around him.

It is this type of detail that I've sought to provide a soldier's eye view of the battles in *History's Greatest Wars*, and I've sought it as well when looking into the lives of the generals and leaders whose job it was to make clarity out of this confusion of war. Did Hannibal really swear a curse to destroy the Romans? Was Napoleon Bonaparte driven solely by egomania, or did he attempt in his own way to make a better world for the people of France? Just how did Hernan Cortez walk into the elaborate Mexica empire with a handful of soldiers and take it over—and why did Montezuma allow him to? And how did Mao Zedong go from an awkward young man from the country, who loved spicy hot food and plump peasant girls, to the iron-willed revolutionary who proclaimed, "We know that political power is obtained from the barrel of a gun"?

History's Greatest Wars: The Epic Conflicts that Shaped the Modern World offers a fresh approach that cuts through the confusion that has been aptly called (by Clausewitz) "the fog of war" and provides a fast-moving narrative of the conflicts that made us who we are today.

1

THE GRECO-PERSIAN WARS

500–449 BCE

A LONG-RUNNING CONFLICT BETWEEN GREEK CITY-STATES
AND THE PERSIAN EMPIRE, WHICH CULMINATED WITH THE GREEKS
REPELLING A MAJOR PERSIAN INVASION

TURNING BACK THE PERSIAN TIDE—AND SAVING A CIVILIZATION

Started in 559 BCE by Cyrus the Great, the Persian Empire arose rapidly out of the grasslands of what is now Iran. By 500 BCE, it was a domain that extended from Pakistan in the east, westward through Central Asia to Macedonia in the north, and to Egypt in the south. It was home to twenty million people, out of an estimated world population of one hundred million.

The Greeks spoke of the Persians as barbarians, but they were generally quite civilized. They established roads and fine palaces, brought peace to outlying areas, and introduced the world's first large-scale coinage system. The Persian aristocracy adhered to knightly ideals of honor, courage, and chivalry. Persia was, however, an autocracy; even more significantly for its neighbors, the Persians believed that their ruler, whom they called the "One King" or "Great King," governed all the world's peoples.

In contrast, what is now the nation of Greece was divided into numerous city-states. Although they sometimes had fractious relationships with each other, these states shared a strong sense of a common kinship, as Greeks or Hellenes. Moreover, they shared a democratic spirit, permitting open political debate and favoring forms of representative government based on majority rule. Indeed, they were passionately opposed to rule by one individual and clung fiercely to their freedom.

These contrasting political philosophies set the two cultures on a collision course. The first clash occurred in 500 BCE in Ionia, now western Turkey, which the Persians had steadily conquered during the preceding half-century. The Greek city-states of that region rose up against the Persians and received support from Athens and Sparta. It took the Persians, under King Darius, six years to suppress the revolt and left Darius determined to seek revenge on the Greeks.

In 492, Darius sent his nephew and son-in-law Mardonius to invade Thrace and Macedonia; Mardonius was able to subdue these northern Greek provinces with relative ease. However, a storm then wrecked his fleet near Cape Athos, and he was forced to retreat to Persia. In 490, a dissatisfied Darius sent his nephew Datis to invade Attica. But a small force of Athenians defeated a much larger Persian army on the plains of Marathon, mainly as a result of superior armaments and tactics, and the Persians were forced to retire without properly punishing Athens. For the Greeks, this was an extraordinary, morale-boosting victory; for the Persians, it was a vexing but not catastrophic loss.

After the death of Darius in 486, his son Xerxes became king and carefully began planning an invasion of Greece. Xerxes' ambitions were not only to punish the Greeks for their upstart victory at Marathon, but also to use Greece as a launching point for a larger push to the west. He sent emissaries to Athens and Sparta, demanding the Greek states submit to his authority; the Athenians threw the emissaries into a pit, the Spartans dropped theirs into a well. Determined to wreak revenge, Xerxes bridged the Hellespont to allow his troops to safely cross that stormy strait leading into the Black Sea, and by 480 had marched a force of perhaps two hundred thousand invaders into mainland Greece while his powerful navy approached by sea.

To oppose the invasion, the Greeks formed an organization of city-states, the Hellenic League, and it was decided to mount a combined land-sea operation to repel the Persians. The navy, to be commanded by the Athenian leader Themistocles and consisting of about 270 wooden battleships called triremes, would row north to meet the Persian fleet, which had about 1,200 triremes. Meanwhile, King Leonidas of the Spartans would march north with his small, handpicked army.

At the narrow mountain pass of Thermopylae, Leonidas's three hundred Spartans, leading a force of some eight thousand other Greeks, heroically managed to delay the Persians for three days before being wiped out. At the same time, 40 miles (64 km) away at the north end of the island of Eurobea, the Greek navy engaged the Persian fleet in a series of actions near the harbor of Artemesium, winning a three-day battle, which delayed the Persian fleet but by no means destroyed it.

Despite these setbacks, the Persian army continued to advance. In mid-August, Xerxes marched his force unopposed through Attica and took Athens. The Greeks retreated to the island of Salamis, just off the coast, where Xerxes' Phoenician-led navy prepared to administer the coup de grâce. However, under the leadership of Themistocles, the Greeks won a stunning victory by outwitting and outfighting the Persians in the naval battle of Salamis. With fall storms setting in and fearing that his retreat over the Hellespont might be cut off by the Greeks, Xerxes made his way back to Persia, leaving behind, however, a sizable force under the command of Mardonius, his brother-in-law.

Newly confident, the Greeks overwhelmed Mardonius's forces at the battle of Plataea in August of 479, thus effectively ending Xerxes' attempt to conquer Greece. Intermittent conflict between the two sides continued in Asia Minor, Egypt, and Cyprus for some years, but in 449, with the drawing up of the Peace of Callias, Persia agreed to stay out of the Aegean.

THE BATTLE THAT CHANGED THE COURSE OF THE WAR AND MADE IMMORTALS OF THE SPARTANS
The Battle of Thermopylae, 480 BCE

To a shepherd boy hiding behind a rock, it would have seemed like the entire world was on the move; certainly, so many people had never been seen together at one time in these remote and rocky regions of northeastern Greece. There were bearded Assyrians with iron-studded clubs; Scythians with their short bows; Indians in cotton dhotis; Caspian tribesmen with scimitars; Ethiopians who covered themselves with red-and-white war paint and wore horses' scalps—with the ears and manes still attached—as headdresses; Arabs, Sarangians, Pisidians, Moschians—as Herodotus said, all the ancient nations of Asia.

What would have especially astonished a shepherd boy were the Immortals, King Xerxes' personal guard of ten thousand Persian knights, who wore brightly burnished armored corselets and were accompanied by their own baggage wagons carrying concubines and personal servants. Most impressive of all, appropriately, was the king himself, traveling in his royal chariot, drawn by ten horses specially picked from the Nisaean region of Persia, famous for its equine stock.

Herodotus claimed that this great force numbered three million men, but that is unlikely; modern historians estimate Xerxes had about 210,000 soldiers, including 170,000 infantry, 8,000 cavalry, 2,000 charioteers and camel corps, and 30,000 Thracians and Greeks. Whatever the exact number, all of Greece must have trembled at the approach of the so-called Great King of the East, who was advancing steadily westward, determined to conquer these upstart states—especially Athens and Sparta—once and for all.

The Hot Gates

Almost the only way for Xerxes' army to reach central Greece was via a narrow pass between the mountains and sea, at a place called Thermopylae, meaning "hot gates," for its sulfurous springs. Around August 14, 480, King Leonidas of Sparta arrived here ahead of the Persians, with three hundred of his Spartan warriors and eight thousand other Greeks. Only Spartans who had left sons behind had been allowed to travel with the king, so that their line would be carried on. The troops accompanying the Spartan warriors included their servants, or Helots, as well as many others from central Greece. All were far from their native lands—indeed, here, for the first time, a Greek army was fighting to protect the whole of the Greek homeland.

With the roar of the sea in the background, and their nostrils assailed by the rotten-egg odor of the springs, the Spartan king and his advisors climbed the twisted and rocky pass to its narrowest point, a spot known as the Middle Gate, which was at most 20 yards (18 m) wide. An ancient, tumbling-down wall stood here, and Leonidas carefully set his men to rebuilding it while their Helots unloaded supplies. On their left, towering above the Spartans, were the sheer walls of Mount Kallidromon. To their right was the Aegean Sea, which today is up to 3 miles (5 km) from Thermopylae, but at the time lapped right up to the pass.

Leonidas—whose name means "lion-like" and who was supposedly descended from Hercules—assumed personal direction of the defense, barking orders with an urgency born of both anger and desperation, for he knew that the Persians would soon approach. To hinder their advance, he ordered that a Spartan unit advance into the plains on the other side of the pass, into Thessaly, to burn and lay waste the countryside there and deprive the Persians of supplies.

Meanwhile, Leonidas quickly realized that there was one way he could be outflanked. This was through a rough and narrow track that ran across the ridges of Mount Kallidromon toward the west of his position, emerging at the southern side of the ranges about an hour's march from Thermopylae. Later myths that sprang up about this path claimed

BENEATH THE TOWERING WALLS OF MOUNT KALLIDROMON, BY THE HOT SPRINGS OF THERMOPYLAE, LEONIDAS'S THREE HUNDRED SPARTANS VALIANTLY DELAYED THE ADVANCE OF THE MASSIVE PERSIAN FORCE IN THIS 1823 OIL PAINTING BY MASSIMO TAPARELLI D'AZEGLIO.

The Bridgeman Art Library International

it was a secret route, but in fact it was well known locally and Leonidas immediately understood its importance. Without hesitation, he sent about one thousand Phocians—the local Greeks—to watch the track where it debouched some 6 miles (10 km) to his rear. Unfortunately, because his Spartans were so few, he did not send any of these more robust warriors with the Phocian force.

Grooming for Battle

Xerxes' army arrived on the following day, a huge, earth-trembling procession of men and beasts. The Great King's pavilion tent was set up and he directed his commanders to send out scouts to explore the Spartan positions. When the scouts came back, groveling before Xerxes, they described an extraordinary scene that they had witnessed: the Spartans, as if they did not have a care in the world, were exercising and combing their long hair—in front of their defensive positions.

The Great King could not believe this behavior. Why did these Spartans not tremble before him? Why did they not withdraw?

Accompanying Xerxes that day was Demaratus, a Spartan king who had earlier lost a power struggle in Sparta and fled to Asia and had now returned to Greece with the Persians, hoping to be given Sparta as a prize when Xerxes won. Demaratus was not puzzled by the Spartans' seemingly relaxed behavior, and told Xerxes, "These men are making ready for the coming battle and they are determined to contest our entrance into the pass. It is normal behavior for the Spartans to groom their hair carefully before they prepare themselves for death … If these men can be defeated … then there is no one else in the whole world who will dare lift a hand, or stand against you."

Xerxes decided to wait for a few days before making a move, not because he was afraid of this small and rather strange force, but because he wanted to give his fleet, damaged in a storm, time to catch up with him. But on the morning of August 18, with the fleet still delayed, he ordered a frontal attack on the Spartan line.

A frontal attack was not an ideal approach, and Xerxes and his staff undoubtedly knew this, but there seemed little other way to unseat the Greeks, whose flanks were so well protected. Xerxes sent his Medes, an ancient people from what is now northwestern Iran, in first. They massed a few hundred yards away, wearing dome-shaped helmets of bronze or iron and carrying short spears and bows and arrows, and shot a storm of arrows up into the brilliant morning sky and down upon the Spartans, who covered themselves with their shields. Then the Medes attacked, racing furiously at the huge Spartan shield wall of bronze, out of which poked sharp and lengthy spears. Because of the narrowness of the pass, the Medes could not bring their superior numbers to bear and were slaughtered in the first fighting. So Xerxes sent in a fresh wave of Medes. They

knelt behind piles of bodies and fired arrows at the Spartans, whose line continued to hold and off whose glittering shields the arrows bounced like so many toys.

Thermopylae now quickly became a scene of indescribable chaos as the Medes screamed their battle cries and fought to get at the Spartans in the narrow space, sometimes leaping over their fellow soldiers to slash at the Greeks. The Spartans spitted the Persians on spears, or hacked them down with their swords, and held their ground. They also adopted innovative tactics, for example turning around and pretending to run away, so that the Medes pursued them wildly—until the Spartans stopped in mid-flight and charged back. Finally, as evening came on, Xerxes sent in the first of his Immortals, but not even these elite troops could gain an inch against the Spartans.

Night then descended, and a terrible storm clattered down upon the combatants as they rested.

Path to Victory

Xerxes was certain that the Greeks would be exhausted after the first day, and so at first light he sent in more of his Immortals; but they were again driven back. In fact, because of the narrowness of their lines, the Spartans were able to regularly replace

GREEK AND PERSIAN TRIREMES COLLIDE AT THE BATTLE OF SALAMIS, 480 BCE IN THIS TWENTIETH CENTURY PAINTING BY ANDREW HOWARTH.

Battle of Salamis, Howat, Andrew (20th Century) / Private Collection / © Look and Learn / The Bridgeman Art Library International the men on the front with fresh troops, and thus were far from tired. As the day wore on, Xerxes promised his men anything to get them to crack the Greek lines, but soon even the Immortals were so reluctant to attack the seemingly insurmountable shield wall that they had to be driven forward by officers using whips.

That evening, Xerxes withdrew his men and began to ponder his next move. Held up by this ridiculously small force, he was in a difficult position, for his navy, harried by Themistocles' triremes and battered by repeated storms, had failed to move in close enough to provide supplies.

That night, Xerxes was meeting with his officers when a local named Ephialtes was brought before him. At first Xerxes could not believe his eyes—why was a commoner being shown into his august presence? But then Ephialtes, cowering, was permitted to speak; soon he convinced Xerxes that he had found a way to help the Persian king achieve victory over the Greeks. "In hope of a rich reward," as Herodotus says, Ephialtes offered to guide the Persians along the track that led to the rear of Leonidas's position. Whether or not the Persians already knew of the existence of this track, only a local like Ephialtes could have guided them safely along it.

Xerxes accepted the offer, and a thousand Immortals, given their chance to redeem themselves, followed the traitor across the mountains in darkness.

Unfortunately for the Spartans, the Phocian force sent to guard the pass was an amateur citizen-army, and had not even placed sentries. When the Persians came down from the mountains as dawn was breaking, the Phocians were caught by surprise and retreated to a nearby hillside. The Persians ignored them and immediately headed up the pass, toward Thermopylae. Some Phocian scouts managed to warn Leonidas, bringing him news that could not have been entirely unexpected (and indeed there is a legend that the seer Megistias, traveling with the Spartan forces, had already warned Leonidas that "death was coming with the dawn").

Leonidas was now faced with a difficult decision: he could withdraw his entire force southward, leaving the pass to Xerxes, or he could fight to the death. Apparently without hesitation, he chose the Spartan way: to die with honor. He sent back into Greece almost the entire force he had with him, excepting his three hundred Spartans, their nine hundred Helots, and about four hundred Thebans who chose to stay with him. Then, awaiting attack from both rear and front, his men combed their long hair and sharpened their swords.

When the next Persian assault came, at first just from the front, it was as fierce as ever, with the Persian troops again being driven forward by whips. Many fell into the sea and drowned, while some were trampled by their own comrades and others impaled on the spears and swords of the Greeks. But gradually, the Persians were able to fight their way among the small band of Spartans, knocking off the points of their spears with swords; slashing at their helmets; and battering, denting, and pummeling their armor until the Spartans fell back. At this point, Leonidas was killed and a fierce struggle began over his body. The Greeks drove off the enemy four times, killing numerous noble Persians, including two half-brothers of Xerxes.

Then a cry arose from the Greek rear: "Here they come!" The Immortals were now attacking from behind. Surrounded, the Spartans retreated to a small hillock. "In this place," as Herodotus says, "they defended themselves to the last, with their swords, if they still had them, and, if not, even with their hands and teeth."

Unable to defeat the Spartans in hand-to-hand fighting, the Persians drew back and fired arrows, picking their foes off one by one. A few of the Thebans surrendered, but not one of the Spartans or their Helots.

The Cost of Victory

Xerxes was so enraged by the Spartans' determination to resist that he had Leonidas's head cut off and displayed on a pike for all to see. This was an uncharacteristic act for a king who normally respected a brave enemy, but he seems to have understood at once that, while he had won the battle, the Greeks had won a significant psychological victory. In an attempt to counter this, he had all the Persian dead buried except a thousand or so, and invited sailors from his navy—which had finally arrived—to tour the battlefield, hoping to convince them that his victory had been a less costly one than it really was.

In fact, Thermopylae had cost Xerxes a great deal. Part of it was the loss of a strategic advantage: had Leonidas abandoned Thermopylae, Xerxes could have sent his cavalry and fleet light infantry after the retreating Greek army, destroying them and leaving the rest of Greece defenseless. But the Greek victory was also powerfully symbolic. Leonidas had chosen to die, not just for Sparta, but for all of Greece, a fact that was widely understood immediately after the battle. The Greek forces that would ultimately defeat Xerxes at Salamis and Plataea followed the inspiring example of Leonidas and held together when they could easily have fallen apart in the face of so much danger.

Had there been no stand at Thermopylae, it is almost certain that central and southern Greece would have capitulated to Xerxes. As Ernle Bradford, a historian of the battle of Thermopylae has said, "The death of Leonidas and his three hundred chosen men ... was seen at the time for what it was: a torch, not to light a funeral pyre, but to light the heretofore divided and irresolute Greek people."

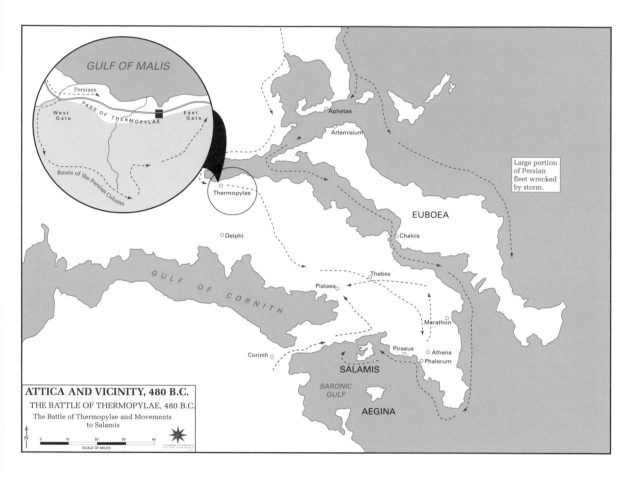

ATTICA AND VICINITY, 480 B.C.
THE BATTLE OF THERMOPYLAE, 480 B.C.
The Battle of Thermopylae and Movements
to Salamis

SCALE OF MILES

THE ROUTE TAKEN BY THE
PERSIAN FORCES AND THE
LOCATIONS OF THE MAJOR
BATTLES OF THE CAMPAIGN.
INSET: THE POSITIONS OF THE
FORCES AT THERMOPYLAE.

THEMISTOCLES: THE UNCOUTH LEADER WHO TRICKED THE MIGHTY PERSIAN FLEET AND SAVED ATHENS

Aside from the fact that he was born in 525 BCE to a foreign mother and a father, Neocles, who was from an aristocratic Athenian family but not wealthy or distinguished, little is known of Themistocles' early life. As an adult, he was probably a merchant for a time, and became a lawyer, a lucrative job in notoriously litigious Athenian society. Historians, including Herodotus, Thucydides, and Plutarch, present Themistocles as a kind of boisterous political boss: gregarious and charming but cunning, a man who knew how to make contacts and use them. Most prominent Athenians shunned him as uncouth (and probably for good reason—he was known not to be above taking bribes and lying and cheating his way to success); so he cultivated the lower classes, whose support helped him get elected to public office.

By the time of the glorious Greek victory at Marathon in 490, Themistocles had become a strategos, or elected general, of a portion of the Athenian forces. Farsighted, he understood that the victory at Marathon, while a great one, had not ended the war against Persia, but was merely the prelude to another, far larger war that would inevitably come. So he pushed successfully to use the profits from a state-owned silver mine to build a formidable Athenian navy and a fortified harbor for the ships at Piraeus. Prominent Athenians scoffed at this—the army was an honorable calling, not the navy, whose oarsmen were traditionally seen as a drunken rabble—but Themistocles knew that the Persian navy must be repulsed if Greece were to remain free. As Plutarch had him say, "I may not know how to tune the lyre or handle the harp but I know / how to take a small and unknown city and make it famous and great." Themistocles undoubtedly did, and his brilliant strategy during the Persian invasion almost certainly saved Greece.

Like many a great wartime leader, however, Themistocles did not fare so well in peacetime. Suspected of taking bribes, he was ostracized at some point between 476 and 471 and retired. After being declared a traitor by the Spartans, and with some suggesting that he was a Persian agent (though there is no hard evidence for this), he fled Greece. Ironically, he turned up in Persia, where he was accepted by the new king, Artaxerxes, and made governor of a Persian province. He died—possibly of illness, although Thucydides claims he committed suicide—in 459.

His end did not become this complicated but brilliant man, but he will always be remembered as the leader who saved his country in time of dire need. "Under Themistocles' leadership," writes the historian Peter Green, "the Athenians ... lived through their finest hour."

THE BATTLE OF SALAMIS

In late September of 480, despite the delays caused by Thermopylae and the Greek victory at Artemesium, Xerxes was ready to savor the taste of victory. His forces had taken Athens, burning the old Acropolis so that black smoke could be seen far and wide, a sobering signal of doom for those who still opposed him. But on the island of Salamis, just over a mile (1.5 km) off the coast of Attica, within sight of the smoke, a group of Greeks were determined to resist. Led by Themistocles, they were sailors and soldiers from various states of the Hellenic League, and at their command they had some 370 triremes—the wooden battleship with three levels of oars and a ram in front that was the mainstay of naval combat in the ancient world.

A short distance away, at the harbor of Phaleron, sat a force of more than seven hundred Persian triremes, which had the potential to easily overwhelm the Greek fleet. Many of the Greek commanders were panicked, but Themistocles stayed calm. Knowing that the key to victory was to force the Persians to fight in the 1-mile (1.5 km) wide Straits of Salamis, where they could not bring their superior numbers to bear, he decided on a daring plan.

On the night of September 24, under cover of darkness, he sent a favored slave, Sicinnus, to penetrate the Persian lines and allow himself to be captured. Sicinnus, claiming to have a message from Themistocles, was taken to see Xerxes. He told the Great King that Themistocles was ready to betray his country and come over to the Persian side, and that the Greeks were getting ready to flee Salamis. If Xerxes sent his triremes out that night, he could capture them.

Perhaps because the information given by the Greek traitor Ephialtes at Thermopylae had been correct and so vital, Xerxes believed Sicinnus, and sent out his triremes. Rowing all night, the Persians tired themselves out, and in the morning they were amazed to see that the Greeks were not retreating, but ready to attack. Trapped in the narrow strait, where, as Themistocles had foreseen, they were unable to exploit their numerical advantage, the exhausted Persians were destroyed by the determined Greeks. The defeat ended Xerxes' attempt to conquer Greece.

SPARTANS: THE MOST EFFICIENT KILLING MACHINE IN THE ANCIENT WORLD

The Spartans were one of the most enigmatic peoples in the world. Although their superb warriors played a crucial role in protecting Greek democracy, their own society was inward-looking, caste-bound, highly stratified, and unsociable.

The city-state of Sparta, at the site of the modern town of Sparti in the southeastern Peloponnese, probably began to take shape around 1000 BCE when waves of Greek-speaking tribes settled in five villages on a fertile plain. These villages joined to form a single city, Sparta, which conquered neighboring tribes in Laconia and Messenia by the eighth century BCE. Then, having acquired substantial human and agricultural resources, the Spartans began developing their curious civilization.

At the top of their social and economic ladder were the Spartiates, the only people who could vote, who lived in what were essentially common military messes in the city. Below them were the Perioikoi, or "Neighbors," free men who marched and fought with the Spartiates but could not vote. At the bottom of the ladder were the Helots, a workforce made up of Laconian and Messenian farmers and their offspring. Not free, but not quite slaves, they had to give half of their produce to the Spartiates. A proud group, Helots had to be watched carefully, lest they rebel, which they did on several occasions.

Historians have estimated that the ratio of free to non-free residents of Sparta was one to fifteen, which may be the reason why the ruling Spartans focused all their efforts on raising fierce warriors. Spartan discipline was extraordinary. Any infant boys with deformities were left in the hills to die of exposure or tossed over a cliff. All others were taken from their parents at the age of seven and raised in large barracks. They were given a meager diet so that they would learn to forage and steal for themselves; at the same time, they might be beaten, sometimes to death, if they were caught stealing. Even the kings of the Spartans subsisted on the same thin black gruel and barley bread as any other Spartan; the fare was so unappealing that one visitor to Sparta exclaimed, "Now I understand why the Spartans do not fear death!"

Politically, the Spartans were rigidly conservative. They had two kings in charge of military affairs, though during times of peace, elected Ephots, or "Overseers", had authority over the kings. There was an assembly and a senate, but debates in these houses were decided by whoever could shout the loudest—a practice endlessly parodied by other Greeks.

After playing such a heroic part in the Greco-Persian Wars, Sparta went to war against and defeated Athens in the Peloponnesian War, which ended in 404 BCE. But Sparta was ultimately defeated by other Greek states, with the help of Persia, and conquered, along with the rest of the known world, by Alexander the Great.

2

THE WARS OF ALEXANDER THE GREAT

336–323 BCE

THE EXTRAORDINARY CAMPAIGN OF CONQUEST THAT SPREAD HELLENIC
CULTURE THROUGHOUT THE MIDDLE EAST AND CENTRAL ASIA

A CAREER OF CONQUEST—PRECEDING THE RAPID DISINTEGRATION OF AN EMPIRE

The wars of Alexander the Great came a century and a half after the Greek city-states warded off the Persian Empire and achieved independence. Athens and allied city-states subsequently fought Sparta and its allies for dominance over Greece in the Peloponnesian War (431–404 BCE), a bloody and devastating conflict that was eventually won by Sparta. These wars so impoverished Greece that Macedonia, the wild and mountainous state to the north led by the gifted general and savage warrior Philip II, was able to conquer most of Greece, with the exception of Sparta, by 338 BCE. Philip then began eyeing up Persian territory in Asia Minor; but in 336 he was assassinated and succeeded by his twenty-year-old son, Alexander.

Alexander III, as he was crowned, then set forth on a career of conquest that has rarely been matched. In part, he was simply following in his father's footsteps and making the most of the superb Macedonian fighting force. But his insatiable desire for conquest perhaps sprung also from his strong feeling that he was heir to the mantle of the ancient Greeks, as well as the fact, as the historian Norman Cantor has put it, that "he was a man dedicated to war." After consolidating his northern borders and savagely putting down a rebellion of Thebans, Alexander crossed the Dardanelles into Asia Minor (modern-day Turkey) in 334. With him initially was an army of thirty-two thousand infantry and five thousand cavalry, composed of Macedonians and allies from other Greek city-states. He defeated Darius III, the Persian Emperor, at the battle of the Granicus that same year and continued down the Ionian coast, capturing numerous Persian-held coastal cities. He entered what is now northern Syria in 333, and within the year defeated Darius for a second time, at the battle of Issus. Though Darius escaped the battle, he was forced to leave his mother, wife, and children in Alexander's hands.

In 332, to protect his western flanks, Alexander turned along the Mediterranean coast and conquered Phoenician ports, including Tyre, thus removing the threat of attack from the Persian fleet. He continued south to liberate Egypt from Persian rule, and there was crowned pharaoh and declared a son of Amon, the Egyptian king of the gods, after a visit to the oracle of Amon at Siwah. He also founded the city of Alexandria, on the mouth of the Nile.

Alexander then returned to Mesopotamia to deal with the Persians. He defeated Darius at the battle of Gaugamela, then seized the Persian strongholds of Babylon, Susa, and Persepolis, sealing the defeat of the Persian Empire. In mid-330, Darius was murdered by his cousin and former advisor, Bessus; Alexander found Darius's body and ensured he received a royal burial.

Beginning in 330, accompanied by about fifty thousand men, Alexander pushed east then north, conquering much of Central Asia. In Bactria (now part of Afghanistan), Bessus tried to raise a mass rebellion. Alexander not only outmaneuvered and defeated him, but also had him captured and executed in 329. He then pushed northward to Maracanda (now Samarkand), where he famously killed his general Cleitus in a drunken quarrel. This angered many of his soldiers, who already resented his absolutism and adoption of Persian customs.

Alexander's army then returned south again, quelling further rebellions along the way. After defeating a chief called Oxyartes, Alexander married his daughter, Roxana, in an attempt to win over local leaders. That didn't detain him long, however, and soon he was leading a huge army back across the Hindu Kush toward India. To the ancient Greeks, India was the end of the world—they had no notion of the existence of China or any lands farther east.

Alexander won major battles against Indian forces at Aornos in 327 and in the following year at the Hydaspes River. But his troops were weary, and in September 326, at the Hyphasis River, they refused to go any farther. Veering southwest along the Indus valley, Alexander was wounded in a battle near the Hydraotes River. He then divided his forces, leading some on an epic trek across the forbidding Makran desert back to his capital city of Susa, while another group returned by ship via the Arabian Sea and the Persian Gulf.

In 324, Alexander went to Babylon to plan the conquest of the last remnants of the Persian Empire, in Arabia. But there he contracted a fever and died at the age of thirty-two, in 323 BCE. After his death, his empire rapidly disintegrated.

SUPERIOR MANUEVERING LED TO THE END OF THE PERSIAN EMPIRE
The Battle of Gaugamela, 331 BCE

For weeks, since early summer 331 BCE, the Macedonian army had been marching through Syria in heat that reached 110 degrees Fahrenheit (43°C), men and horses withering under the onslaught of the punishing sun. They were on their way to Mesopotamia, heartland of the Persian enemy and home of the legendary Darius III, the "Great King." Crossing the Euphrates River, they moved northeast and reached the Tigris River on September 18. They waded across the waterway in ranked columns. At one point, a flash flood swept men and horses away. But as the waters subsided, the relentless march resumed. At the head of the immense column was the army's young and charismatic leader, Alexander III. Commanding and single-minded, he drove his men on, never losing sight of his immediate goal: the destruction of the two-hundred-year-old empire of Persia.

Early on the morning of September 29, the Macedonian leader rode ahead of his men with a scouting party of elite horsemen. Climbing slowly, they at last arrived at the crest of the low ridges overlooking the great plain of Gaugamela—and reeled back

AT THE BATTLE OF GAUGAMELA, ALEXANDER'S FORCES SUCCESSFULLY DROVE A WEDGE THROUGH THE MIDDLE OF THE PERSIAN LINES.

The Triumph of Alexander, or the Entrance of Alexander into Babylon, c.1673 (oil on canvas), Le Brun, Charles (1619–90) / Louvre, Paris, France / Peter Willi / The Bridgeman Art Library International

in shock. Even Alexander seemed astonished as he gazed into the distance. Although he had heard about the size of the Persian force, it was different seeing it here before him: two hundred fifty thousand men arrayed as far as the eye could see, in a haze of heat and dust. Not only that, but Darius had at least forty thousand heavily armored cavalry, and Alexander could also see chariots and fifteen or so war elephants.

Alexander had with him forty thousand infantry and about seven thousand cavalry. All were Macedonian veterans hardened by four years of battle. But they were so outnumbered that it seemed certain they would be crushed.

At the battle of Issus, two years earlier, Alexander had defeated Darius in part because the Persian King had foolishly chosen to do battle on a narrow coastal strip—a front only 3 miles (5 km) wide—where he could not bring to bear the strength of his far superior

numbers. This time, knowing that his army outnumbered the Macedonians five to one, Darius had deliberately maneuvered his forces to bring Alexander to this great plain. In addition, during the week since he had arrived, he had prepared the battlefield , planting hidden traps (pits full of sharpened stakes) and carefully tamping down wide, smooth areas on which he planned to use a most formidable weapon: chariots with scythes attached to their wheels, which would mow down the Macedonian infantry like bloody wheat.

Yet, despite holding the upper hand, Darius had attempted to parley with Alexander. His peace offering, greater than any previous one, was this: aside from paying thirty thousand silver talents in ransom for his mother and children, he also offered Alexander all the territories west of the Euphrates. When the Great King's emissaries brought Alexander this offer, however, a famous exchange occurred with his chief general, Parmenio: "If I were Alexander," Parmenio said, "I would accept this offer." "So would I," Alexander replied, "if I were Parmenio."

Alexander, being Alexander, refused Darius's overtures.

A Tight Position

Alexander spent the day after his arrival at Gaugamela riding around the edges of the battlefield, formulating his plans. Through Persian deserters he pinpointed the locations of the hidden pits, and also discovered why Darius had cleared large areas of the plains. It was apparent to the Macedonians that they were in an extremely tight position, bound to be outflanked and possibly encircled no matter where they placed their forces.

Parmenio suggested to Alexander that the Macedonians try a night attack, to surprise and panic the Persian forces, but Alexander rejected this idea. Not only did he consider night attacks dishonorable—"Alexander must defeat his enemies openly and without subterfuge," he told Parmenio—but also he knew that such operations were highly unpredictable and chaotic.

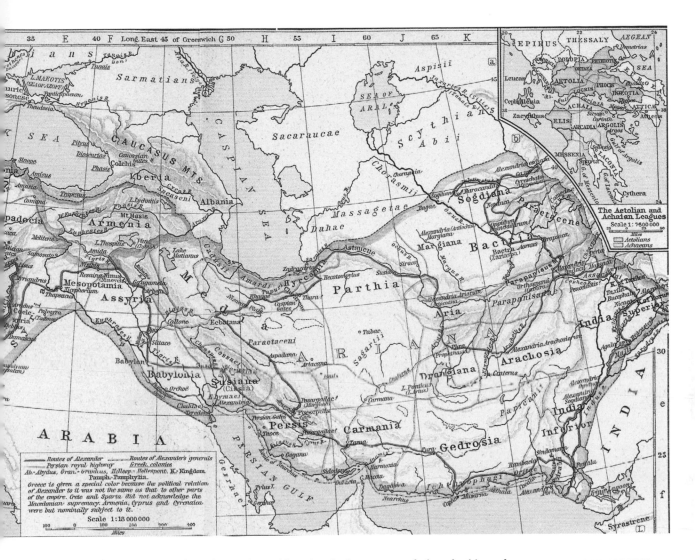

Still, the rumor of a night attack would not be a bad one to spread, thought Alexander, and he instructed his spies to let it be known that he was considering it. As a result, Darius kept a good portion of his army up all night waiting for an assault that never came.

Alexander, meanwhile, sat down in his tent, by himself, and planned.

Wheeling Forces

The next morning, September 30, the sun rose and the Macedonian army woke up, had breakfast, and donned arms. About two miles (3.2 km) away, the Persian army, many of its soldiers yawning from their all-night vigil, did the same. Extraordinarily, Alexander slept on, until, finally, Parmenio woke him up. Amazed at his leader's sangfroid on the morning of the most important battle of his life, especially with the odds so heavily stacked against him, Parmenio

THE ROUTES OF ALEXANDER THE GREAT ARE HIGHLIGHTED IN PINK IN THIS 1920S MAP OF THE MACEDONIAN EMPIRE, 336 TO 323 BCE. AFTER ALEXANDER'S DEATH, HIS FAR-REACHING EMPIRE QUICKLY DISINTEGRATED.

ALEXANDER, AS DEPICTED IN A
MOSAIC IN THE HOUSE OF THE
FAUN IN POMPEII, ITALY.

Museo Archeologico Nazionale,
Naples, Italy / Giraudon / The
Bridgeman Art Library International

expressed his surprise. Alexander merely replied that Darius had done just what he wanted him to do: put himself in the position of having to fight a pitched battle against the Macedonians.

Assembling and directing his forces, he then revealed a plan that was at once simple and brilliant and showed his unparalleled grasp of military tactics. Knowing that he would be outflanked (in the event, Persian lines overlapped his by about 1 mile [1.6 km]), Alexander ordered his forces to line up off center, well off the Persian left flank. He next stationed cavalry on both of his wings, a veteran reserve force in the rear, and the mass of Macedonian infantry at the center. The soldiers then advanced—or rather, shuffled sideways at an angle—torward the Persian force, their great pikes, or sarissas, gleaming.

Alexander kept his troops moving at an oblique angle, to his right, offering his left flank as an inviting target to the massed Persian forces, but keeping the center of his army slightly withdrawn. As Alexander's army advanced to its right, the Persian army—like a dancing partner—advanced to its right, attempting to outflank Alexander. The farther Alexander moved to his right, the farther away he got from Darius's cleared chariot runs, which was one of his intentions.

Realizing what was happening, Darius ordered the cavalry on his right wing to attack the Macedonian left. In a thundering charge, the well-trained Persian riders sped across the open ground, screaming battle cries and waving their banners. But they had a long way to go to hit the Macedonian lines, and Alexander's own flanking cavalry, although greatly outnumbered, counter charged into the weary Persians, slowing down their onslaught and sending them reeling back in disarray.

At the same time, hoping to disrupt Alexander's center, Darius ordered that his scythed chariots be unleashed against the main Macedonian phalanx of infantry. But the Macedonians were prepared for them. Alexander had placed a screen of light infantry at his front, which parted to let the chariots through, but then hurled javelins at them as they sped past, toppling both horses and drivers. When the remaining chariots reached the main Macedonian phalanx, the infantry, too, formed lanes, and the chariots sped harmlessly by, to be dealt with at the rear.

Pitched Battle

The flanks and the centers of both armies now engaged in a frenzied battle. Despite Alexander's clever distribution of his forces, Darius's numerical superiority began to show, and Alexander's center soon seemed in danger of being overwhelmed. But then Alexander, in the thick of the fighting, surrounded by his bodyguards, the Companions, detected a gap in the left center of Darius's line. He formed his reserve forces into a gigantic wedge, with himself at its point, and charged. Smashing through the weak spot, the Macedonians made straight for Darius's personal guard, routing them. In the space of a few minutes, the fortunes of the battle had changed. Alexander's men wheeled and attacked the Persian rear, relieving the pressure on their main force.

What happened next is the subject of numerous legends. Some ancient sources have Darius charging Alexander, only to have Alexander kill Darius's charioteer with a spear, and a false rumor then spreading that Darius was dead, which caused the Persian forces to begin to retreat in disarray. Others say that Darius, seeing he was in danger of being cut off and encircled, fled before he could be captured. However it happened, the result was the same: the Great King of the Persians raced for his life across the vast plain that was supposed to be the scene of his victory, and most of his army broke off and followed him.

Seeing Darius flee, the Macedonians, particularly the forces of Parmenio, who had fought fiercely all day, began to give chase. The slaughter was great; some historians state tens of thousands of Persians were killed during this pursuit alone, which lasted at least until midnight.

By day's end, Alexander had defeated a massive army that had far outnumbered his, inflicting up to fifty thousand casualties, while losing only between five hundred and fifteen hundred men himself. The Persian Empire was at an end, and Alexander was now the undisputed Lord of Asia.

ALEXANDER THE GREAT: THE SON OF A GOD WHOSE ACHIEVEMENTS HAVE NEVER BEEN EQUALED

As an adult, Alexander liked to claim that he had been sired by the god Zeus. His mother, Olympias, backed him up, asserting that the night before her wedding to King Philip II of Macedonia she had been sexually penetrated by a thunderbolt and that fire had flamed from her womb. This was typical of the beautiful but decidedly odd Olympias—a member of a Dionysian sect of snake-worshippers, she liked to take large reptiles to bed with her—and her influence loomed large over the young Alexander.

Yet it was Philip who provided Alexander's most powerful weapon, the crack Macedonian army, and his extraordinary education. For a tutor, Alexander had no less a figure than the great philosopher Aristotle. He fueled the young man's dreams, giving him a copy of the Iliad, which Alexander took wherever he went, dreaming of the large and fabulous world beyond the mountains that ringed Macedonia.

By the time Alexander was twenty, in 336, he was immensely learned and had seen combat in his father's wars against Greece. He was handsome, although a bit on the short side, with curly reddish hair and a ruddy complexion; he was also, like his mother, intuitive, volatile, and superstitious. The death of his father in that year, granted Alexander the opportunity to greatly expand his horizons. During his subsequent conquests, he led by example, fighting hand-to-hand with the enemy. His ego was so large that everything became personal—in his battles against Darius III, he sought to close with his foe in single combat—and he took enormous risks; this may have been because he continued to think that he was a god. Two oracles—one at Delphi in Greece, the other the oracle of Amon at Siwah in Egypt—had told him this. Moreover, he strongly believed that it was his destiny to conquer Asia.

Yet after he defeated Darius and created his empire, Alexander went into a steep decline, in part because there were now no worlds left to conquer and because his victories had exacerbated a growing tendency toward megalomania. He gave himself over to drinking and, to his army's dismay, became "orientalized," wearing Persian robes and insisting on the adoption of Persian practices such as hand-kissing to show obeisance. Later, he would even order mass marriages of his officers to Persian women, hoping to promulgate better relations between the Macedonians and Persians. (Most of the marriages dissolved soon after Alexander's death.)

After the rebellion of his troops and the death of his devoted friend Hephaestion, Alexander drank even more excessively and became increasingly paranoid. He took ill and died on June 13, 323. Ever intuitive, his last words were, "I foresee a great funeral contest over me."

Whether Alexander was a tyrant and butcher or a glorious megalomaniac on a journey of personal conquest, his achievements have never been equaled.

ALEXANDER'S TAUNTING LETTER TO DARIUS TURNS THE TABLES ON THE PERSIAN KING

In 332 BCE, after Alexander captured Darius's mother, wife, and children at the battle of Issus, the Persian king tried to make a deal to get them back. He sent an emissary to the Macedonian leader, who was then heading for Egypt, with a message stating that if Alexander would return his family, the Great King would pay a suitable ransom. Not only that, but if Alexander signed a peace treaty with Darius, he would cede him "the territories and cities of Asia west of the Halys River [in Asia Minor]."

In what may have been a grand bluff, and certainly smacks of his characteristic arrogance, Alexander wrote Darius back, beginning, cheekily, "King Alexander to Darius." He told him he would be willing to give Darius his family back if the Persian monarch came to him humbly enough. But as for a peace treaty:

Alexander war a Macedonian

In the future, let any communication you wish to make with me be addressed to the King of all Asia. Do not write to me as an equal. Everything you possess is now mine; so, if you should want anything, let me know in the proper terms or I shall take steps to deal with you as a criminal. If, on the other hand, you wish to dispute the throne, stand and fight for it and do not run away. Wherever you may hide yourself, be sure I shall seek you out.

Having read this, Darius understood that there would be no making peace with the young Macedonian.

BUILDING A CAUSEWAY TO DESTRUCTION: THE SIEGE OF TYRUS

An ancient settlement on the coast of present-day Lebanon, the city of Tyre is divided into two parts: one on the mainland and one an island about a half-mile (0.8 km) out in the Mediterranean. When Alexander besieged it in 332 BCE, the fortress of Tyre was on the island, protected by walls up to 150 feet (46 m) high, and Alexander had no navy with which to assault it. How could he conquer this stronghold?

First he tried diplomacy, sending two envoys to suggest an alliance. The Tyrians killed the men and threw their bodies into the ocean. Incensed, Alexander came up with a daring plan. He decided to build a causeway between the mainland and the island, an extraordinary undertaking when you realize that the waters in between were 20 feet (6 m) deep and often lashed by winds. Yet build it he did, demolishing the mainland part of the city to obtain materials and creating a roadway 200 feet (61 m) wide, so that he could march his phalanxes over it in breadth as well as depth.

The Tyrians sent out vessels filled with archers and light catapults and rained destruction down upon Alexander's workmen; but still the causeway advanced. The defenders then launched an unmanned ship full of flaming pitch and tar into the causeway, setting it on fire. Yet still the work continued.

After seven months, the causeway was completed and Alexander launched his attack. The Tyrians put up a desperate and ferocious defense, but finally the city fell and Alexander ordered his men to murder its inhabitants. Seven thousand Tyrians died.

Today, although it is part of a later, wider causeway, you can still make out the stones of Alexander's amazing road across the ocean.

3

THE PUNIC WARS

264–146 BCE

A LENGTHY AND SAVAGE CONFLICT FOUGHT BETWEEN ROME AND
CARTHAGE FOR DOMINANCE OF THE ENTIRE MEDITERRANEAN BASIN

AFTER CARTHAGE AND ROME CLASHED, THE VICTOR RULED THE WESTERN WORLD

The city of Carthage was founded in what is now Tunisia, probably in the eighth century BCE, by Phoenicians, the great sailing adventurers of the ancient world (indeed the name Punic comes from the Latin Punicus, which derives from the Greek Phoinix, meaning "Phoenician"). At first, Carthage was a Phoenician mercantile outpost, but by about the third century BCE, Carthaginians, ambitious and excellent traders, had founded trading settlements in North Africa, Spain, Sardinia, Cyprus, Malta, and on the west coast of Sicily (Greek settlements dominated the east). Carthage thus became the preeminent power in the western Mediterranean.

Carthage itself was not just a trading center; it also had an agricultural base of rich land (which was apparently much more fertile than it is today). The city was a wonder of engineering, with an extraordinary circular inner harbor and numerous temples and fine homes. But Carthage had a dark side. Corruption was endemic, and any high political office could be obtained by bribery. And among the numerous gods worshiped by the Carthaginians were some with a hunger for human flesh: indeed, although the evidence is still controversial among scholars, infant sacrifice may have been practiced.

In character, Carthage was almost the exact opposite of the young republic of Rome, a considerably more staid place, at least as compared to the Rome of later centuries. Founded in about 750 BCE, Rome occupied a position astride several important trade routes, at a defensible position on the Tiber River. It was at first ruled by kings, but eventually became a republic. The Romans were strong, family-oriented, deeply conservative, and set on continually expanding their territory. By the end of the fourth century BCE, Rome had annexed much of Italy, and during the third century BCE it conquered the last Greek strongholds in southern Italy as well as other Greek settlements in Sicily. This brought it into direct competition with Carthage.

The spark that set the First Punic War (264–241 BCE) ablaze was the Carthaginian attempt, in 264 BCE, to seize Messana (modern-day Messina) in Sicily, which occupied a strategically vital position close to the Italian mainland. Fearing that control of Messana would give Carthage a stranglehold on Sicily and allow it to mount an invasion of Italy, Rome sent troops to fight the Carthaginian initiative. Then, in the kind of escalating warfare we are familiar with today, each side sent in more and more troops. At the battle of Agrigentum in 262, Rome soundly defeated the Carthaginian army.

Thereafter, Carthage decided to rely on its superiority at sea, which was initially a successful strategy, for Rome, at the time, had almost no navy at all. But after Rome hastily built a fleet, it won a series of naval engagements, practically destroying the Carthaginian fleet. However, a Roman attempt to invade North Africa ended in defeat at Tunis in 255, and in 241 a peace treaty was signed between the warring nations, which gave Rome complete control of Sicily.

No longer able to challenge Rome at sea, Carthage sought other venues for expansion. The Carthaginian commander Hamilcar Barca conquered much of the southern Iberian Peninsula, creating a power base that Rome saw as a threat. When Hamilcar's son, Hannibal besieged the Roman city of Saguntum (now Sagunto) in 218, the Second Punic War (218–201 BCE) began. Going on the offensive, Hannibal led an army of mercenaries across the Alps and down through the Italian Peninsula, defeating the Romans at the battles of the Ticino River, Trebia River, and Lake Trasimene. In 216, at Cannae in southern Italy, Hannibal famously enveloped and destroyed a Roman force, killing upward of fifty thousand Roman soldiers—the most killed in combat in a single day until the battle of the Somme during World War I.

Hannibal's intention was not to conquer Rome—he knew his vastly outnumbered forces could not achieve this—but to break up the relatively new confederation of Roman states by blooding and weakening it in numerous battles. And indeed, as a direct result of his resounding victory at Cannae, most southern Italian provinces went over to the Carthaginian side, as did Greek cities in Sicily, including the largest, Syracuse. But the large Italian provinces of Latium, Umbria, and Etruria remained loyal to Rome, and gradually, the tide turned as the Romans learned how best to fight Hannibal—essentially, by avoiding pitched battles with him and letting him run out of supplies. Meanwhile, the Roman commander Scipio Africanus conquered Spain. Lacking reinforcements from Carthage, Hannibal retreated to North Africa, where he was defeated by Scipio Africanus at the battle of Zama in 202. Carthage sued for peace; Rome agreed, but forced its enemy to pay a huge indemnity over fifty years and stripped it of all its foreign colonies.

But in 151, having finished paying its debt, Carthage started to prosper again. Roman mistrust of an independent Carthage was fueled by alarmists, notably Senator Marcus Porcius Cato who, after a visit to the North African port, returned to Rome full of tales of the city's resurgence. Thereafter, Cato ended every single speech he delivered, no matter what the topic, with the words "Carthago est delenda!"—"Carthage must be destroyed!" Finally, Cato's supporters found an excuse to declare war when Carthage, in a technical breach of its truce with Rome, armed itself to resist an encroachment on Carthaginian territory by the Numidian king Masinissa, a Roman ally.

The Third Punic War (149–146 BCE) lasted three years, with all the fighting taking place around Carthage. There was never any doubt about the outcome. Still, the Carthaginians held out for two years, until Scipio Aemilianus, Scipio Africanus's adopted grandson, took over in 147 BCE and, mounting a final assault, managed to breach Carthage's walls and reduce the city to ashes.

In the Punic wars—3rd one—Hannibal faced Scipio of Rome

A YOUNG COMMANDER DEFEATS THE AGING HANNIBAL—AND CHANGES THE COURSE OF THE WAR
The Battle of Zama, 202 BCE

In September of 202, two men rode slowly out to meet each other on a dusty North African plain. Although the meeting was a private one, it took place in the full view of thousands of armed men—Carthaginians and Romans—all of whom held their breath as the legendary Carthaginian leader Hannibal and the thirty-seven-year-old Roman consul and general Publius Cornelius Scipio the Younger halted their horses at the center of the plain. Sitting astride their mounts, the two longstanding and bitter foes sized each other up. Older and more grizzled, Hannibal wore an eyepatch where he had lost an eye to conjunctivitis during his Italian campaign. Scipio was young, not tall, but clean-cut and stoic.

Tantalizingly, no verifiable record exists of their conversation. We know from later developments that these men had enormous respect for each other, but we cannot know, for sure, even the gist of their exchange. Legend has it that Hannibal reminded Scipio that fate took a hand in every encounter of war—perhaps the older man wanted to caution the younger that victory was by no means certain in any endeavor. If so, Scipio would no doubt have nodded at this, for these words applied to Hannibal as equally as himself.

Whatever they said, after a few moments, each of the leaders turned back, heading for their waiting armies. Nothing would be settled by words that day.

Sacrifice to the Gods

The fateful meeting of these two great rivals had its origins in a late spring day in 204 BCE, when a Roman army of thirty thousand men, headed by Scipio, stood on the coast of Sicily. Riding the waves offshore were some four hundred transports and forty quinquereme warships (ships with five banks of oars), ready to carry this huge invasion force to Carthage. Before any legionnaire could move to board the ships, sacrifices to Mars, the Roman god of War, and Victoria, the goddess of Victory, had to be made. So a sheep was brought forward, and its throat and belly were cut. Scipio reached inside the sheep's belly, pulled out the animals steaming entrails, and flung them into the choppy waves of the Mediterranean. At this, the thousands of soldiers watching cheered and beat their shields and moved to board the ships.

By this point, the Second Punic War had been going on for fourteen years. Despite the fact that Hannibal, Rome's mortal enemy, was still in southern Italy, still undefeated, and still dangerous, and that Romans still remembered an earlier disastrous invasion in 255 BCE, Scipio, fresh from victories that had won back the Iberian Peninsula, was determined to take the battle to the Carthaginians and secure victory for Rome.

After successfully crossing to North Africa, Scipio's forces ravaged much of the abundant Bagradas valley and, in the late summer of 204, successfully laid siege to Utica. Scipio had help in this, for the all-important allies of the Carthaginians, the Numidians, had a new leader named Masinissa, who had switched his allegiance to Rome, bringing his considerable cavalry forces with him. At the same time, there was a power shift in Carthage. Wealthy landowners and merchants ousted the Barcid dynasty (Hannibal's family), which had been in power since the beginning of the war, and sent a delegation to Scipio to beg for peace. Cravenly, they blamed Hannibal and the Barcids for the entire war.

Scipio agreed and gave them terms: all Roman prisoners of war were to be released; all Carthaginian armies were to be withdrawn from Italy; all claims to Spain, Sicily, and the Mediterranean islands were to be renounced; and a large indemnity was to be paid each year to Rome. In addition, Carthage was to provide supplies for the Roman army in North Africa. The Carthaginians agreed. Hannibal's army was recalled from Italy. It appeared peace had arrived.

But then Carthage blundered. In the spring of 203 BCE, a Roman supply fleet ran aground off Carthage. The Carthaginians, whose own supplies may have been running low, could not resist the temptation to loot the ships and take them as prizes. When Scipio heard the news, he was enraged. He began campaigning again, ruthlessly capturing town after Carthaginian town. Even if the towns surrendered, he sold their citizens into slavery. Meanwhile the Carthaginians begged Hannibal to come to their aid, and, in the summer of 202, he did so, with an army of perhaps forty thousand men. Marching five days, or about 100 miles (160 km), west of Carthage, he encountered Scipio's force on a great plain near what would later become the Roman town of Zama (though the exact location of the battlefield has not been discovered).

THE CARTHAGINIANS, HEADED
BY THEIR WAR ELEPHANTS,
COLLIDE WITH THE ROMAN
ARMY AT THE BATTLE OF ZAMA,
AS IMAGINED BY ITALIAN
PAINTER GIULIO ROMANO
(1492–1546)

The Battle of Zama, 202 BCE, 1570–80
(oil on canvas), Romano, Giulio
(1492–1546) (school of) Romano,
Giulio (1492–1546) / Pushkin
Museum, Moscow, Russia / The
Bridgeman Art Library International.

Charge of the Elephants

When the two leaders returned to the ranks of their armies, each of them surveyed his forces carefully. The Carthaginian army outnumbered Scipio's force by some ten thousand men and included in its ranks many hardened veterans of Hannibal's Italian campaigns. But it also included many newer, untried soldiers recently recruited in Carthage—this was not same superb force that had destroyed the Romans at Cannae. Hannibal did, however, have eighty war elephants (although some sources suggest that such a great number would have meant that some of the elephants were poorly trained) and had bought himself a small force of Numidian cavalry.

The Romans were, in contrast, almost all veterans, mainly of the war in Spain. Scipio was Rome's finest tactician and had made sure that his men were superbly trained. And his Numidian cavalry under Masinissa—who had ridden dramatically into Scipio's camp at the last minute, throwing up huge clouds of dust, their faces painted and javelins gleaming—numbered perhaps three times as many as Hannibal's Numidian force.

The two sides faced off against each other, blowing on bugles and shouting and banging on their shields—the usual din that preceded ancient combat. Having insufficient men to attempt the kind of pincer movement he had used so effectively at

Cannae, Hannibal decided to send his elephants straight at the Roman lines. Startled by the noise, some of the animals charged prematurely—perhaps a sign that they were poorly trained—and then the rest followed, trumpeting.

Their approach must have been terrifying—war elephants could kill five men in an instant by trampling them or tossing them high with their tusks—but Scipio was prepared. As the elephants reached them, the Roman soldiers formed narrow corridors, which the elephants naturally raced down. Most of them were speared to death at the rear of the Roman army; some turned and charged back into the Carthaginian lines.

A Bloody Melee

While this was taking place, Masinissa's Numidians charged Hannibal's Numidian force, chasing them off the battlefield. The fight then turned into a hard, bloody struggle between opposing infantries. The first two lines of the Carthaginian infantry, made up mainly of Gauls and Ligurians, advanced across the plain—Hannibal kept his most experienced troops in reserve for the moment—where they clashed with the Roman front line. The fight was fierce, with men colliding, battling in small clumps, retreating slightly to rest, then coming on again, all the time shouting to keep their spirits up and to frighten the enemy.

Using their heavy shields and armor and supported by the arrival of an experienced backup force, the Roman infantry gradually managed to push the Carthaginian first line back. But the Carthaginians' resistance was stiffened by the veterans of Hannibal's reserve, and the Romans were forced to sound a recall and reform their lines—a difficult and risky maneuver in the middle of a battle. The Carthaginians then attacked en masse, and the armies joined in a ferocious bloody melee, hacking each other with swords and spears. Soon the ground was covered with corpses and slick with gore.

While the outcome of the fight was still in doubt, Masinissa's Numidians returned and charged into the rear of the Carthaginian forces. It was a devastating attack, and the Carthaginians broke and ran off to the flanks. The victorious Romans sped after them, cutting them down even as they pleaded for mercy. The Carthaginian camp was sacked; cries of Roman triumph, as well as the screams of the wounded and dying, rang out over the plain.

Perhaps twenty thousand Carthaginians died in the battle; thousands more were killed, wounded, or captured. The Romans lost only fifteen hundred men.

Hannibal was able to escape back to Carthage with his staff, but the war was now at an end, and even the most bitter Carthaginian had to accept it. Perhaps because he knew his relatively small force could not besiege Carthage easily, Scipio—who would return to Rome in triumph, to be dubbed Scipio Africanus—agreed to a peace treaty.

It was harsher than before, however, and included the confiscation of all Carthaginian warships except for ten light triremes, and a heavy indemnity of ten thousand silver talents, to be paid annually over fifty years.

In a final scene of humiliation, five hundred of Carthage's great quinquereme warships were rowed out into the Bay of Tunis and there burned, the fires sending a great pall of smoke over the ancient city—one that presaged its ultimate fate almost fifty years later.

HANNIBAL: THE CHARISMATIC LEADER WHO WAS ROME'S ETERNAL ENEMY

It's fair to say that Hannibal Barca inherited the Punic Wars, the way one might inherit property or a particularly troublesome set of personality attributes. His father, Hamilcar, was particularly bitter after the Carthaginian defeat in the First Punic War. Just six years old at the time, Hannibal must have sensed his wrath; it's said that when he was nine Hamilcar had him swear an oath on an animal sacrifice that he would "never be a friend of the Romans."

After Hamilcar died during an ambush in 229, he was succeeded by his son-in-law Hasdrubal, who conquered much of northern Spain but was assassinated in 220. At the age of twenty-five, Hannibal was elected as the Carthaginian army's new commander by the soldiers themselves, which shows how much faith the troops already had in the young man. Hannibal continued the Carthaginian course of expansion in Spain, which in turn triggered the Second Punic War. He then famously marched his forces over the Alps and into Italy in 218, beginning an extraordinary campaign that would last seventeen years and display his genius as a commander.

Famously, he brought together a polyglot force and commanded it with both strict discipline and an understanding of its strengths and limitations. He also—unlike many Roman generals—led from the front, and there was no hardship he would not share with his troops. Yet he also knew how to delegate, relying on skilled generals such as his brothers Hasdrubal and Hanno, and his great Numidian cavalry leaders Carthalo and Maharbal, who were instrumental in the victory at Cannae.

Many Roman sources portray Hannibal as a cruel man, a liar, and a cheat. But these allegations could just be Roman propaganda, and little is known about Hannibal's personality.

After his defeat at Zama in 202, Hannibal involved himself in internal Carthaginian politics, but made enemies, who accused him of plotting against Rome. Whether or not this was true, Hannibal deemed it wise to flee Carthage in 195 and headed for the court of the head of the Syrian Empire, Antiochus III, in Asia Minor. He commanded a fleet for Antiochus in the latter's war against Rome; when Antiochus made peace with Rome, one of the stipulations was that he turn

Hannibal over. But by then Hannibal was on the run again, this time to the kingdom of Bithynia, near the Black Sea. There, as the Greek historian Plutarch has it, he was trapped "like a bird that has grown too old to fly" and, with the Romans closing in, killed himself by taking poison. It was 183 BCE and he was sixty-four years old.

ROME'S BREAKTHROUGH WEAPON THAT WON CONTROL OF THE SEA

At the time of the First Punic War, the Romans had little or no experience of fighting at sea, whereas the Carthaginians were experienced sea-farers and naval fighters. The Romans tended to look down upon naval power—as the Greeks had done before the Greco-Persian Wars—and considered pitched land battles far more noble. But it became evident that the Carthaginian superiority at sea had to be dealt with or Carthage would have the ability to simply blockade Roman ports and carry troops deep behind Roman lines.

IT WAS SAID THAT AT JUST NINE YEARS OF AGE HANNIBAL SWORE AN OATH OF ETERNAL ENMITY TO ROME, AS DEPICTED IN THIS PAINTING BY JACOPO AMIGONI (1675–1752).

Hannibal swearing eternal enmity to Rome (oil on canvas), Amigoni, Jacopo (1675-1752) / Private Collection / Photo © Agnew's, London, UK / The Bridgeman Art Library International

Once this was realized, the Romans acted with Roman practicality and efficiency. Having captured a Carthaginian quinquereme—an oar-powered battleship that had five banks of oars, as opposed to three in the earlier Greek trireme—they constructed one hundred of these ships within two months, an amazing achievement that would have required, historians estimate, the efforts of thirty-five thousand men.

The Carthaginians remained more adept, however, at maneuvering their craft in close battles. But then the Romans came up with the idea of the corvus. Essentially a moveable wooden bridge, roughly 4 feet (1.2 m) wide and 36 feet (11 m) long, with railings on each side, it was attached by pulleys to a long mast at the front of each warship. At its tip was a huge three-tipped spike, which looked something like a cor-vus, or raven, hence the name. When a Roman warship was able to get close enough to a Carthaginian vessel, it would drop the corvus onto the opposing vessel so that the spike embedded itself in the deck. Roman soldiers would then charge across the bridge and engage the enemy, much as they were used to doing on land.

Although the corvus made vessels unstable in rough weather and was eventually abandoned as Roman naval tactics and experience improved, it helped turn the tide of the First Punic War and make the Romans masters of the sea. As Nigel Bagnall, a noted historian of the Punic Wars, has written, the corvus was "an example of a technical innovation which led to a precipitous reversal of battlefield superiority that had endured for centuries."

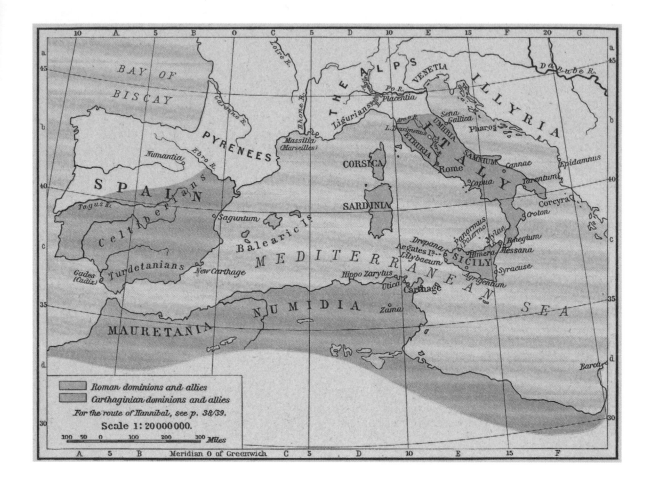

CROSSING THE ALPS WITH ELEPHANTS—AND MAKING HISTORY

For the route of Hannibal, see p. 38/39.

THE ROMAN AND CARTHAGE EMPIRES ARE SHOWN DURING THE BEGINNING OF THE SECOND PUNIC WAR. AFTER THE PUNIC WARS, ROME WOULD OBLITERATE CARTHAGE IN WHAT HAS BEEN CALLED "THE FIRST GENOCIDE."

While Hannibal is revered by military historians for his tactics, most people remember him for taking his army, with elephants, across the Alps. This was truly an extraordinary undertaking—no large body of men had ever made this perilous journey before—and it was a sign of Hannibal's boldness, vision, and self-confidence that he was even willing to attempt it.

With an army of between forty and fifty thousand men, including ten thousand cavalry and perhaps forty war elephants, Hannibal set off from New Carthage (Cartagena in present-day Spain), crossed over the Pyrenees into Gaul (present-day southern France), and fought and finagled his way past hostile Gallic tribes to reach the foothills of the Alps. Here he made an epic speech to his men, seeking to reassure them in the face of this daunting obstacle. "What do you think the Alps are?" he asked them. "They are nothing more than high mountains, [and] no height is insurmountable to men of determination."

Encouraged, the army began its climb, most likely via the forbidding, 9,000-feet (2,750 m)-high Col de la Traversette. They were ambushed by a hostile tribe, the Allobroges, causing numerous casualties. Avalanches, the severe cold, and treacherous tracks were other dangers. Men, horses, and elephants tumbled, screaming, from narrow paths, were swept off the mountains by avalanches, or froze to death on icy slopes. All the while, Hannibal moved among his men, urging them on.

At last, after fifteen long days, the fertile valleys of Italy appeared before them like a mirage. The entire march from Carthage had taken five months; Hannibal had lost twelve thousand men and most of his fabled war elephants. But he was now in Italy, ready to bring the war to Rome.

THE ROMANS DESTROY CARTHAGE AND END AN EMPIRE FOREVER

The final conquest of Carthage in 146 was a brutal affair. After surrounding the city, the Romans, led by Scipio Aemilianus, launched a major assault from the harbor area, eventually breaking through the city walls and swarming into the vast dock areas. The Carthaginians set the buildings here afire and retreated into the inner city. In six days of street-by-street, house by house fighting, most of it uphill, the defenders made the Romans pay for every bit of ground. At one point, tired of fighting on the narrow streets, the Romans leveled rows of houses to create a wide road leading up to a holy citadel that was the Carthaginians' last refuge; the Carthaginian dead were simply built into the road as paving material, according to Polybius—something recent archaeological finds, which have uncovered human bones in this area, seem to confirm.

Finally, on the seventh day, the Carthaginians offered to surrender if Scipio Aemilianus would spare their lives. This he agreed to do, and fifty thousand gaunt and starving men, women, and children were taken into slavery. But the fight wasn't over. Left in the citadel were nine hundred Roman legionnaires who had deserted to Carthage; they knew that to be taken captive would mean certain crucifixion. So they fought on until, surrounded on all sides, they decided to burn the citadel down, immolating themselves.

After plundering the city, the Romans set about with a will to make sure that Carthage was not just defeated, but obliterated. To ensure that Scipio did this properly, a commission of senators (not including Cato, who had died a few years before) was sent out from Rome. Large areas of the city had already been burned in the fighting. Now more of it was set ablaze, and any remaining structures demolished afterward. There is a famous story that the ground was ploughed and sown with salt so that nothing would ever grow there again, but this   probably a later invention. Whatever the case, the destruction of Carthage was complete.

4

THE BARBARIAN INVASIONS

376–553

THE SERIES OF MIGRATIONS AND INCURSIONS OF GERMANIC AND CENTRAL ASIAN PEOPLES INTO WESTERN EUROPE, WHICH STEADILY ERODED THE ROMAN EMPIRE

SUCCEEDING WAVES OF BARBARIANS ULTIMATELY DESTROY THE ONCE MIGHTY ROMAN EMPIRE

At its height in the second and third centuries ad, the Roman Empire controlled 120 million people and extended to the Rhine and Danube rivers in the north, Britain in the northwest, Spain in the west, North Africa in the south, and Asia Minor (present-day Turkey) in the east. So large was this empire that in 285 ad the Emperor Diocletian divided it into two parts to make it easier to govern: the Western Empire, centered on Rome, and the Eastern Empire, with its capital in Constantinople.

The Romans did things that greatly benefited civilization: paved 50,000 miles (80,000 km) of roads, built aqueducts to supply water to cities, and, of course, transformed the architecture, law, languages, and even calendar of future citizens of the world. But, from the point of view of a citizen of the empire, their most important contribution was security. Beyond the boundaries of the Roman realm, especially to the north and east, was a mysterious, untamed world, inhabited by so-called barbarians (from the Latin word for "bearded"). The Pax Romanica kept these dark forces at bay.

Fighting along the fringes of the empire, the Romans managed to conquer and assimilate many barbarian peoples. But toward the end of the fourth century ad, the Western Empire began to weaken. With no new conquests to fill the coffers, the economy went into recession and the army came to depend increasingly on mercenaries.

And then came the Huns. Nomads from Central Asia whose precise origins are unclear, this extraordinary people first emerged north of the Black Sea around 360 ad, swarming east and south. They were skilled warriors, renowned for their ferocity. In Eastern Europe, they clashed with the eastern Goths, or Ostrogoths—ostro is from a German root meaning "eastern"—who at the time were perhaps the most settled of the barbarian tribes. The Ostrogoths had a single king, a Christian religion, a written language, and an agrarian culture, and their territory covered a large area between the Dnieper and Don rivers and the Black and Baltic seas. The arrival of the Huns in 376 ad forced the Ostrogoths to seek refuge inside the Eastern Roman Empire, which led to war with Rome. At the battle of Adrianople on August 9, 378, the Gothic cavalry soundly defeated the Roman infantry, killing two-thirds of the eastern forces and the Eastern Emperor, Valens, and sending shock waves throughout the empire.

Valens's successor, Theodosius I, made peace with the Ostrogoths in 382, ceding them Thrace, or northern Greece, and the Balkans. In 401, however, a new Goth leader, Alaric, arose in the west and led the western Goths, or Visigoths, on an invasion of Italy. He was repelled in northern Italy by the Roman general Stilicho but returned in 408, marched on Rome, and sacked it—the first time the city had felt such an onslaught in seven hundred years. However, Alaric then died of illness, and the Visigoths settled temporarily in Provence.

At the end of 406, another group of barbarians, the Vandals, an ancient Germanic tribe who had been pushed westward by the Huns, invaded Gaul along with two other Germanic tribes, the Alans and the Sueves. Repelled by local tribes, notably the Franks, the Vandals moved on to Iberia, conquering the entire peninsula by 428 ad. However, after doing constant battle with Visigoths entering Spain from the north, the Vandals migrated again, to North Africa.

Meanwhile, the Huns had swollen into a huge and clamorous power on the doorstep of the Eastern Empire. Led by their charismatic general Attila, they appeared along the Danube in 440, destroyed a Roman force outside of Constantinople, and forced the emperor Theodosius II to pay a huge tribute. In 449, having extracted all the wealth they could from the Eastern Empire, they marched across Central Europe and into Gaul. Here, the Huns were defeated at the battle of the Catalaunian Plains in 451 by an army of Romans and Goths under the Roman general Flavius Aetius. But Attila returned to Italy the following year, ravaged the north of the peninsula, and would have sacked Rome had his men not been suffering from an epidemic. He died the following year, after which the Huns evaporated as a power.

The Vandals, having conquered all of North Africa as well as Corsica, Sardinia, and Sicily, sailed to Rome in 455 and sacked the city for two weeks, causing immense damage and bloodshed, before withdrawing. In the following year, the Visigoths conquered the Iberian Peninsula, which they would hold for two hundred years, until the arrival of the forces of Islam. In 476, the last Roman emperor, Romulus Augustus was deposed by the barbarian Odoacer, who took control of the Western Roman Empire, but was subsequently ousted by Theodoric, the Ostrogothic king.

BY 446 AD

The Western Empire was at an end, although the Eastern Empire (also known as the Byzantine Empire) under Justinian would destroy the Vandal Empire in North Africa in 533 and in 535 drive the Ostrogoths out of Italy. Rome continued to be ruled by the Byzantine Empire from afar, but the Lombards and other tribes carved up the rest of Italy between them.

BARBARIANS CLASH WITH BARBARIANS AS THE GOTHS PUSH BACK ATTILA
The Battle of the Catalaunian Plains, 451

The advancing Hun army left behind a great trail of destruction. And there were the terrifying descriptions of these soldiers and their leader, Attila: swarthy, scarred men who rode swift horses and seemed to swoop down out of nowhere to murder and pillage. With his people, the Alans, trembling behind the walls of their city, Orléans, as the Hun forces now approached, and only a small Roman auxiliary force offering protection, Sangiban saw no option but to surrender. With the Hun army already in sight, he sent his men to open the city's massive gates and prepared to plead for mercy.

But Sangiban had reckoned without Flavius Aetius, Rome's wily military commander and the most brilliant leader the empire possessed. Arriving out of nowhere with a ragtag force made up of a bewildering array of Romans, Gallic auxiliaries, and, most astoundingly, rival barbarian groups, he arrived just in time to stop Sangiban from opening the gates. And then he sent his cavalry howling down upon the Huns. Taken by surprise, the Hun warriors, who had been confident of victory, were driven back in disarray, and many slaughtered mercilessly.

Attila's advance westward from the Huns' base in the Eastern Empire had been prompted by an appeal for help from the Western Roman Emperor Valentinian's sister, Honoria. In response, Attila had decided to march on Rome and claim Honoria's hand. But to gather booty to fund his campaign, he and his force of around forty thousand Huns, Ostrogoths, and Burgundians first cut a swath through northwestern Europe, slaughtering and pillaging as they went.

Meanwhile, a Roman force under Flavius Aetius had moved north from Italy to Gaul to meet this threat. Having lived with the Huns and knowing how they did battle, Flavius was undoubtedly the best man to try to stop the onslaught of Attila. But he needed more men than his normal relatively small force of auxiliaries and a few legionaries. Once in Gaul, he attempted to acquire the services of the Visigoths led by Theodoric I, son of Alaric. These Goths had been allowed to settle in Gaul and should have been, theoretically, Rome's vassals. But, aware that the Western Roman Empire was then weakening, Theodoric initially rebelled against the idea until Aetius convinced him that Attila's Huns would devastate the Goths as well as any Romans.

Thus, very typically for the period, Rome prepared to fight the barbarians in a battle where the forces on both sides would consist almost entirely of barbarians. In June of 451, these two forces clashed, momentously, near Orléans.

Grim Omens

Forcing a reluctant Sangiban and his Alans to join them, Aetius and Theodoric followed the Huns as they retreated to an area of low-lying terrain near present-day Châlons-en-Champagne. Whereas many commanders would have been content to let the Huns go, Aetius moved aggressively, determined to pin down the opposing force.

Attila gathered his forces at a large open area known as the Catalaunian Plains, which was almost completely flat except for a hill near Attila's left flank. Clearly, Attila thought his cavalry would be more able to maneuver here and establish superiority.

However, according to certain chroniclers, Attila was nervous about the impending battle. As his men settled into position on the morning of June 20, he called for diviners and had them make animal sacrifices. These foretold disaster for the Huns,

THE COURSE OF EMPIRE: DESTRUCTION, 1836, THOMAS COLE'S APOCALYPTIC IMAGINING OF THE FALL OF CLASSICAL CIVILIZATION, INSPIRED BY THE VANDAL SACK OF ROME IN 455.

The Course of Empire: Destruction, 1836 (oil on canvas), Cole, Thomas (1801–48) / © Collection of the New York Historical Society, USA / The Bridgeman Art Library International although the diviners also said that one of the enemy leaders would be killed. Hoping for the death of Aetius—whom he knew to be his most formidable foe—Attila gave the order for his men to begin the battle.

A Violent Clash of Cavalry

Aetius had placed his best troops on the left side and the weakest, the Alans, at the center. It was at the Alans that the Huns, led by Attila, charged, shooting arrows and screaming their war cries. As a swirling, screaming dust cloud approached across the hot plains, the Alans buckled and made to run but were kept in line by the Visigoths and the other Roman forces. Attila's men slammed into the center of the line with such force that the Alans were sent reeling backward.

But in the meantime, the Visigoths, on the Roman right, had seized the initiative by taking, after a brisk battle, the strategic high ground on the Hun left flank. They then became engaged in a life-and-death contest with the Ostrogoths who had accompanied the Huns. Had the Ostrogoths been able to drive the Visigoths from the field, Attila would almost certainly have won the battle. But Theodoric rallied his forces time and time again, leading his men deep into the Ostrogothic line, swinging his sword in wild circles about his head.

Then, potential disaster struck: Theodoric was knocked from his horse and trampled to death amid thousands of pounding hooves. For a moment, the battle hung in the balance, but then Theodoric's son Thorismund took control and, with renewed fury, attacked the Ostrogoths, who broke and fled to the rear.

The Huns had penetrated so far into the center of the Roman lines that they had opened themselves up to counterattacks from Aetius's forces. Almost surrounded, they attempted to fight their way back to their camp, which, as always, was surrounded by a circle of wagons. But the furious Visigoths fell among them, killing thousands. Finally, under cover of darkness, Attila made it to the safety of his wagons and, for the moment, he could breathe easy. But he was certain that in the morning, his enemies would sweep in to finish him off.

Next day, the sun rose over a scene of incredible carnage, with thousands of corpses rotting across the plain—eyewitnesses said that the dead were stacked 6 feet (1.8 m) high, and that one could not walk across the field anywhere and touch ground. Now, the Romans closed in for the kill. They approached the Hun wagons, men spattered with blood and gore from the previous day's battle, weary and angry, and perhaps fearful as well, for although they had their foes cornered, they knew them to be willing to fight to the death.

Inside the camp, Attila vowed loudly to his bodyguards that he would commit suicide rather than be captured alive. Arming himself with his sword and favorite

bow, he ordered "a funeral pyre of horse saddles" be heaped up, so that he could throw himself on the flames, if necessary.

But it never became necessary. Even though Thorismund, having found his father's body under a pile of corpses, wanted to attack and massacre the Huns, Aetius—ever the politician—realized that a powerful and victorious Gothic army in Gaul, without the threat of the Huns, might be a real menace to the Roman Empire. So he decided to let Attila go. The only problem was deciding how to convince the enraged and grieving Thorismund to accept this.

With typical ingenuity, Aetius quickly came up with an answer. He convinced Thorismund that he needed to return to his home and immediately secure the Visigothic throne for himself, lest his brothers plot to take it from him when they heard of their father's death. Thorismund allowed himself to be convinced, and retreated.

To the disbelieving eyes of Attila, the Roman forces gradually faded away from the encircled wagons. When the way opened for he and his Huns to leave, Attila at first thought it was a trap, but he at last broke camp and headed back east of the Rhine. And there he waited for another year, and another opportunity to claim Honoria and the Western Empire.

A Potential Savior?

Recently, some historians have argued that the battle of the Catalaunian Plains does not deserve its position as the pivotal battle of the barbarian invasions, since, after all, it only delayed the fall of the empire another twenty-five years or so. But the battle remains important for a number of reasons. First of all, it was the first time that a combined force of Romans and Goths had managed to defeat Attila, which in turn showed others that he was a mere mortal after all. Second, it would turn out to be the last-ever victory of the forces of the Western Roman Empire.

What's more, a different outcome at Châlons could have had a much more dramatic impact on subsequent Western history than just a more precipitous decline for Rome. If Attila had won and killed Aetius and Theodoric, he would have been able to advance south through Italy to Rome at his leisure and, quite likely, make himself Western Emperor. And then, instead of dying the next year in his camp, it is possible Attila might have overcome his conventional raiding and pillaging approach and actually ruled his empire, which would then almost certainly not have fallen to succeeding waves of barbarians such as the Vandals who would shortly sack Rome. Might Attila the barbarian have saved Rome from other barbarians?

ATTILA: THE BARBARIAN WHO SWAGGERED HIS WAY TO VICTORY OVER THE ROMANS

It was around 420 that the one thing that had previously held the Huns back—that they were loose bands of nomads, each with its own chieftain—changed, and a Hunnic dynasty began to emerge. It was first ruled by a chieftain named Oktar, who was succeeded by his brother, Rugila, upon whose death two brothers called Attila and Bleda ruled jointly. After Bleda was murdered (supposedly by Attila himself, in 445), Attila became the undisputed head of the huge Hunnic force—and soon emerged as one of the most fearsome figures in history.

There are enough eyewitness accounts of Attila to give us some idea of his character. The Roman historian Profuturus Frigeridus described him as "of middle height and manly aspect … a very practiced horseman and a skilled archer." The Gothic historian Jordanes is less kind, but probably closer to the truth, in depicting Attila as quite short and squat, weather-beaten and swaggering. Most sources agree that he

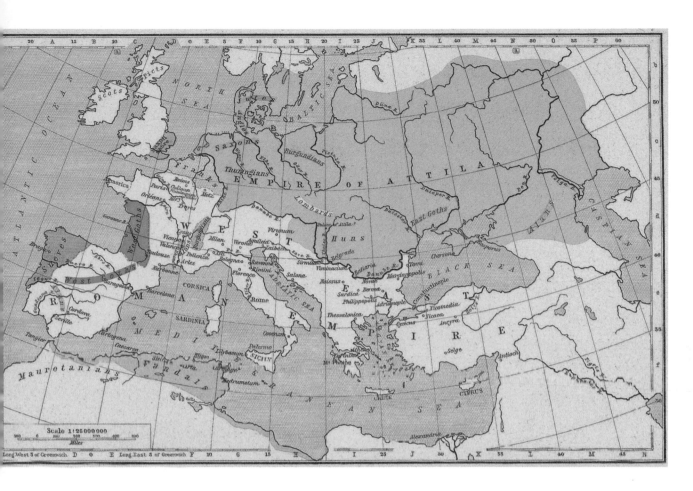

had simple tastes, drinking beer from a wooden bowl rather than a gold cup, and that he was willing to politely receive people of lower rank who came to supplicate him. Whether or not this apparent simplicity was a façade, Attila almost certainly lived his life for power, which, in the world of the Hun, went to the king who could provide his followers with plunder. And that Attila was able to do in spades.

For example, when the Eastern Emperor Theodosius II failed to pay his yearly tribute promptly enough in 440, Attila attacked him again in 441 and took thousands of wagons of booty and long lines of slaves away into the vastness of the Central Asian steppes. And in 449, seeking even greater wealth and power, Attila decided to attack the Western Roman Empire, even though he had until then been on relatively friendly terms with its ruler, Valentinian III.

Attila's excuse for doing so was provided by Honoria, sister of Valentinian. She had been forced by her brother, whom she hated, to become engaged to a Roman senator. In response, the strong-willed Honoria had sent Attila a letter asking him to

LIKE OTHER EMPIRES, THE HUNNIC REALM, SHOWN HERE ABOUT 450 BCE, QUICKLY DISAPPEARED AFTER THE DEATH OF LEADER ATTILA. THE HUNS WERE NOMADS FROM CENTRAL ASIA WHOSE PRECISE ORIGINS REMAIN UNCLEAR.

come and rescue her and enclosing her engagement ring. Honoria meant this merely as a sign that the letter was genuine, but Attila took it—or chose to take it—as a proposal of marriage. Despite Valentinian's attempts to explain that this was not the case, Attila declared that he was accepting the offer and was coming to Rome to marry Honoria and receive his dowry: half the Western Empire.

As this indicates, Attila was a master opportunist. He was evidently a master of propaganda, as well. When, around this time, one of his herdsmen found a rusty sword, Attila claimed it was the sword of the Hunnic God of War, which had previously been lost, and that its discovery made him ruler of the world. Soon he began to refer to himself as "the Scourge of God."

THE SURPRISING NAVY OF THE WORST BARBARIANS IN HISTORY

Although their name is synonymous with mindless destruction and they left no legacy of lasting importance, the Vandals did at least claim the distinction of being the only barbarian force to possess a navy. Moreover, they created an empire that, for a brief period, even outshone Rome.

Originating in Jutland (in present-day Denmark), and moving something the Vandals were, like the other refugees from the Huns, a weak and starving tribe merely seeking shelter in Gaul. But as they fought their way through France and into Spain, ousting other tribes like the Sueves, Alans, and Franks along the way, they became richer, more powerful, and apparently more confident.

In 428, however, when they reached the bottom of the Iberian Peninsula, they found themselves besieged by the Visigoths, who wanted Spain for themselves and were far more numerous. The Vandal leader Gaiseric—one of the great barbarian leaders of his time, although he has received less attention than Alaric or Attila—looked across the Straits of Gibraltar to the shores of Africa, only 7 miles (11 km) distant, and made a momentous decision. He ordered that a fleet of ships be built to take his people, now numbering perhaps eighty thousand, to Africa. No one knows how the Vandals found the skills to do this—perhaps they learned from captive local shipbuilders—but in 429 they ferried themselves across the straits to the vicinity of modern Ceuta, on the Moroccan coast.

Gaiseric, who would go on to reign for forty years, marched his army though North Africa, conquering this rich and fertile land by 442. He expanded his navy to include numerous warships and sent them to seize the islands of Sardinia, Corsica, and the Balearics, which he turned into naval bases. With no other naval power strong enough to stop him, Gaiseric used his fleet to create havoc in the Mediterranean, capturing shipping and raiding the coastal cities of Sicily.

In 455, he used his navy to take his forces to Italy, where he plundered Rome and kidnapped the Empress Eudoxia and her daughters, Eudocia and Placidia. Eudocia was forced to become the wife of Gaiseric's son, Hunneric, but her mother and sister were eventually ransomed by Rome.

The Vandal kingdom of North Africa was destroyed in 533 by the Emperor Justinian. The Vandals, who had never evolved beyond a warrior society, vanished from history.

DID ROME REALLY FALL—OR GRADUALLY FADE AWAY?

A debate currently raging among historians is whether the Western Roman Empire really fell, abruptly and calamitously, to the invading barbarians, or merged more slowly with the incoming cultures, becoming a mix of influences. The first point of view—that the barbarians destroyed the Romans and much of Western civilization with them, precipitating the Dark Ages—was put forth by the eighteenth-century historian Edward Gibbon in his famous masterwork, The History of the Decline and Fall of the Roman Empire. Since then, some historians have questioned his thesis, depicting the period as one of gradual cultural transformation.

The debate will inevitably go on, but it is certainly true that one very real consequence of the barbarian invasions was the destruction of much classical (Greek and Roman) knowledge, as well as the faltering of numerous economies and a precipitous decline in the population of Western Europe. Not quite a "gradual transformation."

5

THE MUSLIM CONQUESTS

632–732

THE CENTURY-LONG CAMPAIGN OF EXPANSION UNDERTAKEN BY ARABIAN FORCES ESPOUSING THE NEW FAITH OF ISLAM

SPREADING THE WORD OF ALLAH, A NEW POWER IS INTRODUCED TO THE WORLD

The Muslim Conquests stemmed from one man, the Prophet Muhammad. Inspired by a series of divine revelations, Muhammad began to espouse a revolutionary new religion, Islam, beginning in 610. Gradually this universal, monotheistic, and egalitarian creed spread across the broad Arabian Peninsula, transforming the social and political status quo among the warring, traditionally polytheistic Bedouin tribes of the deserts and the materialistic, socially competitive merchants of the trading centers. Islam united Arabs of all ranks and persuasions, and by the time of Muhammad's death in 632 it had created a cohesive religious and political force across much of Arabia.

Under Muhammad's appointed successor, or caliph, Abu Bakr, Arab Muslims sought to expand the Islamic state. In part this was for religious reasons, to spread the word of Muhammad; but it was also prompted by the perceived weakness of the Byzantine Empire, which then ruled much of the Middle East, and by a desire to direct the energies of the warlike Arabian tribes outward in order to maintain internal unity.

In 633, a Muslim army led by the military commander Khalid ibn al-Walid began a war against the Byzantine Empire, launching strikes first at forces belonging to the Emperor Heraclitus in what is now Israel and western Jordan. In 634, Abu Bakr died and was succeeded by 'Umar I, who expanded these raids into a full-scale offensive. The Arabs took Damascus in southern Syria and defeated the Byzantine army at the six-day-long battle of the Yarmuk River in 636.

In 637, 'Umar I's forces entered Mesopotamia and successfully destroyed a large Sasanian force at the battle of al-Qadisiyah. In the following year, they conquered Jerusalem. Victory at the battle of Nahavand in 641 brought control of central Persia, and the rest of Persia was under Muslim sway by 651.

After the death of Khalid in 642, a new Muslim commander, Amr ibn el-Ass took the city of Alexandria from the now almost totally defeated Byzantines and within a year, Muslims controlled all of Egypt. They then moved farther into the Byzantine

Empire, seizing Cyprus and Byzantine Armenia in 653, but in 669 failed in the first of a series of unsuccessful attempts to take the Byzantine capital of Constantinople.

After being delayed by the unexpectedly strong resistance of Kahina, Queen of the Berbers, in North Africa, Muslim forces under Tariq ibn Ziyad crossed the Straits of Gibraltar and decisively defeated the Visigothic leader, King Roderick, in 711. Tariq's forces then moved steadily north, conquering all of the Iberian Peninsula by 718 and pushing the remaining Visigoths into the mountainous northwestern province of Asturias.

In 718, Muslim forces crossed the Pyrenees, invading Aquitaine and southern France and capturing the city of Narbonne. By 730, a larger force had advanced as far north as Poitiers, in western-central France, where it was defeated by a Frankish army under Charles Martel in 732.

Thereafter, Islamic domination of the Iberian Peninsula was weakened by a struggle for power between the ruling Umayyad dynasty and a rival dynasty, the Abbasids, who eventually seized control in 750. Though an Umayyad leader 'Abd ar-Rahman established a separate state, centered on the city of Córdoba, in 756, sporadic conflict between Muslims and Christians in the Iberian Peninsula would eventually lead to the Reconquista, or reconquest, of the region by Christian forces.

MUSLIM FORCES UNDER TARIK IBN ZIYAD CROSSED THE STRAITS OF GIBRALTAR IN 711 AND DEFEATED THE GOTHS AND KING RODERICK DURING THE BATTLE OF GUADALETE, AS SHOWN IN THIS NINETEENTH CENTURY OIL PAINTING BY SPANISH ARTIST SALVADOR MARTINEZ CUBELLS.

THE BATTLE THAT PUSHED BACK THE MUSLIM TIDE
The Battle of Poitiers (Tours), 732

By most accounts, the battle took place on a cold Saturday morning in October, which further heightened the symbolism of this controversial encounter, for while the Franks were dressed in their warm animal furs, the Arab and Berber Muslim warriors wore light clothing more appropriate to the Spanish plains or the deserts of North Africa and Arabia. Shivering, they stared up the sloping fields at the heavily armored phalanx of Frankish knights who awaited them in their fox pelts and scale armor, spears and swords glittering.

The battlefield these soldiers stood on lay somewhere between the modern-day towns of Poitiers and Tours in southwestern France, and hence the subsequent clash has come to be known as both the battle of Poitiers and the battle of Tours. Over the centuries, this engagement has gained the status of one of the greatest and most decisive battles in Western history. Here, it is said, the extraordinary advance of Muslim forces, which had begun exactly a century earlier, was finally halted, and Europe was saved from Islamic domination.

But more recent historians have questioned this, postulating that, rather than a full-scale invasion, the Muslim incursion into France was merely a razzia, a large-scale raid, which was casually abandoned after the first serious resistance from the Franks. Whatever the truth, the symbolism of Poitiers, if a little too convenient, remains significant. The Arabs never did penetrate farther into France than Poitiers. And in the main Christian chronicle we have of the battle, a word is used for the first time to describe the Frankish force: Europenses—"Europeans."

The first Muslim raids into what would become France began in 718, soon after the forces of Islam had subdued the Iberian Peninsula, with attacks on the rich lands of Aquitaine in the southwest. Their main opponent here was the Frankish Duke Eudo, who, after several battles, began to lose ground to the Arabs. Trying another approach, he sought to exploit the perennial bad blood between the Berbers and Arabs by marrying his daughter to a disgruntled Berber chief.

In retaliation, in the summer of 732, the Muslim general 'Abd ar-Rahman (not to be confused with the later Umayyad leader of the same name) led a major raid into Aquitaine. Estimates of the size of his force are hard to come by, but range from sixty thousand to eighty thousand cavalry.

This left Duke Eudo with nowhere to turn but to his great rival, Charles Martel, whose attempts to conquer Aquitaine he had fiercely resisted. Recognizing an opportunity to extend his influence, Martel gathered a force of some thirty thousand Franks (along with some Burgundians) and marched it directly into the path of the advancing Muslims.

Martel formed his army into a square on the road between Poitiers and Tours. The Muslim force, having met little or no resistance, had sent smaller parties off on raids to take booty and slaves—one more sign that this was a pillaging force and not an invading army. But the main force, led by 'Abd ar-Rahman, soon came up against Martel's army. Taken by surprise, 'Abd ar-Rahman halted, sent messengers to track down and call in the rest of his men, and then began to study his enemy.

Standing Firm

For a week, 'Abd ar-Rahman and Charles Martel sized each other up, sending out scouting parties, feinting, watching each other closely. The Franks were spread out along a relatively narrow front at the top of a hill, with woods on either side of them. It was a nearly perfect position, with the woods protecting against flank attacks and the steep slope likely to slow down any cavalry charge.

'Abd ar-Rahman was an experienced general, and he probably hesitated to attack such a well-chosen position; on the other hand, his force greatly outnumbered Martel's, and he must have derived confidence from a recent, unbroken string of victories as he marched through Aquitaine—victories that had left his wagons and his camp filled with booty. He would not turn tail.

On that Saturday morning, as the sun rose over the cold and misty fields, the Muslims said their prayers to Mecca and then leaped on their horses. They charged from more than half a mile (0.8 km) away, giving themselves time to gather speed, shouting war cries to Allah and banging drums and clashing cymbals. They continued to scream with a wild fervor as they poured toward the enemy lines.

Martel knew the Frankish cavalry could easily be overwhelmed by this type of attack, so he had his men form an armored square, in emulation of the old Roman fighting formation, spears and swords pointing outward, shields interlocked. With a thundering of hooves and a tremendous clatter of swords and lances, the Muslims crashed into the Frankish lines. And, astonishingly, they broke on the tips of the Frankish swords, spears, and battle-axes, with not one getting through. Charge after charge struck the line, but still it didn't break, the Franks, as one Muslim chronicler wrote, standing there like a "wall of ice." It was one of the few times in history when infantrymen were able to resist such a massed cavalry charge.

Some say the battle lasted only one long day, others two, still others up to seven. The lower estimates are more likely to be correct, but no one knows for sure. What is known is that 'Abd ar-Rahman was killed during one furious attack on the Frankish lines—some say seeking to find Charles Martel and outdo him in individual combat—and the Muslims, deprived of their leader, withdrew to their encampment.

That night on the battlefield, the Franks held their ground in the freezing cold, listening for any sign of attack, and in the morning they stood up, weary, ready to face the expected onslaught. But the forests and fields around them were filled with a strange silence. No attack came. Cautiously, Martel sent out scouts to search the area, expecting an Arab attack the moment he broke ranks. But still no charge came, and no Arab forces were found. Gradually, the Franks realized that the entire Arab army had disappeared during the night, taking its booty but leaving behind the brightly colored tents that had done little to shelter its soldiers from the northern weather.

Martel had won a momentous victory. Whether it was a victory that prevented the Muslim forces from flooding Western Europe or whether, as is more likely, the Arab advance had already begun to slow and lose momentum, we can't be sure. But undoubtedly the Europenses took heart from it and considered it a great triumph against this new and most deadly of enemies.

CHARLES MARTEL: THE CHARISMATIC LEADER WHO UNIFIED THE FRANKS

The Franks were a Germanic tribe that crossed the Rhine and settled in the former Roman province of Gaul in the fifth century, before spreading out to dominate the region. By the late seventh century, the ruling dynasty of the Franks, the Merovingians, had been weakened by internecine conflicts. The resulting power vacuum was filled by administrators previously appointed by the Merovingians and known as Mayors of the Palace. One such man was Pippin of Herstal, who effectively ruled the Frankish kingdoms on behalf of a succession of puppet kings.

As well as a wife and children, Pippin had an illegitimate son, Charles Martel, born around 688. On Pippin's death in 714, a struggle for power broke out among his offspring. Despite the best efforts of Pippin's wife Plectrude and her grandchildren, Martel—whose name means "Charles the Hammer"—triumphed and became Mayor of the Palace, ruler of the Franks, in 719.

Martel was tall and handsome with immense personal strength. Although historians have portrayed him as the savior of Christianity, he was in fact a savage warrior who was not beyond imprisoning anyone—including clerics—who got in his way. Eventually, he conquered a kingdom that covered much of present-day France, western Germany, and the Netherlands.

The main reason Martel agreed to help the Frankish Duke Eudo of Aquitaine oppose Muslim forces at Poitiers in 732 was self-interest. Martel had been raiding Eudo's lands since the 720s, seeking to extend his realm southward, and the alliance was a chance for a breakthrough.

Poitiers was a great triumph, but Martel's military reputation does not rest on that battle alone. He was a brilliant strategist who pioneered the use of the cohesive attack of heavy cavalry, established a system of conscription that created the first standing army in Western Europe since the days of the Romans, and also forged the beginnings of feudalism, by bestowing upon his supporters lands that had been given him by the Catholic church, and creating a hierarchy of barons, counts, and dukes, all loyal to him.

After consolidating his empire through numerous battles after Poitiers, Martel died in 641, but the so-called Carolingian line (from the name Charles) would live on in his son Pippin III and his grandson Charlemagne, the first Holy Roman Emperor.

THE MESSENGER OF GOD WHO CREATED THE NEW RELIGION OF ISLAM

The astonishing prophet who founded the faith of Islam—a religion whose adherents today number more than one billion worldwide—was born in about 570 into the Quraysh tribe of Mecca, an important trading center in the west of the Arabian Peninsula. A young orphan, Muhammad—whose name means "worthy of praise"—was taken in by his Uncle Abu Talib, the head of the Hashimite clan to which Muhammad belonged, and taught how to barter and sell goods in the bustling Mecca marketplace.

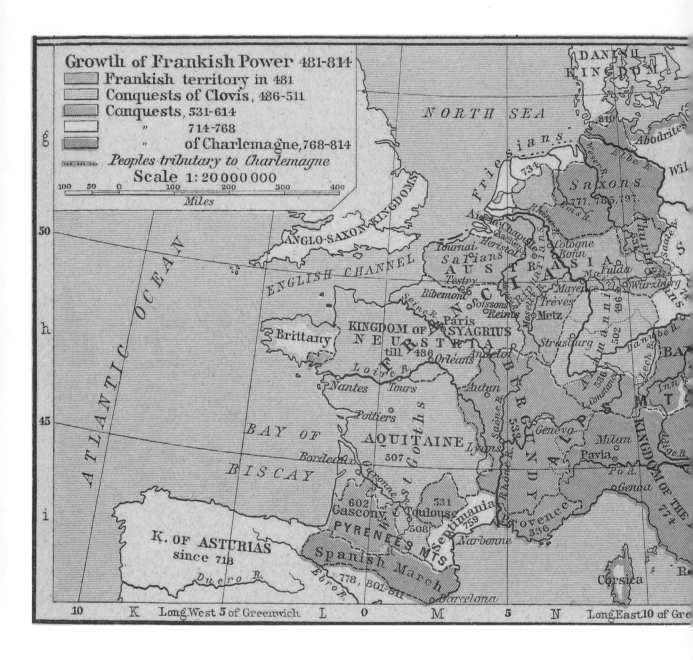

As a young merchant, Muhammad accompanied his uncle on at least one caravan trip to Syria and soon began to lead his own trading expeditions. By the time he was twenty-five, he was working for a rich widow named Khadija, ten years his senior, whom he eventually married and by whom he had six children—two stillborn boy infants, and four girls who lived. Muhammad had a spiritual, contemplative side, often going by himself into the wilderness near Mecca to pray and think. It is possible

that he had conversations with religious Jews and Christians, both present in Arabia at the time, about the shared origins of these religions.

In the year 610, Muhammad had a mystical experience that shook him spiritually and physically. He was visited by the Angel Gabriel, who told him—in the first of the admonitions that would make up the Koran—to "Recite: in the name of thy Lord who created, created man of a blood-clot." The messages continued over the next five years, and Muhammad soon sought to pass them on to others, preaching publicly and drawing a few dozen followers.

The new religion that Muhammad began to call Islam, from an Arabic word meaning "submission" or "surrender," demanded that its followers, no matter what their tribe or clan, lead a life of honor and piety and be brothers in all dealings. This message was threatening to the status quo of those who controlled Mecca, and eventually Muhammad and his followers (known as the Companions) were driven out of the city, to Medina. There, Muhammad garnered support among local Bedouin tribes, then returned to attack Mecca, finally gaining control of it by 630 and then much of the Arabian Peninsula by 632. In that year, he died of natural causes; but his message had already begun to spread across the world.

6

THE RECONQUISTA

722–1492

A LONG SERIES OF CAMPAIGNS AND SPORADIC WARS THAT SAW CHRISTIAN FORCES OUST THE MOORS FROM THE IBERIAN PENINSULA

THE LONG, SLOW EXPULSION OF THE MOORS CREATED MODERN SPAIN

The term Reconquista, though widely used for this epic conflict, is not strictly accurate, for it implies that the Christians were reconquering something that had been theirs in the first place. In fact, by the time they were expelled, the Iberian Muslims, or Moors, had held al-Andalus—the Islamic name for Spain—for centuries and created a vital and stable culture that contrasted sharply with the primitive and corrupt Visigothic society they had displaced. The word also suggests a planned counter-offensive, but the Reconquista consisted of an almost eight-hundred-year series of sporadic and often spontaneous rebellions and battles, and only in its later stages did the Christian campaign become more organized.

The Muslim conquest of the Iberian Peninsula in the early eighth century initially created a fractured and fragile Islamic realm, torn by disputes between the Arab Muslim leaders and the Berber tribesmen who had played a large part in the conquest. Early on, it was troubled by guerilla raids made by Christian Visigoths under a leader called Pelayo, who inhabited the mountainous northwestern province of Asturias, the only part of the peninsula not then controlled by the Muslims. When a Muslim force was sent to root out these rebels, it was destroyed by Pelayo and the Visigoths at the battle of Covadonga in 722. The first major Christian victory against Islam in Iberia, this battle is traditionally said to mark the beginning of the Reconquista.

But further significant rebellions would be a long time in coming. In 756, the last Umayyad prince 'Abd ar-Rahman arrived in Spain and consolidated his power over the warring Muslim and Berber clans. This created the Emirate of Córdoba, a state, centered on the city of Córdoba, that was independent of the rest of the Muslim empire, which had been taken over by the Abbasids. Umayyad rule lasted until 1031, with the emirate becoming a caliphate in 929, and for most of this period there was peace and stability.

However, the Christian foothold in Asturias gradually spread out to include the rocky northern provinces of Castile, Leon, Aragon, and Navarre. In the late tenth century, in response to this expansion, the Muslim leader al-Mansur began a series of incursions into the Christian north. This unsettled the balance of power and drove the Christian provinces to unite. At the battle of Calatañazor in 1002, led by the Christian King of Navarre, Sancho the Great, they defeated the Muslim army and fatally wounded al-Mansur.

The Caliphate of Córdoba then fell apart, and al-Andalus disintegrated into as many as two dozen ta'ifa states, petty kingdoms run by governors. In 1010, Berbers rebelled and overwhelmed Córdoba, burning, killing, and looting. Seeing an opportunity, Sancho the Great besieged Córdoba the following year and installed a puppet ruler. Ferdinand I of Castile captured Seville in 1061; and in 1085, King Alfonso VI of Castile and Leon took the Muslim city of Toledo.

This stirred a response—not within Spain, however, but in North Africa, where a new sect of Islam had arisen. The Almoravids, rigidly puritanical in their interpretation of Islam, arose out of the Atlas Mountains; their ranks were mostly formed by Arabs and Berbers. They crossed into Spain with large armies in 1086, 1088, and 1093 to wage a holy war against the Christians, defeating Alfonso VI at the battle of Sagrajas in 1086 and eventually reclaiming all of al-Andalus except for Valencia, which remained under the control of the legendary Spanish knight known as El Cid.

In the early twelfth century, however, Portugal, under the Burgundian knight, Henry, Count of Portugal, asserted its independence, which was officially recognized by the papacy in 1143, and in 1154 the Almoravids were conquered by another, even stricter Islamic sect from North Africa, the Almohads. But Christian forces continued to advance farther south into al-Andalus, especially after their crushing victory over the Almohads at the battle of Las Navas de Tolosa, in 1212. Their success derived not just from winning battles, but also from their policy of repopulating seized territory with Christian settlers and then creating strongly fortified towns.

From 1230 to 1250, the majority of Spain was retaken by Christians, aided by Christian warrior monks who began arriving from Palestine and the Crusades. These monks—of the Santiago and Calatrava orders—were akin to the Knights Templar and Hospitaller, and instilled a crusading spirit among the Christians fighting in Spain. In 1235, under King Fernando III, a Christian army captured Córdoba and in 1248 Seville.

After this, the only remaining Moorish outpost on the Iberian Peninsula was the city of Granada, in the far south. Crowned by the beautiful Alhambra palace, it had become a tributary state of Spain in the early thirteenth century. It then thrived as a center of Muslim culture and learning for more than 250 years; however, when King Ferdinand and Queen Isabella came to power, they decided that this last Moorish stronghold had to be eliminated, too. During a long and bitter campaign, Muslims from the surrounding countryside were forced to seek refuge in the city itself, which was secretly surrendered to the Christians by the Muslim leader Boabdil in 1492. In that same year, Christopher Columbus discovered the Americas and King Ferdinand and Queen Isabella, by then joint rulers of most of Spain, decreed that all Muslims and Jews must convert or leave the country.

A FIERCE BATTLE, FOUGHT WITH VISIONARY PASSION, ALTERS SPANISH HISTORY
The Battle of Las Navas de Tolosa, 1212

At the height of the fighting, at the most telling point of the battle, some chroniclers recount that a dazzling cross appeared in the sky; others say Saint James was seen hovering over the battlefield. Whether or not this was true, the Christian soldiers at Las Navas de Tolosa, on July 16, 1212, were said to have fought with a heightened fervor, as if possessed by some kind of inspiring power. Their leader, Alfonso VIII, was at the heart of the fray, swinging his sword with such boldness "that a fire seemed to light up the bushes" around him. It was as if the Christian army knew that everything depended on this fight: their lives, of course, but also the future of their kingdoms and the survival of their religion in Spain.

Of course, they could not have known this, and yet the battle they were waging did turn out to be the most pivotal of the eight centuries of warfare that constituted the Reconquista. As a result of Las Navas de Tolosa, the entire history of the Iberian Peninsula, and Western Europe, was changed.

After the Almohad zealots overthrew the Almoravids in 1154, they began attacking the cities that represented the Christian foothold in the southern Iberian Peninsula. And in 1195—taking advantage of the fact that the rulers of Navarre, Castile, and Leon were fighting among themselves—they destroyed the frontier fortress of Alarcos near La Mancha, inflicting a severe defeat on the Castilians.

The young Castilian king, Alfonso VIII, was lucky to escape with his life, and the defeat seems to have had a transformative effect on him. Deciding that his humiliation at the hands of the Muslims was God's punishment for the feckless life he had been leading—in particular, for his affair with a lovely young Jewish girl—he vowed "to straighten out his life and do service to God in every way he could." In fact, he vowed to lead a crusade against the Almohads.

In this he was supported by the new pope, Innocent III, who was eager to restore Christian pride in the aftermath of the disastrous Third Crusade, in which the Crusaders had been badly defeated at the battle of Hattin. In late 1211, Innocent issued a proclamation declaring a holy war in Spain and offering remission of sins to all who flocked to Toledo to join the crusade in May 1212. According to a Christian

chronicler, the large companies of crusaders who subsequently arrived there, mainly from France, "did great harm, for they killed Jews and did many other sorts of misbehavior." But Innocent's proclamation also forced King Sancho II of Navarre and King Pedro II of Aragon to put aside their rivalries and join Alfonso.

This was the first time in the Reconquista that the Christians had waged what could be seen as a holy war rather than a war for territory. To meet this threat, the Almohad Caliph Muhammad an-Nasir gathered a large force. As with the Christians, religion unified and overrode petty rivalries: the army raised by Muhammad—who had red hair and blue eyes and was the son of a Christian concubine—was made up of Berbers, Turkish mounted bowmen, and Arab irregulars from North Africa.

In July 1212, the Muslims headed north as the Christians headed south, each force numbering around thirty thousand soldiers.

The eager French crusaders led the way for the Christians and soon reached the Almohad fortress of Malagon, north of the present-day city of Ciudad Real. Without waiting for the Aragonese or Castilians, they took the fortress and mercilessly butchered its Muslim inhabitants. When Alfonso VIII caught up with the French, he castigated them for this, and at the next siege, of the town of Calatrava, Alfonso offered its Muslim defenders generous terms to leave without a fight, which they did. Offended by this show of mercy, the French crusaders—veterans of the fighting in Palestine, where little such succor was offered defeated enemies—turned around and headed for home. As they passed by the walls of Christian Toledo, its inhabitants pelted the retreating Crusaders with rotting food and dead animals, taunting them as cowards.

Their retreat was not such a great disaster for Alfonso, for while it did reduce his forces, it eliminated a troublesome and disobedient group of knights who had been undermining his campaign. The Christians continued south, until they reached the Sierra Morena mountain range, where they realized that the forces of the Caliph Muhammad had set a trap for them in a narrow valley. With great skill and secrecy, the Christians skirted this trap, came in behind the Moors, and took control of the high ground of a wooded mesa about 6 miles (10 km) from the village of Las Navas de Tolosa, about 40 miles (64 km) north of modern-day Jaén in Andalucia. It was Friday, July 13.

During the next two days, Muhammad tried to force the Christians to attack him, but Alfonso wisely rested his army. Then, on the morning of Monday, July 16, Alfonso went on the offensive.

Divine Inspiration

The Christian battle order placed the three kings who had accompanied the expedition—Alfonso, Pedro, and Sancho—at the rear. In front of them were the warrior monks and citizen militias. In the very front lines were the knights of the Christian army, led by a famous warrior, Diego López de Haro, who began the attack by leading his men in a charge down the sloping sides of the mesa and into the caliph's army. The Moors were advancing, too, but more slowly, and the Spanish knights overwhelmed them and chopped them to pieces in a frenzy of rage.

The Christians then turned to face the main lines of the Alhomads, which were aligned along a slight rise, with the red tent of Muhammad in the center. Now the battle became ferocious, with Berber horsemen racing out, swinging their scimitars

in great circles over their heads, while their infantry hurled javelins at the Christians. Diego's men began to fall back, and the whole Christian line began to falter.

It was at this point that the Christian soldiers, according to some chroniclers, received divine inspiration. Whether a cross lit up the sky or flames really appeared to shoot from Alfonso's sword, his men seem to have been seized by an equal fervor, for by early afternoon they had broken the Almohad army. Legend has it that the caliph himself was surrounded in his tent by slave-warriors chained together to force them to stand their ground, and that King Pedro of Navarre personally leaped between them to try to kill the caliph.

Muhammad managed to flee, however, and eventually ended up back in Seville, lucky to be alive. But his men were hunted down in all the chasms and hollows of this mountainous region and slaughtered, and then Alfonso and his fellow kings—elated by the glory of their victory—went on to attack the Muslim cities of Baeza and Úbeda, deep in al-Andalus.

To celebrate the victory at Tolosa, Pope Innocent ordered that bells be rung in churches throughout Christendom. It was the beginning of the end for Moorish Spain.

ALFONSO VIII, KING OF CASTILE, CAMPAIGNING AGAINST THE MOORS IN SPAIN, AS ILLUSTRATED ON NINETEENTH-CENTURY TILES IN THE PLAZA DE ESPAÑA IN SEVILLE, SPAIN.

Alfonso VIII, King of Castile (c.1155–1214) Subdues Cuenca in 1177, 19th century (glazed ceramic tiles), Mensaque, A (19th century) / Plaza Espana, Seville, Spain / Index / The Bridgeman Art Library International

A PORTRAIT OF AL-MANSUR
BY FRANCISCO DE ZURBARAN
(1598–1664).

Portrait of Almanzor (940–1002) (oil
on canvas), Zurbaran, Francisco de
(1598–1664) / Private Collection /
Index / The Bridgeman Art Library
International

AL-MANSUR: THE ARM OF ALLAH OR THE DEVIL?

Probably no Muslim amir or overlord of the Reconquista stirred more passion than Abu 'Amir al-Mansur. To the Muslims, he was "the arm of Allah," chosen by God to strike at the infidel Christians. To the Christians, he was the Devil himself, the Antichrist.

Al-Mansur was born around 938 into a family of minor nobles, originally from Arabia. During the reign of the Córdoba Caliph al-Hakam II, al-Mansur trained in classics at a university and then went to Córdoba, where he set up shop outside the palace gates, making a living as a scribe.

But al-Mansur was fiercely ambitious and soon found his way inside the palace—popular tradition has it that the handsome young man began an affair with Sudh, the beautiful, slave-born Basque wife of al-Hakam II. However it happened, he soon schemed his way into obtaining no fewer than eight high posts in al-Hakam's government. When al-Hakam died in 976, leaving the rule of Córdoba to his twelve-year-old son, it took al-Mansur only a few years to unseat the boy and become ruler himself.

So far, another petty power grab story. But al-Mansur then changed the landscape of Iberian politics by dedicating himself to a jihad, or holy war, against the Christians. He imported mercenary Berbers from Spain to do much of his fighting and even managed to attract disgruntled Christians to his side. He successfully invested fortresses in the northern Christian kingdom of Leon, sacked Barcelona, and led a brutal raid on one of the most holy of Christian shrines, Santiago de Compostela. Over twenty years, he organized and took part in fifty-eight campaigns against the Christians, particularly those of Leon and Castile, and was victorious in fifty-seven of them.

Al-Mansur sought not to take territory, but to humiliate and discredit Christendom. This finally provoked the Christian kingdoms into a concerted attempt to oppose him. Led by Sancho the Great, the armies of Navarre, Leon, and Castile met the forces of al-Mansur in July of 1002, at a place called Calatañazor in the present-day province of Soria, in north-central Spain. The Christians, one Islamic chronicler wrote, fought like "famished wolves," the Muslims like "raging panthers." After a daylong battle, al-Mansur was forced to retreat, mortally wounded. He died two days later.

All of Moorish Spain mourned. As for the Christians? Well, as one contemporary Spanish monk wrote, "Al-Mansur died in 1002. He was buried in Hell."

THE LEGEND AND REALITY OF EL CID

Probably the most famous figure to come out of the Reconquista, El Cid was born Rodrigo Díaz de Vivar, into a family of minor nobility of Castille, in about 1040. The name "El Cid" comes from the Arabic al sayyid—"master" or "lord"—and it underscores the difficulty of discovering which side El Cid really served. As the historian David Nicolle has written, was the honorific given "in recognition of El Cid's victories against Islam … or because this Castilian nobleman was as content to serve beside the Muslims as to fight them?"

Not a great deal is known for certain about El Cid's early life. He became the chief military commander of King Sancho II of Castile. After Sancho was assassinated during a siege, his brother Alfonso took the throne as Alfonso VI and grew increasingly jealous of El Cid's fame and prowess—according to the account in the El Cantar de mio Cid, The Song of El Cid, a 3,700-line epic poem about the knight that was probably written in the early thirteenth century. This episode may well be true; it is certainly also true that El Cid, sent to Seville to collect tribute from a Muslim ruler there, captured and held for ransom numerous Castilian nobles—a sign of his mercenary tendencies. For this Alfonso exiled him.

Taking his top commanders with him, El Cid then joined forces with the Muslim ruler of the northeastern city of Zaragoza, and fought for him and his successor for five

EL CID (LEFT) WITH HIS FATHER, DON DIEGO RODRIGO DÍAZ DE VIVAR, AS PAINTED BY ALEXANDRE EVARISTE FRAGONARD, C 1827.

Rodrigo de Vivar, "El Cid" (c.1043–99) and his father, Don Diego, c.1827 (oil on canvas), Fragonard, Alexandre Evariste (1780–1850) / Private Collection / © Stair Sainty, London / The Bridgeman Art Library International

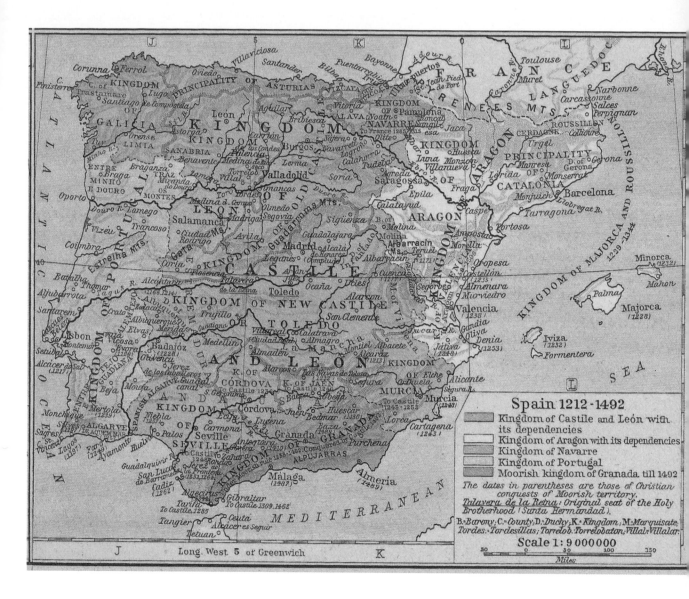

years, defeating Christian armies twice in 1082 and 1084. But when the Almoravid armies of North Africa invaded in 1086, King Alfonso temporarily arranged a truce with El Cid. El Cid then defeated the Almoravids in two battles, one of them an extraordinary victory at Cuarte in 1094, when El Cid feigned retreat and then charged to defeat a larger Islamic force—which took his legend to new heights. Yet, in the same year, El Cid conquered the Muslim-held city of Valencia, from which—ever interested in profit—he extracted a ruthless toll in taxes.

El Cid held Valencia until he passed away in 1099. Even in death, myths surrounded him. According to a thirteenth-century source, his body was embalmed, dressed, placed in armor, and tied upright upon his famous horse, Babieca, at which point it led his troops into victorious battle against the Almoravid foe.

THE KING AND THE QUEEN WHO MADE SPAIN FIRST IN A NEW WORLD

In the last years of the Reconquista, a man and a woman arrived upon the scene in Spain whom some contemporary chroniclers thought were divinely placed—in the right spot, at the right time—to put the finishing touches on the faltering Muslims and lead Spain into the new light of a Christian age.

The marriage of Ferdinand II of Aragon and Princess Isabella of Castile in 1469 united the two most powerful provinces in Spain. Unity, indeed, became the theme of their rule; their motto was "Tanto monta, monta tanto, Isabel como Fernando" ("They amount to the same, Isabella and Ferdinand"). The conquest of Granada, the last Moorish state in Spain, took place under these two monarchs in 1492, as did Columbus's voyage to the Americas—events that signaled a unified Spain's entry onto the world stage.

Unfortunately, while directing Spain toward nationhood, the so-called "Catholic Monarchs" also distanced the country from the religious tolerance that had marked the days of Muslim rule and into an era of pitiless bigotry. The Alhambra Decree, issued by Ferdinand and Isabella in March of 1492, forced all Muslims to convert to Christianity or face death; many did convert, while others fled to North Africa. The same decree ordered the expulsion of all Jews, who had in any event suffered for a decade under the Inquisition, which the same monarchs had instigated, and whose excesses horrified even the pope who had approved it. Eight hundred years after the Visigoths had ruled the country, Spain was finally back in Christian hands, but at a great cost in human life and suffering.

THE RECONQUISTA CONSISTED OF AN ALMOST EIGHT-HUNDRED-YEAR SERIES OF BATTLES IN WHICH CHRISTIAN FORCES OUSTED THE MOORS FROM THE IBERIAN PENINSULA. THE REMAINING MOORISH OUTPOST, THE KINGDOM OF GRANADA IN SOUTHERN SPAIN, THRIVED AS A CENTER OF MUSLIM CULTURE AND LEARNING UNTIL KING FERDINAND AND QUEEN ISABELLA CAME TO POWER. IN 1492, THE SAME YEAR COLUMBUS DISCOVERED THE AMERICAS, SPAIN TOOK OVER GRANADA.

7

THE NORMAN CONQUEST

1066–71

THE INVASION OF ENGLAND—DECIDED BY ONE MOMENTOUS AND
FAMOUS BATTLE—THAT ENTIRELY ALTERED THE COURSE OF
WESTERN EUROPEAN HISTORY

THE NORMANS AND SAXONS CLASH—AND MODERN ENGLAND BEGINS

To a great extent, the history of both England and Normandy over the few hundred years leading up to 1066 was shaped by the activities of the Vikings. These fierce, seafaring people from Scandinavia first raided the British Isles in the late 700s and within about 150 years had destroyed the old culture of Ireland and despoiled much of Britain. They then turned their attention to mainland Europe, where they pushed inland via France's many long waterways, raiding as far as Paris, in 845. In 911, in an attempt to prevent further raids on the French heartland, the King of France, Charles the Simple, ceded the land that would become Normandy to the Vikings, then led by the chieftain Rollo. The bribe worked, and these Normanni, or "Norsemen" or "Northmen," for whom Normandy was eventually named, began to settle down and adopt French customs (though they would continue to participate in raids such as those that later gained them control of Sicily.

Viking raids on England continued, however, and in 1013 Danish King Sweyn I ("Forkbeard") conquered the country, forcing the Anglo-Saxon King Ethelred II—who, significantly, had been married to the daughter of Duke Richard I of Normandy—to flee. Sweyn's son Canute then established a North Sea empire that included England, Denmark, and Norway; but his successors failed to maintain control, and in 1042 England reverted peacefully to Anglo-Saxon rule under Edward the Confessor, who had been in exile in Normandy for some twenty-five years.

On his return to England, Edward brought his Norman advisors with him, which did not sit well with some Anglo-Saxon nobles. One of the most powerful, Godwine, Earl of Essex, and his son Harold Godwinson led a rebellion against Edward. Though he remained as king, Edward was forced to cede a great deal of power to these men, and when Edward died in January of 1066, Harold Godwinson became king.

Harold immediately had to face two rival claimants to the throne. One was the Norwegian King Harald III Sigurdsson (Harald the Ruthless), who claimed a tenuous relationship with the English throne but mainly saw a chance to take advantage of a weakened England. His cause was bolstered when he was joined by Harold's traitorous brother, Tostig. The other, more serious claimant was William the Bastard of Normandy. William's great-aunt Emma had been King Ethelred II's third wife; he also claimed that King Edward had promised him the throne in return for his help in quelling the rebellion led by Godwine. What's more, he asserted that Harold Godwinson, after being shipwrecked in Normandy in 1064, had sworn an oath on a saint's relic

THE BODY OF HAROLD BROUGHT BEFORE WILLIAM THE CONQUEROR (1844–61), BY FORD MADOX BROWN.

The Body of Harold Brought Before William the Conqueror, 1844–61 (oil on canvas), Brown, Ford Madox (1821–93) / Manchester Art Gallery, UK / The Bridgeman Art Library International Brown, Ford Madox (1821–93) / Manchester Art Gallery, UK / The Bridgeman Art Library International

that he would help William gain the throne of England after Edward died. Harold, however, denied that this had occurred (and some historians think the story may simply have been made up by the Normans as propaganda, to discredit Harold).

Whatever the truth, the die was cast in the fateful year of 1066. When Harald III Sigurdsson and Tostig invaded the north of England in September, Harold Godwinson defeated them at the battle of Stamford Bridge. But shortly thereafter, William landed in the south of England with his Norman army of about six to eight thousand men and defeated the Anglo-Saxon forces at the battle of Hastings, on October 14, killing Harold.

William the Conqueror was crowned King of England on Christmas Day, 1066, but the battle wasn't over. Rebellion would continue in England—William faced opposition from two northern earls, Edwin and Morkere, and brutally put down the uprising they led in 1069–70. The last major rebellion, led by Hereward of Wake, took place in 1071, and ended with the Normans' successful siege of Hereward's stronghold on the island of Ely. After this, the war was over.

Surrounded by the Anglo-Saxon majority, Norman lords took land grants from William and put strongholds and castles. William spent a good deal of time away from England, whose climate and customs he is said to have disliked, but his lords kept a firm hold on the country. Gradually, through intermarriage and the imposition of new laws and customs, the old Anglo-Saxon culture was superseded by the new Anglo-Norman mix. English history had changed forever.

SHIELD WALL MEETS CAVALRY CHARGE—AND INVADERS TURNED THE TIDE
The Battle of Hastings, 1066

He must have viewed his triumph with mixed emotions. King Harold Godwinson had won a great military victory, leading an army almost 200 miles (320 km) northward from London to halt a large Norwegian invasion force under Harald III Sigurdsson on the banks of the Derwent River. But it was a victory that had killed his own brother, Tostig, who had joined the rebellion against Harold and whose corpse now lay before him.

Harold had offered Tostig an amnesty if he surrendered, and Tostig had refused, thus sealing his own fate. What more could Harold have done? He had to secure his kingdom, and that is what he had achieved, emphatically. No time for sadness then. Shaking off his sorrow, Harold mounted his horse and headed a march of his loyal warriors to York, there to celebrate the great victory at Stamford Bridge.

But it was in York, a few days later, that he received the news that dashed whatever feelings he had about Stamford Bridge from his soul. For there, on or about

A NINETEENTH-CENTURY
FRENCH DEPICTION OF THE
BATTLE OF HASTINGS, BY
FRANÇOIS HIPPOLYTE DEBON

The Battle of Hastings in 1066 (oil on
canvas), Debon, Francois Hippolyte
(1807–72) / Musee des Beaux-Arts,
Caen, France / Giraudon / The
Bridgeman Art Library International

October 1, 1066, he was brought the news that William, Duke of Normandy, had landed a great invasion force on the south coast of England, posing an even more ominous threat to Harold's rule and his realm.

Harold immediately made haste to retrace his steps to London. Speed had won him one great victory against Harald; now, he was sure, it would give him another over his archrival William. Covering the distance in four or five days—an incredible rate of march—he arrived in London on or about October 6, gathered reinforcements, and, on October 11, set out to march south to the coast through the thick forest of the Weald. Exhausted but determined, Harold and his army emerged from the forest on the night of October 13 and encamped along the ridge of Senlac Hill, about 8 miles (13 km) from the port town of Hastings, astride the Hastings-to-London road.

William was aware of Harold's approach because he had sent out scouts. In the early hours of October 14, he quietly countermarched his men into position at the base of the hill. When dawn broke, the two armies found themselves staring at each other across a gently sloping expanse of ground, over which hovered a ghostly October mist.

The exact numbers of the combatants at the battle of Hastings are still disputed, but each force probably had around six to eight thousand men. At first light, the Anglo-Saxons arrayed themselves into their fearsome shield wall on the crest of the hill, their heavy, semicircular shields interlocked on the ground in front of them, their deadly battle-axes at the ready. Staring down at the Normans, they banged their fists on their shields, crying "Ut! Ut!"—"Out! Out!"—hoping to exorcise these French demons from their homeland.

William held a couple of significant advantages. His men were rested and fresh, whereas Harold's were worn out from marching for days, and may have included many walking wounded from the battle of Stamford Bridge. Furthermore, while the center of the English line was held by a powerful thousand of King Harold's thanes, his loyal nobles, and his housecarls or bodyguards, the flanks were secured by levies, men who had been conscripted to fight and, who, in some cases at least, were armed only with farm implements and piles of stones. In contrast, William's fighting force was, to a man, superbly drilled, well armed, and efficient, especially its heavily armored cavalry, which, according to one historian was then "the most superb fighting force in Europe since the time of Charlemagne" some 250 years earlier. A thundering charge of Norman horse, one contemporary chronicler wrote, "could pierce the walls of Babylon."

These horsemen were now aligned at the bottom of what came to be known as Battle Hill, awaiting word from their king to unleash their fearsome power.

"Rooted to the Soil"

William rode at the center of his lines with his Norman cavalry; to his right and left were his Breton, Flemish, and Bolognese allies. In front of him were the Norman archers and mainly Breton infantrymen. William gave a great shout, and there was a rustling as arrows were fitted on bows, then a sibilant hiss as the archers let loose a shower of arrows. Given that they had to shoot uphill, this was probably ineffective. Then the mainly Breton infantry attacked. They were quickly repulsed, but the Norman commanders noted with interest that the Anglo-Saxon shield wall broke as some overenthusiastic English soldiers chased the retreating Bretons down the hill and had to be regrouped by their commanders.

Next came the first Norman cavalry charge of the day. The Norman infantry lines parted, and the Norman horse charged thunderously up the hill and struck the shield wall on the Saxon right flank. After much carnage, this charge was repelled, as were several more charges that William sent into the Saxon lines over the next several hours. Though bloodied and wavering, the shield wall stood up to the punishment. And this despite the fact that the battle had by now gone on longer than most medieval clashes of the time, and despite the fact that the English soldiers were exhausted from weeks of marching and fighting.

THE MARCHES OF WILLIAM THE CONQUEROR AND KING HAROLD ARE DEPICTED ON THE MAP, AS IS THE DECISIVE LOCATION OF HASTINGS IN SOUTHERN ENGLAND, WHERE HISTORY WAS CHANGED FOREVER IN ONE BATTLE. WILLIAM THE CONQUEROR WAS CROWNED KING OF ENGLAND ON CHRISTMAS DAY IN 1066, AND GRADUALLY, THROUGH INTERMARRIAGE AND IMPOSITION OF NEW LAWS AND CUSTOMS, THE OLD ANGLO-SAXON CULTURE WAS SUPERSEDED BY THE NEW ANGLO-NORMAN MIX.

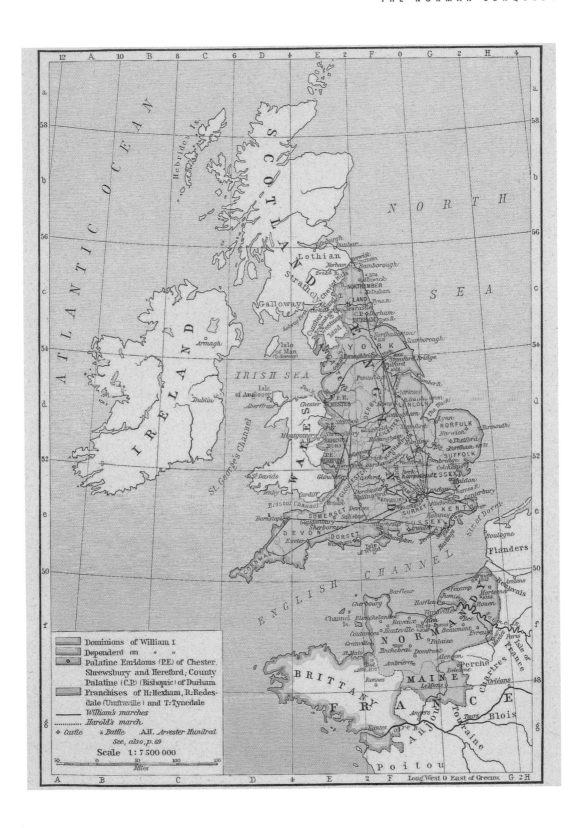

Harold, stationed behind the lines at the center, must have been extraordinarily proud that his men could fend off such a determined adversary. It was the Saxon shield wall at its finest, entrenched and immoveable. William of Poiters, a chronicler who supposedly was an eyewitness to the battle, wrote that "this was a strange kind of battle, one side with all the mobility and the initiative, and the other just resisting as though rooted to the soil."

A Norman Breakthrough

Despite repeated cavalry charges—and no one is sure exactly how many took place—the shield wall held fast for most of the day. As with many clashes of the period, relatively few men were killed or seriously wounded in this early part of the encounter, when the aim was to break the enemy's lines; the slaughter really began during the pursuit of the fleeing foe.

In the afternoon, a wild rumor spread through the French lines that William had been killed. William's death would have caused his troops to abandon the field and put an end to Norman hopes in England; so William took off his helmet and rode in front of the French lines to reassure his men.

Some time after that, he ordered one more cavalry charge. At this point, the Normans, recalling how the English had earlier attempted to pursue retreating French soldiers, decided to adopt the tactic of the feigned retreat. They tried one, which sent a few Saxons running after them, and then another in a different part of the line, and this one produced the breakthrough William had been waiting for. A surge of English soldiers raced down the hill after the retreating French cavalry, only to be cut down and butchered when the horses wheeled on them and caught them, virtually defenseless, on the slope.

The battle changed very quickly after this. The shield wall, seriously broken, closed in protectively around King Harold as more and more of his thanes fell to Norman sword and lance. As evening was coming in, William ordered one last great assault, heralded by a shower of arrows from his archers. The arrows flew through the pale evening sky, arching high over the Saxon lines, as the houses carls ducked beneath their shields. King Harold, who was rallying his troops, looked up into the sky and at that precise moment was pierced through the right eye by an arrow. Some accounts say that he wrenched it out and continued fighting, spurting blood, until he was finally cut down by a Norman knight who had penetrated his weakened circle of guards.

William had won the greatest battle of his life. But it had been a very near thing. Had Harold's men not been exhausted from their previous battle and long marches, had they kept the discipline of their shield wall, the United Kingdom might be a very different country today.

HAROLD II: THE LAST ANGLO-SAXON KING OF ENGLAND

Harold Godwinson, King Harold II, comes down in history as the man who reigned for less than a year before William the Conqueror snatched his kingdom. This makes him seem like a bit of a weakling, but Harold was in fact an able, intelligent, and courageous soldier, who, had he lived, might have made a powerful king.

Harold was born about 1022, the son of Godwine of Wessex, the most influential earl in England. Harold was a formidable military campaigner, a tall man, and a fierce fighter. In 1063, with his brother Tostig, Earl of Northumbria, he had defeated the Welsh under Gruffydd ap Llewellyn, subsequently taking Gruffydd's widow, Ealdgyth, as his wife. But then he fell out with Tostig, forcing him into exile following an uprising in Northumbria.

The year 1066 was a momentous one for Harold and England. After King Edward died in January, Harold was crowned king. But almost immediately he had to fight off the rival claims of Harald III Sigurdsson—backed by his own brother—and William of Normandy. Though Harold responded swiftly and assertively to these threats, he was overwhelmed at Hastings and died on the battlefield.

In death, Harold's face was supposedly so disfigured as to be unrecognizable; tradition has it that his wife, Queen Edith Swan-neck, identified the body by a mark known only to her. Harold's mother offered the dead king's weight in gold if William would release the corpse to her, but the Norman ruler, as a sign of respect, wanted the body to be buried where Harold had died.

A legend subsequently sprang up that Harold had not died at all, but lived on in secret as a hermit—for many in England simply could not accept the fact that their last native king was gone.

WILLIAM I: THE DETERMINED MAN WHO CONQUERED ENGLAND

Until 1066, William the Conqueror, as William I is widely known, labored under a much less grandiose sobriquet, for most of the people in his home region of Normandy knew him as William the Bastard. He was born around 1028, the son of a Norman adventurer known as Robert the Magnificent or Robert the Cruel, who inherited the rule of Normandy after he (or so it was rumored) poisoned his elder brother Richard. The unmarried Robert died of natural causes in 1035, on his way home from a pilgrimage to Jerusalem, leaving seven-year-old William, whose mother was probably the daughter of a tanner, as his sole heir.

William was supported by regents, but naturally enough in the violent and scheming world of the Norman nobility, there were rival claimants to the throne. One by one, William's regents were killed, until, at the age of nineteen, he was forced to escape to a safe refuge offered by King Henry of France. However, in 1047, with Henry's aid, William defeated his rivals at the battle of Val-es-Dunes to become Norman ruler.

There are no authenticated portraits of William, but he was said to be a tall, well-built man with a receding hairline. He married his cousin Matilda of Flanders, a union that was frowned upon by the Church, but that lasted and produced ten children—four boys and six girls.

NORMANS AND ANGLO-SAXONS CLASH IN A SCENE FROM THE BAYEUX TAPESTRY

Bishop Odo Holding a Baton Urges on the Young Soldiers, from The Bayeux Tapestry (wool embroidery on linen), French School, (11th century) / Musee de la Tapisserie, Bayeux, France / With special authorization of the city of Bayeux / The Bridgeman Art Library International

Used to defending himself against enemies from early on—"I was brought up in arms from childhood," he claimed—William became a formidable and courageous adversary. He took an enormous chance invading England when he did, but this was part of the Norman character—to risk all for great rewards.

And England was William's shining reward. Governing the country adroitly, he showed mercy to his new subjects whenever possible, but was extraordinarily brutal when he felt the occasion called for it. He put down a major revolt of northern Anglo-Saxon

lords in 1069–70 with such ferocity—murdering men and boys in and around York—that some historians have termed what is known as "the harrying of York" a genocide.

William died on September 9, 1087, of wounds received ear0lier in the summer at the siege of Mantes, in France. He was buried in St. Stephen's Abbey, in Caen.

THE BAYEUX TAPESTRY CAPTURED A MOMENTOUS HAPPENING

Like The Domesday Book, the Bayeux Tapestry, now preserved in a museum in the town of Bayeux, France, opens a window onto medieval life in England—in this case, life in 1066. Commissioned in the 1070s by Bishop Odo, William's half-brother, to commemorate the conquest, this remarkable work is actually a series of embroidered linen panels made in six sections that were carefully stitched together to form a winding river of chronology, 20 inches (50 cm) wide by 230 feet (70 m) long.

Each panel shows a particular event, but the overall theme is the story of William the Conqueror and King Harold. It begins with Harold, then Earl of Wessex, taking leave of Edward the Confessor, setting sail for Normandy, being imprisoned by another Norman noble, and finally being taken before William, whom Harold then swears he will support. The last part of the tapestry is missing, but it probably would have shown the coronation of William the Conqueror as King of England on December 25, 1066.

With its dramatic events, betrayals, and personality clashes, the story is like a glorious soap opera. Except that it wasn't a soap opera, but a clever piece of propaganda that was put on display, around the nave of the cathedral, on feast days, to show what would happen to a man who broke an oath, as Harold had done: his death by an arrow through the eye is another vivid scene in the tapestry.

Propaganda or not, the tapestry is a gold mine of information for historians of the period: 623 persons have been counted in it, as well as hundreds of animals, 37 buildings, and 47 ships and boats. Brought to life right before our eyes is a vanished world.

8

THE CRUSADES

1095–1291

AN EXTENDED RELIGIOUS WAR FOUGHT BETWEEN CHRISTIAN AND
MUSLIM FORCES FOR POSSESSION OF JERUSALEM AND THE HOLY LAND

THE PIVOTAL STRUGGLE BETWEEN TWO RELIGIONS
FOR THE HOLY LAND

After centuries of Christian control, the city of Jerusalem fell to Islamic forces in 638 and from the late eleventh century it was ruled by the Seljuk Turks. As well as taking control of Syria and Palestine (the next century would see them controlling Egypt, too), the Seljuks struck north into the Byzantine Empire, destroying a Byzantine army in 1071 in what is now Armenia.

In 1095, threatened by the Seljuks from without and by civil war from within, the Byzantine Emperor Alexius I Comnenus sent the West an urgent plea for help. Despite the fact that his Orthodox Christian Church was in open schism with the Roman Catholic Church of Pope Urban II, he begged Urban to help him raise military aid to beat back the Turks. Urban sensed an opportunity. He had heard that Christians were suffering in the Muslims' internal wars and he also wanted the warring knights of Europe to turn their aggression outward, instead of at each other. So in November of 1095, he made a speech at the Council of Clermont in France, exhorting Christians to fight the Muslim threat—not only in Byzantium, however, but throughout the Middle East.

The result was the First Crusade (1095–99). In response to Urban's call, perhaps one hundred thousand people began to move east across Europe in a human wave motivated by a combination of religious hysteria, greed for plunder, and a yearning to ensure salvation—Urban had offered "immediate remission of sins" to all who died in the crusade.

The first wave, made up mainly of peasants—the so-called People's Crusade—reached Constantinople in the summer of 1096, but was soundly defeated by an experienced Seljuk army. But the main crusading force of knights, led by European nobles including Count Robert II of Flanders; Count Stephen of Blois; and Godfrey of Bouillon, the Duke of Lorraine, then made its way, via Constantinople, to the Holy Land. There it allied itself with the former Muslim rulers of Jerusalem, the

Fatimids of Egypt, captured Antioch, and stormed and captured Jerusalem in 1099. Godfrey of Bouillon then governed Jerusalem and created three fiefdoms—Edessa, Tripoli, and Antioch—that, along with Jerusalem, would become known as the Latin or Crusader States.

After the Seljuk Turks under Imad ad-Din Zangi recaptured Edessa in 1144, the Second Crusade (1147–49) was declared. Spearheaded by French and German armies under King Louis VII and the Holy Roman Emperor Conrad III, the Christian forces made an ill-advised attack on Damascus, and were ultimately forced to retreat in disarray. Encouraged by these successes, the great Muslim warrior Saladin took Damascus from the Christians and defeated them decisively at the battle of Hattin in 1187. He then reclaimed most of the Holy Land.

The Third Crusade (1189–92) was urged by Pope Gregory VIII and led by the Holy Roman Emperor Frederick I Barbarossa, King Richard I (the Lionheart) of England, and King Philip II of France. However, Barbarossa drowned while crossing the River Saleph in Anatolia, and Philip left after falling out with Richard, leaving Richard alone at the head of the crusade. But Richard was unable to recapture Jerusalem and was forced to conclude a truce with Saladin and depart.

The Fourth Crusade (1198–1204) was declared by Pope Innocent III, but was diverted to Constantinople when Alexius IV, son of the deposed Byzantine emperor, offered the Crusaders money to help him oust his uncle, the usurper Alexius III Angelus. The Crusaders ended up sacking Constantinople, killing thousands, and establishing the Latin Church in Byzantium. This was against the wishes of the pope and it made reconciliation between the Catholic Church and the Eastern Orthodox Church impossible. And the Crusaders never reached the Holy Land.

Promised support by the Holy Roman Emperor Frederick II, the Catholic Church soon launched the Fifth Crusade (1217–21). The Crusaders attacked Egypt hoping to take control of the eastern Mediterranean and then attack Jerusalem by sea. But Frederick's Christian forces were delayed by an epidemic and the Crusaders, and after taking Damietta and seeking to advance on Cairo, were trapped by Nile floods and forced to accept unfavorable peace terms.

To make amends for his failure to join the Fifth Crusade, Frederick led the Sixth Crusade (1228–29). This was more of a diplomatic mission than a military one; in negotiations with the Egyptian Sultan al-Malik al-Kamil, Frederick obtained control of Jerusalem, Bethlehem, and a stretch of land extending from Jerusalem to the Mediterranean, though the Muslims retained control of Jerusalem's holy sites.

After numerous minor crusades led by various European knights, Jerusalem was captured once again by the Muslims in 1244, prompting King Louis IX to launch the Seventh Crusade (1248–54), which again attacked Egypt but was defeated. Louis then launched the Eighth Crusade in 1270, this time striking at North Africa, but died there of disease, halting his army's advance. The Ninth Crusade (1271–72) was led by Prince Edward of England, who hoped to help King Louis IX, but arrived too late, accomplished nothing, and returned home upon succeeding to the throne as Edward I.

After the fall of Tripoli in 1289 and Acre—the last Christian stronghold—in 1291 to the powerful Mamluks of Egypt and Syria, the Crusades were effectively over.

THE BATTLE THAT ENDED A CENTURY OF CHRISTIAN CONTROL OF JERUSALEM
The Battle of Hattin, 1187

At last the long-awaited opportunity to confront the Christian forces had come. For four years, while he had sought to consolidate his victory over the forces loyal to Nur al-Din and become undisputed lord of Syria and Egypt, Saladin had maintained a series of truces of convenience with the Crusader States. The death of King Baldwin IV of Jerusalem in 1185 and Guy of Lusignan's subsequent seizure of the throne from his rival Raymond of Tripoli had revealed weakness and division in the Christian realm. But Saladin, ever a man of honor, had remained true to his agreements.

Since early 1187, however, one of Guy's most ardent supporters, Reginald of Châtillon, lord of the castles of Kerak and Montreal, had been brazenly attacking Saladin's caravans—a clear breach of the treaties. A demand for redress had brought

THE CRUSADES OF KING RICHARD THE LIONHEART ARE DEPICTED ON THE MAP. MOST HISTORIANS RATE RICHARD A POOR KING—HE SPENT JUST SIX MONTHS OF HIS REIGN IN ENGLAND—BUT A MAGNIFICENT WARRIOR AND MILITARY LEADER. LEGEND HAS IT HE EARNED HIS NICKNAME AFTER SINGLE-HANDEDLY SLAYING A LION IN COMBAT, BUT IT IS MORE LIKELY DERIVED FROM HIS BRAVERY IN BATTLE.

NINE (9) CRUSADES 1095–1272

Guelf, Hohenstaufen and Ascanian domains in Germany about 1176
Guelf   Hohenstaufen   Ascanian
Scale 1:15 000 000
The dark coloring indicates hereditary or imperial domains; light coloring, feudal territories, and border coloring, suzerainty.

an arrogant refusal from Reginald. Saladin's hand was thus forced, and the fate of Reginald and the rest of the Christian armies was sealed.

On April 30, 1187, Saladin sent a large Saracen raiding party to annihilate a group of 150 Knights Templar at the Springs of Cresson, near Nazareth in Judaea. And after this prelude, in July, the new champion of Islam marched into the Holy Land with thirty thousand Saracen warriors, ready to do battle.

The Saracen army first laid siege to the city of Tiberias, a relatively unimportant place—except for the fact that it housed Raymond of Tripoli's wife, Eschiva, while Raymond himself, now rejoined with King Guy to face this threat to the kingdom, was 16 miles (26 km) to the west, at the springs of Saffuriyah, a strong position with ample water. Saladin's move displayed him at his most brilliant: knowing the divisions between the Christian forces, he had deliberately trapped Eschiva, thereby making the issue a personal one. Raymond would have to choose whether to leave with his men and go to his wife's aid. And Guy would have to decide, too: whether to follow his ally or hold fast in a place of safety.

Angry Council

In all, the forces of Guy and Raymond, along with that of Reginald of Châtillon and a small force of Knights Templar, numbered about 1,300 knights and 12,000 infantry. They were vastly outnumbered by Saladin, who now sent elements of his army to Saffuriyah, hoping to tempt the Christians into moving.

On the night of July 2, there was an angry council in the Christian camp—guards and those nearby could hear shouting inside Guy's tent as figures gestured frantically inside, silhouetted by firelight. Raymond of Tripoli was thinking with his head not his heart: his advice was not to move on Tiberias—after all, he could always ransom his wife back—but to stay where there was ample water and a good defensive position and wait for the Islamic forces to wilt in the heat and go back to Egypt. Reginald of Châtillon, in contrast, argued passionately for attack. This was the largest force the Christian kingdom could muster; although they were outnumbered, now was the time to destroy Saladin and win a victory of great prestige for the Christians.

In the end, King Guy—a new ruler who had in the past been accused of moving too cautiously in the face of Saracen aggression—stifled the arguing voices by making a decision. The next day, they would march to Tiberias and lift the siege of the city.

Historians have long been baffled by Guy's plan, for he seems to have been intent on leaving the only source of water for miles around and marching 16 miles (26 km) through blistering heat in one day. In any event, he never got to Tiberias. While he marched at the head of his army—his 1,300 knights forming the core, surrounded by infantry—Saladin's cavalry encircled them and attacked their rearguard as they struggled on the mainly uphill march.

On the evening of July 3, Guy stopped, his army spread out around him, his soldiers parched and exhausted. Even the notoriously tough Templars could not take a step farther. There followed a night of horror for the Franks. They could hear the Muslim forces moving in the dark, occasionally coming in to pick off stragglers—the screams of the doomed Franks sent chills down the spines of those who lay in the dark, waiting. Many of them clustered around a sliver of wood—said to be a splinter from the True Cross—which they had carried with them to ensure their safety.

On July 4, the Saracens waited until the sun had risen high and the heat was ferocious, and then attacked. While there are few accounts of the actual fighting, it appears that the Christian infantry was driven onto a particularly bleak piece of ground: a hill topped with two stony promontories known as the Horns of Hattin. The Saracens set fire to the dry grass that covered the hill, then attacked through the smoke, loosing arrows and shouting war cries. The Christian knights, left at the bottom of the hill without the protection of the infantry, fought ferociously but were cut down, one by one, by the Muslim archers. King Guy led two savage charges trying to break through the Saracen lines but failed, although Raymond managed to escape with perhaps three thousand men.

"Like Stones among Stones"

The aftermath of the battle was terrible. An Arab onlooker wrote, "The plain was covered with prisoners and corpses, disclosed by the dust as it settled and victory became clear. The dead were scattered over the mountains and valleys, lying immobile on their sides, lacerated and disjointed, with heads cracked open, throats split, spines shattered, bones broken, tunics torn off, faces lifeless, wounds gaping, skin flayed … like stones among stones."

Captured by the Saracens, Reginald of Châtillon and King Guy were brought to Saladin's tent. The Muslim ruler asked Reginald how he could justify having broken his treaty; Reginald answered arrogantly that he was a king (in fact, he was only a lord) who had acted as kings always acted. Hearing this, Saladin offered Guy a cup of iced water, which meant, according to the Middle Eastern rules of hospitality, that he could not take his life. Guy drank and offered the cup to Reginald, who also drank, but Saladin told Reginald, "It is not I who have given you the drink," rose, and cut off his head. He then imprisoned Guy, holding him for ransom, and moved up the coast to take Jerusalem, which he recaptured that fall.

Saladin's victory at the Horns of Hattin ended nearly a century of Crusader control of Jerusalem. And although the battle set the scene for the Third Crusade and the legendary confrontation between the armies of Richard I and Saladin, in a sense, after Hattin, the Crusades were already over. Saladin's triumph had ensured Islamic control of the Middle East for centuries to come.

KING RICHARD I: THE LEGENDARY LIONHEART—GREAT LEADER, POOR KING

King Richard I of England lived to be only forty-two years old, but like his counterpart, Saladin, he cast a long shadow down through the ages. Born in 1157, the third son of Henry II and Eleanor of Aquitaine, Richard became heir to the throne after his two elder brothers died. After his coronation, he vowed to keep his father's unfulfilled promise to recapture Jerusalem, and set out on the Third Crusade on July 4, 1190. After the death of Frederick I and the departure from the Holy Land of Philip II, Richard began the campaign that can be said to have created the legend of the Lionheart, leading his men to victory after victory over the Saracens as he marched south toward Jerusalem. For a time, it seemed that nothing could stop him; indeed, many of his men believed that he was ordained by God to become the King of the Holy City. Richard himself was motivated less by piety, it seems, than by a desire for glory and victory, as well as a powerful love of battle. But Richard met his match in Saladin and was eventually forced to sue for peace.

In 1192, having heard that his younger brother John was scheming to take over the throne of England, Richard headed back home. Rough seas forced him to land in Corfu and make passage overland through Central Europe, where he was captured and imprisoned by Leopold V of Austria. Leopold handed him over, as a prisoner, to the Holy Roman Emperor Henry VI, who wanted to use Richard as leverage in a power struggle with England. Finally, Richard was ransomed by his mother, Eleanor, for the astronomical sum of one hundred thousand marks—perhaps two times the annual annual income to the English crown.

KING RICHARD LION-HEART WON MANY BATTLES IN 3RD CRUSADE BUT COULD NOT TAKE BACK THE HOLY LAND

Supposedly, Richard's brother John offered Henry VI half that amount again to keep Richard prisoner until September 1194, but Henry released him in February of that year.

Richard returned to his kingdom in England and, out of political necessity, reconciled with John, although, naturally, he never trusted his brother again. He spent much of his remaining years campaigning in France against Philip II; during one relatively unimportant siege in 1199, he was struck by an arrow and killed.

Most historians rate Richard a poor king—he spent perhaps just six months of his reign in England—but a magnificent warrior and military leader. One of the legends that sprang up around him after the Third Crusade was that he had received his nickname after single-handedly slaying a lion in combat; but, in fact, the name derived from his bravery on the battlefield (though he had once been attacked by a huge wild boar and killed it with his knife). And Richard's enemies rated him highly. A contemporary Muslim historian, Ibn al-Athir, called him "the most remarkable man of his time for his bravery, cunning, activity, and prudence."

SALADIN: THE ISLAMIC HERO WHO UNIFIED THE MUSLIM WORLD AGAINST THE CHRISTIANS

The Muslim ruler whose full name was Salah al-Din Yusuf Ibn Ayyud, but is known to history as Saladin, was born in 1138 to Kurdish military aristocracy—his father was a provincial governor and his uncle was the Kurdish general Shurkuh, the most trusted officer of the Muslim ruler Nur al-Din. After Shurkuh became vizier of Egypt, and then died a few weeks later, the ambitious Saladin took control of the country and subsequently vied with Nur al-Din for mastery of the Middle East. Nur al-Din's death in 1174 saved them from an open power struggle, and Saladin, having unified the forces of Egypt and Syria, turned to face the Crusader States.

It was Saladin's genius to unite the Muslim world behind the idea of a unified jihad, or holy war, against the invaders. Yet while his ultimate goal was the ouster of the Christians, in reality he spent much of his time fighting other Muslims, in particular Nur al-Din's followers and family in Syria, which in turn led him to make temporary truces with the Christians. It was the breaking of one such truce, by Reginald of Châtillon, the principal general and advisor to King Baldwin IV (the king of Jerusalem who was, famously, afflicted with leprosy), that prompted Saladin to finally confront the Christian armies in 1187. By then ready, as one contemporary Islamic historian put it, "to bring Christian death to the blue-eyed enemy," he won a decisive victory at the battle of Hattin and went on to recapture most of the Holy Land.

Saladin's strategy against Richard I during the Third Crusade further confirmed his military genius. Having suffered one defeat at the battle of Arsuf in 1191, Saladin cleverly withdrew his forces into the Judaean hills. As Richard's army moved toward Jerusalem,

Saladin burnt crops and dammed the springs that ran down to the coast. Eventually, Richard ran out of supplies and was forced to withdraw.

Despite this deadly rivalry, and Saladin's reputation for ruthlessness and his fierce adherence to the notion of a holy war, the Muslim leader displayed great courtesy toward Richard during their struggle. When Richard's steed was killed, Saladin sent him another; when Richard was ill with a fever, Saladin sent him snow from the mountains to cool his brow. Partly as a result of this, Christians became so enamored of Saladin that legends were invented around him—for example, that he had secretly allowed himself to be knighted by Richard I and that he had had an affair with the Queen of France.

Five months after reaching a truce with Richard, in March 1193, Saladin died of illness in Damascus. Interestingly, because he was a Kurd from Iraq who had fought the ruling Seljuk family, many Muslim historians continued to see him as a usurper. His reputation did not fare well with them until the twentieth century, when he was reassessed as a jihad hero who had turned back the West.

THE FIERCE WARRIOR MONKS WHO TERRIFIED ISLAM

As the Crusades wore on, two unique Christian military orders arose: the Knights Templars and Knights Hospitallers, fighting men who were also monks. Both began in Jerusalem as religious brotherhoods that cared for pilgrims. The Hospitallers were based in a hospice near a Catholic abbey, the Templars in a house near a structure that was thought to be Solomon's Temple. The Templars were knights, as well as religious brothers, who patrolled the roads near Jerusalem to keep pilgrims safe; but by the 1130s, they had become fighting men first, religious second. With the continuing Islamic threat, the Hospitallers morphed into militant fighters about twenty years later.

Both orders accepted knights from all over Europe who sought salvation, and the orders grew rich with donations, so that their holdings soon extended across the Holy Land. Individual knights, however, lived a simple and austere existence as befitting "warrior monks."

In Jerusalem, the two orders together totaled perhaps just six hundred knights at any given time, but these were fierce fighters who were feared far and wide in the Muslim world. After the battle of Hattin, Saladin supposedly said, "I shall purify the land of these two impure races!" and ordered the execution of all his Hospitaller and Templar prisoners.

The two knightly orders lived on, however, and were the last Crusader forces manning Acre before it fell in 1291. Later, the Hospitallers settled in Rhodes, then Malta, where they built the capital Valletta; ousted by Napoleon, they shifted to Rome, where the order of the Knights of Malta still exists. The Templars, however, were forcibly disbanded in the early fourteenth century by King Philip IV of France, who feared their power and desired their property.

THE STEALTHY ASSASSINS WHO BROUGHT FEAR TO FRIEND AND FOE ALIKE

From the early twelfth century, both Muslim and Christian forces were terrorized by a radical Islamic sect known as the Assassins. Shiite Muslims who followed the teachings of a grand master, or iman, called Hasan-e Sabbah, the Assassins spread across Persia in the eleventh century and occupied fortresses in northern Syria in the early twelfth century. There, a Syrian grand master known as the Old Man of the Mountain ruled the Assassins from the fortress of Masyaf.

While the Assassins' exact religious beliefs are not known, it was their desire that everyone follow their iman; they set out to kill anyone who refused. Normally they achieved this not by fighting in groups on a battlefield, but by murdering the leaders of their rivals; and they were masters of stealth, disguise, and poisons. They even got close to Saladin, who was almost always well guarded—one morning in 1175, he awoke in his tent to discover a poisoned dagger beside him on his pillow, a grisly Assassin warning of imminent death.

But Saladin lived on, probably because he paid off the Assassins. Most Crusader leaders did the same thing. The only Europeans who refused were the Templars and Hospitallers. But they had such a fearsome reputation themselves that it was rumored that the Assassins bought them off with a yearly tribute. Later, after being conquered by the Mongols after they had tried to kill Khan Möngke, the Assassins were suppressed by the ruling Mamluks.

Supposedly, the Assassins performed their killings while high on hashish, from which word the name "assassin" derives—a name that the Crusaders, who were terrified of these fanatical men, first brought into popular usage.

9

THE MONGOL CONQUESTS

1206–81 AD

A HALF-CENTURY OF SPECTACULAR VICTORIES ACROSS ASIA,
WHICH CREATED A VAST EMPIRE SPANNING THE ENTIRE CONTINENT

THE MONGOLS SWEPT THROUGH ASIA—AND NEARLY CONQUERED THE KNOWN WORLD

Before the birth of Temujin, later known as Genghis Khan, in 1162, the Mongols were a disparate group of warring tribes. They lived a nomadic, herding existence on the Central Asian plateau, an area some 3,000–5,000 feet (900–1,500 m) high that encompasses the northern plain of Outer Mongolia, the Gobi Desert, and the vast steppes of Inner Mongolia. After conquering and uniting the tribes around him and being named Genghis Khan (Great Leader) in 1206, the ambitious and ruthless Temujin set about conquering China, then ruled by the Jin dynasty. China was a traditional enemy—the Great Wall had been built in part to keep the Mongols out—but it had never experienced such an organized Mongol attack, and the northern part of the country fell in 1210 (though it would take until 1234 to force the total capitulation of the Jin).

In 1217, Genghis Khan ordered the invasion of the Muslim country of Khwarezm, which covered much of Persia, Afghanistan, and eastern India. Millions were killed in a three-year campaign, and the country became a Mongol possession.

In 1220, Genghis Khan sent out his top commanders, Subotai and Jebe, along with thirty thousand men, on a "reconnaissance in force" into Eastern Europe. They entered Armenia and Georgia, defeated the Christian King George IV and his army of ten thousand knights, then headed north, overcoming the Kipchak Turks on the Volga steppes and the Bulgars on the Upper Volga. In a battle near the Kalka River, they destroyed an eighty-thousand-man force sent out by the Prince of Kiev to meet them.

Genghis Khan died in 1227 and bequeathed his kingdom to Ögödei, the third of his four sons. Ögödei continued Mongol expansion in China, subjugated Korea, and moved into eastern Persia in preparation for a campaign against the Muslim Middle East.

In 1236, Ögödei sent Subotai and a Mongol force west. They first tore a swathe through Russia, destroying Moscow and Kiev by 1240. Then they defeated Hungarian and Polish forces arrayed against them at the battles of Mohi and Liegnitz in 1241, at which point Europe lay open for the taking. But then Ögödei died unexpectedly, and

GENGHIS KHAN LEADS HIS
TROOPS INTO BATTLE, IN THIS
FOURTEENTH-CENTURY PERSIAN
ILLUSTRATION.

Genghis Khan (c.1162-1227) in Battle,
from a book by Rashid-al-Din (1247–
1318) (gouache), Persian School, (14th
century) / Bibliotheque Nationale,
Paris, France / The Bridgeman Art
Library International

Mongol forces, by custom, were forced to return and elect a new khan. This turned out to be Ögödei's son Güyük, who would be replaced by his cousin, Möngke, in 1251.

Under Möngke, the Mongols pursued their campaign of expansion. Möngke's brother Kublai conquered much of southern China, while another brother, Hülegü, conquered much of Syria and Persia, destroying the Assassins sect and ravaging Baghad, Aleppo, and Damascus. In 1259, a three-hundred-thousand-man force of Mongols under Hülegü was poised to invade Egypt, which would have opened the door to North Africa and expansion into Europe through Spain, but Möngke died and, once again, the Mongol forces were obliged to return to Mongolia elect a new khan. Hülegü left a force of twenty thousand behind to await his return; but this force was annihilated by the Mamluk soldiers of Egypt at the battle of Ain Jalut, and the Mongols were never again able to gain a foothold in the Middle East.

However, as a result of a series of conquests, Kublai Khan managed to finally conquer the old Sung dynasty of China by 1279, establishing the Yüan dynasty. Kublai's Mongol forces even made modestly successful expansions into Burma and Vietnam. But two invasions of Japan staged from Korea in 1280 and 1281 failed when typhoons destroyed Mongol ships, costing more than one hundred thousand lives.

In the late thirteenth century, the Mongols continued to dominate western and central Asia. However, the empire split into separate provinces, known as khanates and ruled by descendants of the Great Khan. By the 1350s, with the Mongols showing more inclination for warfare than governing, these provinces fell into a state of near dissolution and eventually formed separate states: the Il-Khanate, which covered modern-day Iran; the Chagatai Khanate in Central Asia; the Yüan dynasty in China; and the Golden Horde in what is now central and western Russia.

THE BATTLE THAT STOPPED THE MONGOLS FROM CONQUERING EUROPE
The Battle of Ain Jalut, 1260

In the mid-thirteenth century, not far from the town of Nazareth, in Judaea, was a fresh-water spring that satisfied the thirst of weary travelers on their way to and from the sacred sites of the region, including Bethlehem and Jerusalem. The Arab name for the place was Wadi Ain Jalut, which means "the Spring of Goliath," because this was supposedly the place where David slew Goliath. In fact, numerous historic battles had occurred here, because the flat, 3-mile (5-km)-wide plain and the abundance of water made it an obvious meeting point for conflicting armies. In the twelfth century, it had been the site of at least two skirmishes between the Islamic forces of Saladin and the Crusader armies. And in September of 1260, during the Muslim holy month of Ramadan, Ain Jalut was to become the scene of one of the most momentous encounters of all: an epic battle between the invading Mongols and the Mamluk rulers of the Middle East, which would determine the future not just of the region, but of the known world.

In the spring of 1260, Sultan al Muzaffar Sayf ad-Din Qutuz, the Mamluk slave-warrior who had recently overthrown the young ruler of Cairo to become Sultan of Egypt was visited by four emissaries of the Mongol khan Hülegü, grandson of Genghis Khan, who was in command of the Mongol forces then marauding through the Middle East. They read him a note from Hülegü, a note that was couched in the kind of language that had already made strong rulers quiver throughout Asia, the Middle East, and Europe:

You should think of what happened to other countries … and submit to us. Where will you flee? What road will you use to escape us? Our horses are swift, our arrows sharp, our swords like thunderbolts, our hearts hard as mountains … Your prayers to God will not avail against us. We will shatter your mosques and reveal the weakness of your God, and then we will kill your children and your old men together.

Having heard them out, Qutuz asked for the note and examined it for a moment. Then, courteously, he asked the Mongols for some time alone with his advisors. In a

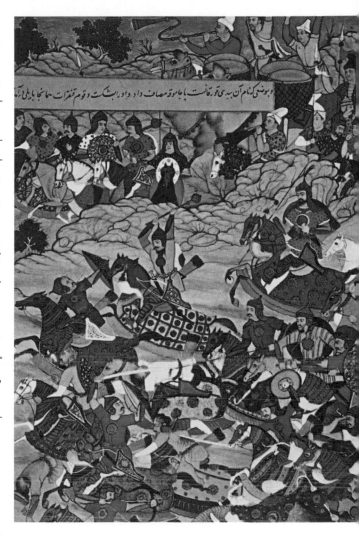

private room, he met with several of his principal Mamluk lieutenants, all of whom begged him to send back a message to Hülegü capitulating without reservation. For these men knew well the extraordinary power of the Mongols.

With an army numbering around three hundred thousand men, Hülegü had been advancing across the Middle East since 1253, when his cousin, the Great Khan Möngke, had ordered him to take an invasion force "as far as the borders of Egypt." In Persia, in 1256, he had destroyed the castles of the dreaded Assassin sect, one of whose members had tried to assassinate Möngke. Then he had razed Baghdad, massacring its entire population except for the Christians (whom the Mongols had realized might be a valuable ally against the Mamluks)—an event that had a profound effect on the Muslims of the Middle East, for while Egypt had become the center of Muslim political power, Baghdad had remained the spiritual and intellectual heart of Islam.

Mongol forces had then crossed the Tigris and Euphrates rivers and staged a bloody assault on the city of Aleppo in January of 1260. Damascus had then surrendered, and Hülegü had marched triumphantly into the city—accompanied by Bohemond VI, the Crusader Prince of Antioch, who was convinced the Mongols would convert to Christianity, submit to the pope, and help Europe destroy Islam.

It was from Damascus that Hülegü had sent his terrifying missive to Qutuz.

TREMENDOUSLY SKILLED RIDERS, THE MONGOLS USED RAPID CAVALRY CHARGES TO OVERWHELM OPPONENTS.
The Bridgeman Art Library International

A Forceful Response

After listening to his panicky advisors for a few hours, Qutuz made up his mind. He strode back into his throne room, where the Mongol ambassadors waited, and smiled at them. Next he ordered his guards to take the ambassadors out into the courtyard and cut off their heads, which he then placed on pikes above the city's main gates.

Killing a Mongol ambassador was the worst possible insult to the Mongol throne—one that could see the perpetrators erased from the face of the earth. But

Qutuz had grown up as a slave, and he had resolved that he would die a free man before living as a Mongol vassal.

Qutuz began strengthening the defenses of Cairo, preparing the city and its inhabitants to defend themselves to the death. But then extraordinary news came: the Great Khan Möngke had died and Hülegü had withdrawn the bulk of his forces in order to return to Asia and claim the throne. Hülegü intended to return, finish off Egypt, and personally decapitate Qutuz; but, for the time being, he had left behind his chief lieutenant, Kitbuga, in charge of a holding force of about twenty thousand handpicked warriors.

Immediately, Qutuz saw that he had a chance to strike.

Gathering an army of about 120,000 and enlisting the aid of his arch-rival, a Mamluk warrior called Baybars, Qutuz marched northeast from Egypt as Kitbuga headed south. The two forces converged in early September, at Ain Jalut. Qutuz arrived just ahead of the Mongols and sent his cavalry units into the hills that overlooked the plains. Then he instructed Baybars to advance with a large part of the Egyptian force.

On the other side of the plains, Kitbuga carefully observed the Egyptians approaching. An interesting figure, Kitbuga was a Turk and a Christian convert who believed he was a direct descendant of one of the three magi, or holy men, who had brought gifts to the infant Jesus. He had operated as Hülegü's liaison with the Crusader community, which nervously awaited the outcome of this encounter at its last remaining stronghold, Acre.

Kitbuga watched the Mamluk cavalry thunder forward, trailing a huge cloud of dust, and heard the sounds of the Mamluk yells and trumpets. The arrogance of these Muslim fighters offended him, both as a Mongol warrior and as a Christian. Ignoring the fact that he was outnumbered, he ordered his men to charge straight ahead, leading them into battle himself.

The two forces struck at each other with a murderous clash, the Mongols shooting a steady stream of arrows and the Mamluks swinging their glistening curved scimitars. After a bloody half-hour of fighting, Baybars gave the order for the Mamluk cavalry to retreat and they turned tail and fled back across the plain.

A Taste of Their Own Medicine

Kitbuga, thinking that the entire Mamluk army was retreating, ordered his forces to follow, and they chased the Egyptians all the way to the springs themselves. There, Baybars suddenly ordered his men to wheel about and charge back at the Mongols. At the same time, Qutuz, positioned in the surrounding hills, sent his cavalry down on Kitbuga's men on either side, trapping them.

Kitbuga had fallen for a trick right out of the Mongol playbook—the feigned retreat. Even so, as fiercely proud as any Mongol warrior, he refused to give up.

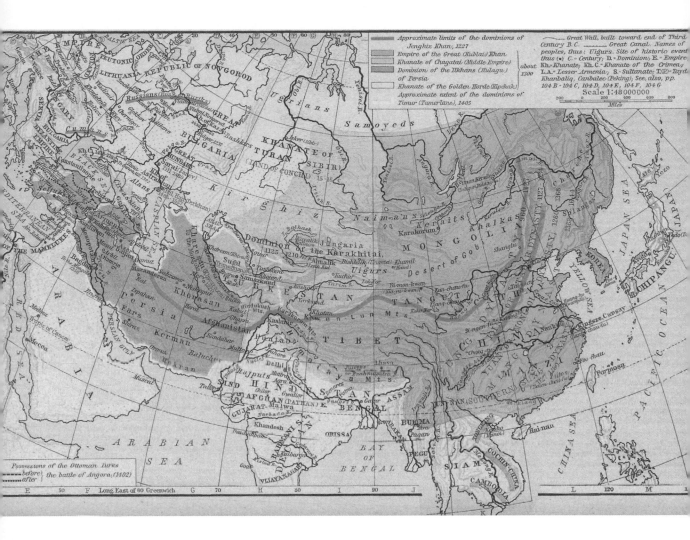

Marshaling his men, he ordered a charge at the Mamluk left wing, which, in the desperate fighting that ensued, began to waver.

At this point, Qutuz rode out in front of his men, tore off his helmet so that they could see his face, and cried out, "O Muslims! O Muslims! O Muslims!"—a phrase with which he has been associated ever since in Islamic history. He then led a countercharge that finally scattered the Mongols.

Kitbuga was captured, brought in front of Qutuz, and beheaded. The rest of the Mongols fled eastward, across Syria and across the Euphrates. Days later, Qutuz liberated Damascus and the other captive Syrian cities.

Although Qutuz was later murdered by Baybars, his victory was an extraordinary one. One seldom sees Ain Jalut mentioned in Western history books, but some

THE MONGOL EMPIRE FROM 1227–1405, SHOWN ON THE MAP, COVERED ALMOST ONE-SIXTH OF THE EARTH'S LAND MASS, FROM EASTERN EUROPE TO THE EASTERN SHORE OF ASIA. THE EMPIRE ENCOMPASSED ABOUT 110 MILLION PEOPLE, SURPASSED ONLY IN OVERALL SIZE AND REACH BY THE BRITISH EMPIRE.

historians think the battle is every bit as important as Thermopylae or Poitiers. For had the Mongols been able to conquer Egypt, they would easily have swept through North Africa and from there into Spain, and would most likely have taken Europe, too. Qutuz's victory not only prevented this, but also shattered the myth of Mongol invincibility—and the Mongols' self-belief. After Ain Jalut, they made only a few small invasions into Syria, and never again threatened the Mamluks, who would continue to rule Egypt until the eighteenth century.

GENGHIS KHAN: THE GREAT RULER WHO CHANGED THE COURSE OF WORLD HISTORY

When a child named Temujin was born to a family of nomads in 1162—according to legend, clutching a blood clot in his tiny fist—the Mongols numbered perhaps two million, and were divided into countless clans, each with its own khan, or leader, that fought continuously. About sixty years before Temujin's birth, his ancestor Kubal Khan attempted to unite these tribes, but his confederation fell apart after its army was defeated by the Chinese.

When Temujin was nine, his father was killed by rivals, and Temujin and his family were forced to wander in the wilderness. But Temujin grew into a strong, charismatic, and ambitious young man who was able to vanquish his enemies ruthlessly and rally other clans to his banner. By 1206, he had conquered all the tribes of Central Asia—the Naimans, Merkits, and Tatars—and been named Genghis Khan or "Great Ruler."

It was at this point that Genghis Khan then set out on a campaign of global conquest, attacking China, Khwarezm, Russia, and eastern Europe in succession. Genghis Khan and his Mongols soon gained a reputation for being almost supernatural, seeming to appear out of nowhere in front of the gates of any city. Mercy might be given to those who surrendered immediately, but woe betide any rulers or peoples who defied them, for they were usually decimated.

Genghis Khan said himself that "the greatest joy a man can have is victory," and he probably believed that it was his divine destiny to fulfill the unrealized ambitions of his ancestor Kubal Khan. Yet Genghis Khan was a fairly modest person who lived in a nomad's ger, or round hut; preferred to spend time with the people of his immediate clan; shunned titles; and showed an interest in creating laws to govern and benefit his subjects. And although he demanded total temporal loyalty from conquered peoples, he was tolerant of other religions and customs. He himself took more than five hundred wives and was a father many times over; indeed, scientists estimate that his DNA is carried by some sixteen million people living today.

In 1227, the Great Khan, nearly seventy years of age, died of natural causes. His body was taken to a secret location in his Mongolian homeland, where it was buried without markers. The Mongols believed that after a man's death his body should be left undisturbed, so an area of several hundred square miles around the grave was marked off and guarded by specially trained warriors. For centuries afterward, no one was allowed to enter this area of the Ikh Khorig, or "Great Taboo." Even in the twentieth century, the Soviet Union restricted access to the area, to prevent nationalists using it as a rallying point. Such was the lasting power of the Great Khan.

A MAMLUK HORSEMAN IS SHOWN IN THIS NINETEENTH CENTURY ARTWORK BY ROBERT BOWYER, AN ENGLISH BOOKSELLER, PUBLISHER, AND PRINTER.

A Mameluke Exercising, published by R Bowyer, 1802 / Private Collection / Photo © Bonhams, London, UK / The Bridgeman Art Library International

THE MAMLUKS—THE ONLY WARRIORS WHO COULD MATCH THE MUSLIMS IN FEROCITY

The term mamluk is Turkic for "owned" and was originally applied to boys from Central Asian tribes who were enslaved and bought by the caliphs of Syria and Egypt to be raised as soldiers. When Saladin toppled the Fatimid dynasty in 1174 and supplanted it with the Ayyubid reign, he replaced the often-unreliable African infantry used by the Fatimids with a corps of Mamluk warriors, whom he dressed in distinctive, bright-yellow uniforms. His successors kept up the practice, until eventually these warriors did all the fighting for Egypt and Syria. Not surprisingly, the Mamluks grew more powerful until, not long before the Mongols marched on Egypt, the Mamluk leader Qutuz deposed a weak fifteen-year-old Ayyubid sultan and became head of Egypt himself.

The Mamluks who fought the Mongols in 1260 were mainly members of the Turkish Kipchak tribe who had been sold into slavery by Mongol slave traders; converted to Sunni Islam; and taught to speak, read, and write Arabic. Typically, the Mamluk was utterly devoted to his master, whom he addressed as "father," and whose life he placed before his own. In return, masters treated Mamluks less like slaves and more like members of their families.

The Mamluks were honed, and honed themselves, into superior fighters. They were provided with manuals covering everything from archery, spear-play, and battle tactics, to horsemanship, the use of chemicals to spread poisonous fire, and the best ways to treat wounds—even what magic spells to cast on the enemy, when all else failed. Fearsome swordsmen, they strengthened their arms through such exercises as slicing through lead bars or heaps of clay, sometimes hundreds of times a day, using a special, heavyweight sword.

Perfectly disciplined and living, as a contemporary wrote, "only for raiding, hunting, horsemanship … taking booty, and invading other countries," the Mamluks in many ways mirrored the Mongols—which may be why they were ultimately able to defeat them.

THE EXTRAORDINARY SECRET HISTORY OF THE MONGOLS

The sole source of information on the early life of Genghis Khan is The Secret History of the Mongols, written perhaps twenty years after his death and considered by scholars to be part epic poem, part creation myth, part richly detailed history.

The Secret History was written in the Uighur script, which the Mongols had adopted from the Turks, although the only copies that survive appear to be transliterations by Chinese scholars of the Ming Dynasty. The Secret History starts long before Genghis Khan was born, with the creation myths of the Mongol people: "At the beginning there was a blue-grey wolf born with his Destiny ordained by Heaven Above." But it also captures extraordinary scenes from the Great Khan's life, such as the moment in 1206 when three of the greatest chieftains of the Mongols paid obeisance to him as Great Khan:

A general council of all the chieftains was called, and the three most notable men among them, Prince Altan, Khuchar, and Sacha Beki, came forward. They addressed Temujin formally, in the following manner:

We will make you khan; you shall ride at our head, against our foes. We will throw ourselves like lightning on your enemies. We will bring you their finest women and girls, their rich tents like palaces. From all the peoples and nations we will bring you the fair girls and the high-stepping horses. When you hunt wild beasts, we will drive them toward you; we will encircle them, pressing hard at their heels. If on the day of battle we disobey you, take our flocks from us, our women and children, and cast our worthless heads on the steppe. If in times of peace we disobey you, part us from our men and our servants, our wives and our sons. Abandon us and cast us out, masterless, on the forsaken earth …

10

THE HUNDRED YEARS' WAR

1337–1453

A SERIES OF WARS FOUGHT BETWEEN FRANCE AND ENGLAND
OVER THE COURSE OF MORE THAN A CENTURY, WHICH SIGNALED
THE END OF THE MIDDLE AGES

GENERATIONS OF CONFLICT BETWEEN FRANCE AND ENGLAND USHER IN A NEW ERA IN HISTORY

The Hundred Years' War was not given that name until the nineteenth century, and in fact, these wars lasted one hundred sixteen years. But it is an appropriate enough title for the long-drawn-out series of conflicts that took place between France and England from 1337 to 1453. The war was fought essentially for dynastic reasons: to determine which royal family would control France. Ever since the Norman Conquest, the English royals had retained extensive lands in France and increasingly this became a bone of contention. When the French King Charles IV died in 1328, the English King Edward IV, grandson of former French King Philip IV and ruler of the duchy of Guyenne—in the region of Aquitaine in southwestern France—laid claim to the French throne. However, a French assembly gave the crown to the rival French claimant, Philip, Count of Valois. Subsequently crowned Philip VI, he declared Guyenne confiscate in 1337, triggering hostilities.

Historians traditionally divide the war into four phases. In the first phase (1337–60), the English were surprisingly successful, given that their country was poorer and less populous than France, they were fighting abroad, and their forces were smaller than their enemy's. In part, this success was due to the English men-at-arms, who were particularly well disciplined and were accompanied by longbowmen, whose fearsome fire-power helped make up for their army's lack of numbers.

France also had a larger navy, but at sea, too, the English triumphed initially, winning a great naval victory at Sluys in 1340 that neutralized the French fleet for the remainder of the war. In 1346, Edward scored another major victory at the battle of Crécy, and in 1347 he captured the port of Calais. At this point, a truce was arranged with the help of the pope, both armies by then war-weary and affected by bubonic plague. Three years later, however, Philip died, to be succeeded by John II. In 1356, Edward's son, Edward Woodstock, known to history as the Black Prince

launched an attack on France, reigniting the conflict. Within the year, he defeated King John II at Poitiers and took him hostage, forcing the French to sue for peace. The Treaty of Brétigny of 1360 obliged the French to pay three million gold crowns to the English—John II's ransom—and gave England control of nearly half of France. In return, Edward renounced his claim to the French throne.

However, John died in captivity before the terms of the treaty were fulfilled, and his son and successor Charles V soon reopened hostilities, beginning the second phase of the war (1369–99). At last providing France with effective leadership, Charles first invaded Aquitaine, whose inhabitants were being heavily taxed by the Black Prince. Then, under the brilliant general Bertrand du Guesclin, the French took Poitiers, Poitou, and La Rochelle by 1372, and Aquitaine and Brittany by

THE BATTLE OF NÁJERA, 1367, TOOK PLACE IN NORTHERN SPAIN BETWEEN ENGLAND AND FRANCE AND THEIR RESPECTIVE SPANISH ALLIES.

Battle of Najera, 1367, from Froissart's Chronicle (vellum), French School, (15th century) / Bibliotheque Nationale, Paris, France / The Bridgeman Art Library International

1374, thus regaining all of the land ceded under the Treaty of Brétigny and leaving England with only Gascony and Calais. The Black Prince died in 1376, Edward III in the following year, and the second phase of the war became almost entirely a French victory. But then Charles died of a heart attack in 1380 and the conflict petered out. The Truce of Leulinghen of 1389 allowed the two sides to recover and regroup.

The third phase of the war (1399–1429) has been compared to a "cold war" by some historians, for following the 1399 deposition of the unpopular Richard II in England, who had succeeded Edward III, and the French King Charles VI's descent into madness around the same time, factions on both sides began trying to undermine the other country. And even though the Truce of Leulinghen officially remained in place, English raids resumed during the short reign of Henry IV (1399–1413). In 1415, Henry V captured the port of Harfleur, then won a great and famous victory at Agincourt; by 1419, he had conquered all of Normandy. The Treaty of Troyes of 1420 made Henry heir and regent of France. But in 1422, before he could assume the throne, he died (just a few weeks before Charles), leaving John, Duke of Bedford, to rule as regent for his six-year-old son, Henry VI. The new English king was recognized as King of France north of the Loire River. South of the Loire, however, the French population continued to support Charles VI's son, Charles, who initially remained uncrowned, with the title of dauphin, or heir. So English forces laid siege to the dauphin's stronghold of Orléans in 1428 in an attempt to gain control of the rest of France.

The fourth phase of the war began in 1429, when the charismatic Joan of Arc rallied French forces to lift the siege. The dauphin was crowned Charles VII at Reims in the same year, and the French then achieved a series of victories, liberating Paris and the Ile-de-France (1445–48), Normandy in 1450, and Aquitaine in 1453, and crushing a major English force at the battle of Castillon, also in 1453. No formal peace treaty ended hostilities between the two countries: England simply recognized that France was now too strong to attack successfully.

By the end of the war, the English government was nearly bankrupt. A series of civil wars ensued in England, fought between rival claimants to the throne and known as the Wars of the Roses. Of their lands in France, the English retained only Calais, which they were forced to relinquish in 1558. Despite the defeat, successive English monarchs referred to themselves as the King or Queen of France until 1802. The French, though victorious, bore the scars of English depredations, and the resulting resentment and enmity between the two countries lasted for centuries.

ONE WOMAN SAVES A BESIEGED CITY—AND CHANGES THE OUTCOME OF A WAR

The Siege of Orléans, 1428-29

To the besieged French looking down from the walls of the city of Orléans on that bright, cold spring day of April 29, 1429, the woman astride the white charger must have seemed like an apparition. Tiny and black-haired, she was dressed in a suit of shining white enamel armor made especially for her, and she held aloft her pennon, a narrow banner of blue and white emblazoned with two angels and a single word: Jesus.

Following behind Joan of Arc—as we know her today, although the French at the time called her "the Maid," or la Pucelle, the Virgin— was a processional force of some two hundred lancers. And encamped outside the walls of the city were

JOAN OF ARC (C 1864), BY DANTE GABRIEL ROSSETTI. THE MAID, AS SHE WAS KNOWN TO THE FRENCH, BECAME A NEAR-MYTHICAL FIGURE IN EUROPEAN HISTORY.

Joan of Arc, 1882 (oil on panel), Rossetti, Dante Charles Gabriel (1828–82) / Fitzwilliam Museum, University of Cambridge, UK / The Bridgeman Art Library International

another five thousand men, who had followed Joan across France in order to save the city of Orléans—and the entire country—from the English.

The Maid was the strangest commander these men had ever had. She attacked the prostitutes who followed the army with the flat of her sword, forbade the men to swear, and wore her heavy armor at all times, to the amazement of at least one knight: "She bears the weight and burden of her armor incredibly well, to such a point that she has remained fully armed for six days and nights."

And magic seemed to follow the Maid. At the town of Ferbois, along the army's route, a town she had never before entered, she ordered the clergy at St. Catherine's Church to dig up a stone at the rear of the altar. They would find a sword there, she told them. And they did, a rusting relic of some bygone century. The soldiers were astonished, although those who knew Joan a little better understood that St. Catherine was one of the trio of saints who spoke to her almost daily.

When Joan of Arc entered Orléans with her lancers on that evening in April, a huge crowd of men, women, and children gathered, carrying torches, shouting and laughing. For, as one chronicler wrote, "they felt themselves already comforted and as if no longer besieged, by the divine virtue which they were told was in this simple maid."

The Last Stronghold

Joan of Arc had arrived on the scene at one of the most critical junctures of the Hundred Years' War. Responding to the refusal of the French population south of the Loire River to accept the rule of their young king, Henry VI, English forces, under the Duke of Bedford and his field commander, the Earl of Salisbury, had begun a major southward offensive in 1422. Routing the French as they went, they advanced steadily and by 1428 were on the brink of victory.

In October, Bedford sent Salisbury, at the head of five thousand men, to capture the city of Orléans, on the north bank of the Loire. This city controlled the chief passage to this important waterway and was the last stronghold of the French forces loyal to the dauphin.

Despite their previous victories, the English had no assurances of conquering Orléans. The city was formidable. Situated on the north bank of the river, it was surrounded by walls 30 feet (9 m) high surmounted by at least seventy cannons, some of which shot stones weighing 200 pounds (90 kg). Inside were 2,500 troops and 3,000 militia—a force that outnumbered the English because Salisbury had lost at least 1,000 of his men through desertion on the way to Orléans.

Salisbury could not possibly blockade Orléans or even surround it, given his small force. So, he set up a strong infantry position on the south bank of the river and fortified the gatehouse known as Les Tourelles at a bridge leading to the city. On the north bank, east and west along the river, he placed a semicircle of six stockades.

In mid-October English gunners sent cannon shots into the streets, scattering its inhabitants. The battle was on. And if Orléans fell, France would fall, too.

There then ensued one of the strangest sieges of the war, a haphazard and oddly leisurely affair for both sides. Soon after it began, Salisbury was killed by a lucky French cannon shot and replaced by the Earl of Suffolk. Far less aggressive than Salisbury, he took most of his troops into winter quarters, leaving only a small force at Les Tourelles. Suffolk's superiors then forced him to bring his men back and create a network of sixty breastworks, topped by palisades and connected by communications trenches. But Suffolk left a wide gap in the defenses to the northeast, through which the French could receive supplies. He also neglected to block river traffic, and thus troops and supplies could move into Orléans by boat almost at will.

As a result, the defenders of the city, well fed and feeling no particular urgency to either attack or escape, simply bided their time. And the English did much the same. On Christmas Day, a truce was called from 9 a.m. to 3 p.m., and French musicians came through the gates of Orléans to play music for the English troops.

After her arrival, Joan, having rested a night and prayed at the cathedral, tried to convince the commander of the garrison, the Comte de Dunois, otherwise known as the Bastard of Orléans, that he should foray out to attack the English. Dunois, still mistrustful of this strange and charismatic young woman, refused, and instead set out to seek reinforcements. After he left, Joan—trying to raise the spirits of the French garrison—rode out to within shouting distance of the English forces. She was enraged because she had earlier sent the English a note carried by her herald, Guyenne, whom the English had taken prisoner, in contravention of the knightly code of conduct, and were now threatening to burn at the stake, on the basis that he was a familiar of the "witch," Joan.

A FIFTEENTH-CENTURY FRENCH ILLUSTRATION OF THE SIEGE OF ORLÉANS. FRANCE'S SUCCESSFUL DEFENSE OF THE CITY GAVE IT A HUGE MILITARY AND PSYCHOLOGICAL BOOST.

The Bridgeman Art Library International

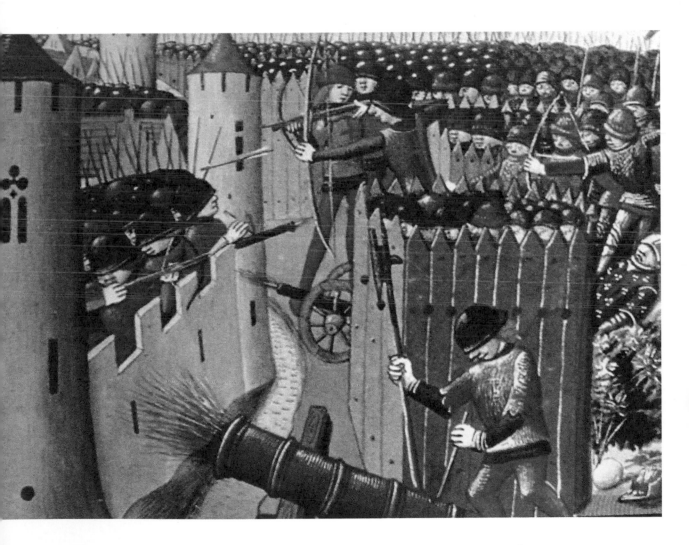

When Joan shouted at the English to surrender, they merely laughed at her, calling her a "cow-girl" (even though Joan had herded sheep, not cows) and the French who were with her "pimps." They threatened to have her burned when they caught her.

When Dunois returned on May 4 with reinforcements, Joan "sprang to her horse," as one of the knights present said, and galloped to meet him outside the city. Finally they could attack the English, she urged Dunois. When he would still not lead a large-scale attack against the enemy, Joan went to her chambers to take a nap, but after a short time awoke and told her aide, "In God's name, my counsel has told me to go out against the English." Joan's "counsel" was her trio of saints, and when they spoke to her she could not be stopped. She put on her armor and raced out of Orléans.

A small French force was skirmishing with the enemy outside the English bastion of St. Loup; Joan stormed into the melee and ferociously led a charge that caused the fortress to fall. But she was now confronted, for the first time, with the carnage of war. Appalled by the sufferings of the dead and dying—both French and English—she began to weep, distraught that these men had not made a confession before they died. She took one Englishman who had been run through by a sword and cradled him in her arms until he passed away.

A Frenzied Attack

Reading the story of Joan at Orléans—much of it in the form of testimony at the trial for heresy that resulted in her execution at the stake—one is struck by the contrast between Joan's energy and fervor and the cautiousness of the leaders around her. After resting on the Feast of the Ascension, Joan made another attempt to rescue Guyenne, writing a note to the English and having it attached to an arrow and shot into the enemy camp. It read, in part, "You, Englishmen, who have no right in this Kingdom of France, the King of Heaven orders and commands you, through Joan the Maid, that you quit your fortresses and return to your own country ... You [hold] my herald named Guyenne. Be so good as to send him back."

The English responded by shouting that Joan was a whore. When she heard this, she began to cry, as she did on many occasions when insulted. But the next day, she rose early, confessed her sins, and took her men out of the city to attack another bastion, St.-Jean-le-Blanc, which covered the approaches to Les Tourelles. The English were so surprised that they abandoned the bastion immediately, fleeing toward a stronger and far larger fortress, a monastery called Les Augustins. In a wild frenzy of fighting, with Joan alternately shouting to the Lord and weeping, the French gave chase and took Les Augustins as well, tearing down the English banners and replacing them with French ones. A great cheer arose from the city of Orléans as the English retreated now to Les Tourelles, their strongpoint on the bridge.

An Inspiring Tableau

The next day, May 7, at about 8 a.m., Joan led a force in a direct frontal attack on the fortified towers of Les Tourelles. This was perhaps her greatest act of bravery. The evening before, she had predicted to her confessor that she would be wounded in the assault—"tomorrow the blood will flow out of my body above my breast," she said—but despite the fact that she was clearly terrified, she mounted her horse and led the men in the first attack. She was soon struck just below the shoulder by an arrow, as she had predicted, and the English archers on the walls laughed and shouted curses as she was carried off the field. Some of the Frenchmen handed her magic amulets to protect her, but she shoved these away angrily and had her wound—which was not deep—treated with lard and olive oil. Her armor dirty and her hair disheveled, she then gave confession to her priest in a highly emotional state before resting.

Repeated French assaults failed to dislodge the English, and the Bastard of Orléans decided to call off the attack for the day. When Joan heard this, she refused to allow him to give the order and prepared to return to battle.

There now occurred one of the most extraordinary moments in French history. Joan's standard-bearer, exhausted after the day-long fighting, had given Joan's pennon to a soldier known to history only as the Basque. The Basque and another brave French knight had reached the base of the bridge across the Loire, near the bottom of the towers of Les Tourelles, and found a wooden ladder they could climb to the bridge's roadway. As they started to climb, Joan arrived and demanded her banner back, crying, "My standard! My standard!" But instead of handing it over, the Basque raised it higher.

The French soldiers saw this tableau—Joan reaching for her banner, the Basque holding it up in the air—and, shouting almost as one voice, raced for the bridge with their assault ladders. Joan was on the first one placed there. Despite heavy fire from Les Tourelles, the French swarmed up to the roadway and attacked the English soldiers there, with Joan crying out, "Classidas, Classidas [the English commander] yield thee, yield thee to the King of Heaven, thou [who] has called me 'whore.'"

Classidas, fully armored, fell into the river and drowned during the chaos of the assault. Hundreds of other Englishmen also died at the hands of their foes or in the river, before the French, led by the triumphant Maid, finally carried the day.

The siege was broken. The next day, the English burned their stockades and marched away. And the French people, according to French knight Jean d'Aulon, who was there and later testified at Joan's trial, "made great joy, giving marvelous praises to their valiant defenders and above all others to Joan the Maid."

EDWARD WOODSTOCK: THE BLACK PRINCE WHO FOUGHT LIKE A LION

Edward of Woodstock, the Prince of Wales, is one of the most colorful figures in a century's worth of colorful men and women. He also ranks alongside King Henry V as England's greatest warrior hero of the Hundred Years' War. Born in 1330, Edward was seven years old when his father, Edward III, first joined battle with France in 1337. When the younger Edward was just sixteen, he took part in the battle of Crécy, where he showed himself to be a fearsome warrior. Fighting in the middle of the action, he was knocked to the ground, but, protected by a nobleman in his retinue, managed to regain his feet and fight off French attacks. When his father sent a group of knights to relieve his son, they found Edward and his companion standing erect amid a pile of French corpses.

Although Edward did not gain the glamorous nickname of the Black Prince until a few hundred years after his death (it derived from the color of the cuirass, or chest armor, presented to him by his father after his heroism at Crécy), he was a renowned and popular figure in England during his lifetime. He displayed a combination of chivalry—when he captured the French King John II at Poitiers, he made a point of serving the king dinner on his knees—and callousness, which manifested itself in the violent attacks he authorized on French civilians during English raids into the countryside. But, as Edward III aged, he became a superior commander of English forces. As well as his notable victory against the odds at Poitiers, he conquered an army of French veterans at the battle of Nájera in northern Spain in 1367, where the French and English fought in support of rival claimants to the crown of Castile.

However, the Black Prince—as so often happens with military commanders—was a far poorer administrator than he was a battlefield leader, and it was his harsh taxation of the province of Aquitaine that caused its citizens to join forces with Charles V.

Struck by illness, the Black Prince died in 1376, a year before his father's death, becoming the first and, so far, last Prince of Wales never to rule as king.

THE LONGBOW—THE MACHINE-GUN OF THE HUNDRED YEARS' WAR

ENGLAND AND FRANCE ARE SHOWN IN 1453 AT THE END OF THE HUNDRED YEARS' WAR. HISTORIANS RECOGNIZE FOUR PHASES OF THESE SERIES OF WARS, WHICH ENDED AFTER JOAN OF ARC RALLIED FRENCH FORCES TO DEFEAT THE ENGLISH AT ORLEANS IN 1428–29. NO FORMAL PEACE TREATY ENDED THE WARS; ENGLAND SIMPLY RECOGNIZED THAT FRANCE WAS TOO STRONG TO ATTACK SUCCESSFULLY.

The longbow revolutionized military tactics during the Hundred Years' War. A Welsh innovation, the English adopted it during the twelfth century and immediately became adept at using it. Its potential—it could put an arrow through a thick church door—became so apparent that during the reign of Edward I (1272–1307) each village in England was ordered to contribute men to a national pool of archers. Peasants practiced on the village green Sunday morning. By the time Edward III led the English into battle against the French, each English force usually carried with it some five hundred longbowmen.

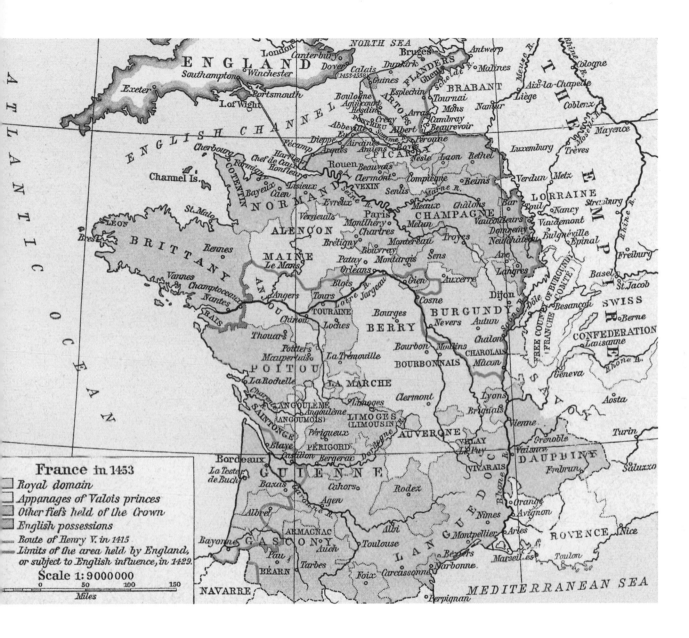

The longbow was made of strong and flexible yew, and ranged in height from about five and a half to six and a half feet (170–190 cm), depending on the height of the archer. It could draw about 100 pounds (45 kg) in weight; it would kill accurately at 150 yards (137 m), and pierce plate armor at 60 yards (55 m). Each archer carried a quiver containing two-dozen arrows, and carts followed into battle carrying more. A single archer could shoot a dozen arrows in the space of two minutes; five hundred could make the sky black as night with deadly missiles.

The longbow altered military tactics in much the same way that the machine gun changed tactics in later centuries: by breaking up enemy charges at a distance. At Crécy, in 1346, where French troops under King Philip outnumbered the English three to one, English longbowmen rained arrows down on the flower of French knighthood, aiming especially at the horses, causing them to fall one atop the other like "a litter of piglets." Agincourt, in 1415, was a similar story: an outnumbered English army, on French territory, shot a storm of arrows into French lines killing horses, driving men mad, and ultimately forcing the French to charge before they were ready.

The coming of cannon at the end of the conflict made longbows obsolete, but their power as a battle-winning weapon during the Hundred Years' War cannot be overestimated.

JOAN OF ARC—THE ENIGMA WHO SAVED AN ENTIRE PEOPLE

Even today, it is not clearly understood how Joan of Arc, an illiterate shepherd girl, managed to turn the tide of the chaotic and bloody war against the English and help the Dauphin Charles ascend the throne and unite France behind him.

Joan (Jeanne d'Arc) was born in January of 1412, to Jacques d'Arc and Isabelle Romée, at Domrémy, on the River Meuse, in eastern Champagne. At around thirteen years of age, she began hearing heavenly voices—in particular those of a trio of saints: St. Michael, St. Catherine, and St. Margaret. Whether these were a manifestation of mental illness or a genuine religious experience, no one will ever know, but eventually the voices instructed Joan to save her country from the English.

In 1428, Joan undertook an extraordinary journey to the court of the dauphin, where she somehow convinced Charles that God had ordered her to lead a relief force against the English forces then besieging Orléans and to have Charles crowned king at Reims. Charles, who was superstitious and dabbled in astrology, seems to have thought she was a witch. When Joan came to meet him, he dressed as an ordinary civilian and hid among his advisors, but Joan picked him out immediately, saying, "Very noble Lord Dauphin, I am come and I am sent by God to bring succor to you and your kingdom." The calmness with which she said this appears to have both impressed and frightened Charles. After having her quizzed by theologians, who decided that whatever she was she was not a witch, he allowed her to lead his troops to Orléans.

After raising the siege, Joan continued to campaign against the English, enraging them with the letters she sent them ("I have been sent by God, the King of Heaven, to throw you out of all France") and with the powerful effect she had on the French army. However, in May of 1430, she was captured at Compiègne and put on trial. Found guilty of being a heretic and for wearing men's clothing ("a thing displeasing and abominable to God"), she was burned at the stake in the marketplace in Rouen in 1431. But for successive generations of French people, however, she remained a symbol of a pure and united France, and in 1920 she was declared a saint by the Catholic Church.

In 1920 Joan of Arc declared a saint by the Catholic

11

THE SPANISH CONQUEST
OF MEXICO

1519–21

THE INVASION THAT DESTROYED THE ANCIENT MEXICA (AZTEC)
CULTURE, ENRICHED SPAIN, AND OPENED CENTRAL AND SOUTH
AMERICA TO EUROPEAN DOMINATION

TWO CULTURES COLLIDE AND SPAIN DESTROYS A POWERFUL
NEW WORLD EMPIRE

The conquest of Mexico was a clash between two glittering empires. Spain, following its consolidation of most of the Iberian Peninsula after the Reconquista and Columbus's 1492 voyage to the Americas, had steadily tightened its grasp on the New World. By 1510 or so, it had gained control of Cuba, Hispaniola, Puerto Rico, and other Caribbean islands and was poised to move west, toward the sun and a rumor of gold. There it came upon the empire of the Mexica, who had only recently completed their own territorial conquests.

The Mexica (pronounced Me-*shee*-ca) were traditionally a wandering people, but following the collapse of the Toltec civilization at the beginning of the thirteenth century, brought on by a vast drought and crop failure, the Mexica had moved south from their homeland in the north of present-day Mexico into the Valley of Mexico. There they fought other tribes for control of the region and in 1428, led by King Iztcóatl, now thought of as the founder of the Mexica Empire, ruthlessly conquered a territory stretching from the Gulf of Mexico to the Pacific Ocean and covering 80,000 square miles (200,000 sq km). By the time the Spaniards arrived, this territory consisted of a loose confederation of about fifty small states, inhabited by eight million people, as well as a magnificent capital at Tenochtitlán, where merchants came to trade fine cloth, silver, ornaments, and wood and obsidian tools.

One of the strongest influences on the subsequent development of Mexica culture was Iztcóatl's nephew and royal counselor Tlacaelel. As well as reforming the army and the judicial system, he reshaped the Mexica religion. In particular, he placed great emphasis on the need to feed human blood to the warrior god Huitzilopochtli, which resulted in human sacrifice becoming a distinctive feature of Mexica civilization.

In early 1519, the Spanish adventurer Hernán Cortés led an eleven-ship expedition from Cuba to the Yucatán Peninsula. Cortés set sail despite receiving an order from the governor of Cuba, Diego Velázquez, to relinquish the expedition's leadership. Previously, other Spanish explorers had landed in the Yucatán and at points along the Mexican coast and had reported back rumors of a rich civilization, though none had seen Tenochtitlán. Sailing west across the Gulf of Mexico, Cortés landed on the east coast in April and founded the settlement of Veracruz. He then headed toward the Mexica capital of Tenochtitlán on Lake Texcoco. Along the way, he defeated several of the Mexica's great rivals, notably the Tlaxcala, who became Cortés's most important allies. The Spanish force entered Tenochtitlán on November 8. Within a week, Cortés, through cunning and superior weaponry had trumped a passive and superstitious ancient culture, taken the Mexica ruler Montezuma captive, and was running the country through him.

In the spring of 1520, Governor Velázquez of Cuba sent a large force under Pánfilo de Narváez to arrest Cortés for disobeying his orders. Cortés marched east to meet and defeat Narváez, leaving Tenochtitlán under the control of his lieutenant, Pedro de Alvarado. When trouble flared at a local festival, Alvarado led a massacre of thousands of Mexica, sparking a widespread rebellion. When Cortés returned, Tenochtitlán was in chaos, and he and his men were cornered by the Mexica. Fighting his way out during a driving rainstorm, Cortés lost eight hundred conquistadors and several thousand Indian allies, and Montezuma was killed, possibly stoned to death by his own people or murdered by the Spaniards.

However, early in 1521, Cortés returned to Tenochtitlán with thousands of his Indian allies. Having first cutting off supplies to the city, which had already suffered a devastating smallpox epidemic, Cortés then attacked, using small sailing ships he had had built especially. After a battle that lasted three months, he finally recaptured the city and the empire of the Mexica.

Though estimates vary wildly, it is thought that the population of Mexico subsequently fell from 8 million in 1518 to a low of 2.6 million in 1560.

A SMALL GROUP OF DARING MEN CONQUER A FABLED CITY
The Fall of Tenochtitlán, 1521

At first, everything had gone Hernán Cortés's way. His daring gambit—to take five hundred men, plus a few thousand Indian allies, and strike at Tenochtitlán, the heart of the mighty Mexica Empire—had paid off. He had easily captured the Mexica ruler Montezuma II, had issued edicts banning human sacrifice, exiled Mexica priests, and

THE CONQUEST OF MEXICO BY THE SPANISH IN THE EARLY 1500S IS SHOWN ON THE MAP, WITH THE RED LINE DEPICTING A PORTION OF THE ROUTE HERNÁN CORTÉS TOOK OVER THE MOUNTAINS TO TENOCHTITLÁN. THOUGH ESTIMATES VARY WILDLY, IT IS THOUGHT THAT THE POPULATION OF MEXICO SUBSEQUENTLY FELL DRAMATICALLY DURING THIS PERIOD OF WARFARE, FROM 8 MILLION IN 1518 TO 2.6 MILLION IN 1560.

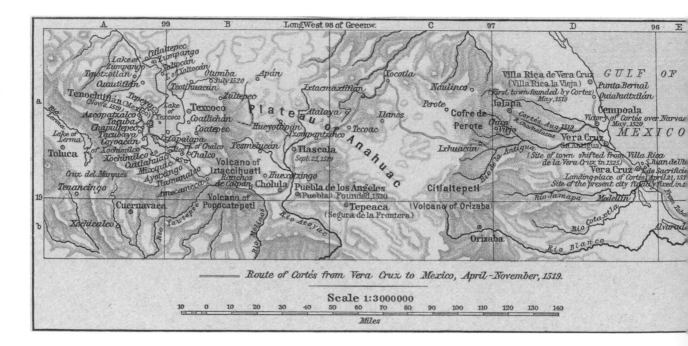

installed Christian gods in Tenochtitlán's temples. Montezuma had even handed over huge quantities of finely wrought bracelets and necklaces in an attempt to buy his freedom—which he, Cortés, had immediately melted down for bullion, saving the finest pieces for his king, Charles V of Spain. Then he had triumphed over his old rival, Velázquez, not only defeating the force under Narváez sent to arrest him, but also managing to persuade its soldiers to join him.

But then things had started to go horribly wrong. He had blundered by leaving Alvarado in charge of Tenochtitlán while he dealt with Narváez. His hot-headed lieutenant had lost control and turned the whole city against him, undone all his careful planning. He had been lucky to get out of there alive, had lost hundreds of men and, worst of all, had lost Montezuma.

Now, in August of 1520, resting in Tlaxcala, capital city of his allies the Tlaxcalans, he counted his losses. His forces were exhausted from their ordeal, barely in fighting condition. Despite this, he knew he had to strike again. He needed to come up with a new plan—and soon.

In September, he got a lucky, if macabre, break. A smallpox epidemic—almost certainly brought by Narváez and his men—broke out in Tenochtitlán. Thousands died—"we were covered with agonizing sores from head to foot," one Mexican remembered later—including the new ruler of only eighty days, Cuitláhuac. The next emperor, Cuauhtémoc, was known to be a brave warrior. But with the city weakened and its population decimated by illness, Cortés, the master opportunist, saw another door opening before him.

In December of 1520, Cortés gathered his small force and twenty thousand of his Tlaxcalan allies and attacked the city of Texcoco, on the lakeshore to the northeast of Tenochtitlán. This ally of the Mexica was quickly subjugated after its king fled to Tenochtitlán. Cortés then used Texcoco as a base to assemble a fleet of small, two-masted sailing vessels, known as brigantines, the materials for which he had the Tlaxcalans transport from coastal forests.

From January through May, Cortés advanced around the shores of Lake Texcoco, conquering cities that were loyal to the Mexica and adding forces to his growing army. Many of the locals thought that here, at last, was the chance to overthrow the yoke of Mexica oppression. Then Cortés had his men destroy the main aqueduct that carried fresh water to Tenochtitlán. His plan was to make sure that the city was completely isolated before he attacked it. And, despite repeated Mexica canoe raids, he soon succeeded.

An Amphibious Offensive

In late April 1521, Cortés finally launched his offensive. Down each of the three major causeways that connected Tenochtitlán to the mainland, he sent an army of

Indians numbering between twenty thousand and twenty-five thousand, led by two hundred or so Spaniards. Meanwhile, he launched his thirteen brigantines, each of which carried twelve crossbowmen, twelve arquebusiers, and one cannon. While fighting off a flotilla of war canoes, these small ships pinned down the main Mexica force, preventing it from counterattacking along the causeways; they also began bombarding the defensive walls the Mexica had placed around the shores of their city.

The fighting was ferocious. The Mexica were no longer as afraid of the Spanish guns as they had once been, and had at least learned how to deal with them, as Díaz recorded: "When the Aztecs … discovered that the shots always flew in a straight line, they no longer ran away in the line of fire. They flew to the left or the right."

After the initial assaults, which lasted through the month of May, hand-to-hand street fighting went on for almost three months in Tenochtitlán. Cortés realized from the Mexica's stiff resistance that they would never surrender, so he began to destroy the city, burning down the buildings block by block, as the screams of those caught in the fires echoed through the city. It was slow progress. Advancing from house to house, the Spaniards and their allies forged their way through Tenochtitlán, mercilessly murdering any foes they captured. The Mexica resisted fiercely and responded in kind. Whenever they caught Spanish soldiers, they would force them to climb the steps of the main temple at Tlatelolco—in full view of the Spanish forces—before sacrificing them, cutting out their hearts and tossing them down the temple steps. It was a horrible sight. The Mexica later told Spanish friars that "some of the [Spanish] captives were weeping, some were keening, and others were beating their palms against their mouths." Twice, the Mexica narrowly missed capturing their main target, Cortés.

But finally outnumbered and starving, the Mexica were forced to retreat. They made a last stand in Tlatelolco, the market district of the city, where they were overwhelmed. As their Indian allies finished off the Mexica force, the Spaniards set fire to the great temple. The brigantines caught Cuauhtémoc's canoe as the ruler tried to flee. He surrendered to Cortés, saying, "I can do no more. I have been brought before you by force as prisoner. Take that dagger from your belt and kill me with it quickly." Then he began to weep. Cortés spared Cuauhtémoc for the moment, but was later to execute him after torturing him to find out whether he knew the locations of stores of gold.

It was August 13, 1521. Around two hundred thousand Mexica had died in Tenochtitlán. The smell of the dead, wrote Bernal Díaz, was awful: "even Cortés was sick from the stink in the nostrils."

But it was the smell of conquest.

HERNÁN CORTÉS: A SINGLE-MINDED FORTUNE-SEEKER WHOSE DETERMINATION OVERCAME ALL

Numerous stories attest to Hernán Cortés's arrogance, but one is particularly revealing. When Cortés landed at Veracruz in April of 1519, the Mexica emperor, Montezuma, became convinced that the Spaniard was the returning white, bearded god Quetzalcóatl; he ordered messengers to take appropriately regal finery to the new arrival, including a diadem made of jaguar skin and pheasant feathers, pendant earrings of gold, a cloak adorned with tiny gold bells, and a gold shield rimmed with mother of pearl. Admitted into Cortés's presence, the messengers dressed the Spanish leader in these clothes. And Cortés—who could have only had the most rudimentary idea of what Quetzalcóatl meant to the Mexica—said, "And is this all? Is this your gift of welcome? Is this how you greet people?" Then he ordered that the messengers be chained by the hands and feet, and he fired the ship's cannons, which so frightened the messengers that they fainted and had to be revived with wine.

Hernán Cortés knew the value of always taking control of a situation. He was a man who dominated the action rather than waiting for events to overtake him—and in this he was the polar opposite of Montezuma. But he was also a man many of his contemporaries loathed and mistrusted.

Cortés was born in 1485, in Medellín in southwestern Spain, and briefly studied law before sailing for the New World to seek his fortune. In 1511, he joined Diego Velázquez's expedition to conquer Cuba, and he later married Veláquez's sister-in-law. When he heard about the rich treasures of the Mexica, he made up his mind to go to Mexico—and nothing was going to stop him, not even an order from Velázquez withdrawing his permission for Cortés to set sail.

Arriving at Veracruz, Cortés burned his ships on the shore to banish any thought of retreat or withdrawal from the minds of his men. Then he made his way across a rugged mountain range and prepared to enter a city where he was outnumbered by hundreds of thousands. Along the way, he displayed guile and strong powers of persuasion, convincing the defeated Tlaxcalans and several other tribes to become his allies. And he was perceptive about the vulnerability of the Mexica, recognizing immediately that Montezuma was weak-willed and irrational.

After his great victory in August of 1521, Cortés sent the myriad treasures of the Mexica back to Spain, claiming all his efforts had been on behalf of King Charles V. The latter forgave him his original disobedience toward Velázquez and rewarded him handsomely, although Cortés was later to fall out of favor with the Spanish crown. Cortés stayed in Mexico until 1528, when he returned to Spain to look after his affairs, but he then went back to Mexico, where he lived on a great estate from 1530 to 1541. Moving back to Spain, he fought against the Turks in Algiers, then died of dysentery in his homeland in 1547.

MONTEZUMA II: THE LAST MEXICA RULER, BROUGHT DOWN BY SUPERSTITION

The Mexica ruler Montezuma is one of the most tragic figures in the early history of the Americas. Head of a mighty and sophisticated empire, he possessed immense power but was paralyzed by fear and superstition.

Born around 1466, Montezuma was invested as leader of the Mexica in 1502, sixty years after the investiture of his great-grandfather. His people regarded him with awe—years later, Mexica were unable to describe his appearance to Spanish friars, because any commoner who dared look at him was put to death. He wore the finest clothes available, lived in a palace with hundreds of rooms, and, according to Bernal Díaz, "his cooks prepared thirty kinds of dishes for every meal." If anyone—from a noble to a layperson—committed any act that offended him, a Spanish friar of the early fifteenth century wrote, "he would have them pierced with arrows or burned alive."

In this, Montezuma was no different from any previous Mexica ruler. But he was also a man with a contemplative side, who was said to be scholarly, and who believed firmly in predictions. In particular, he believed the prediction that foretold the return to Earth of the god Quetzalcóatl in the year I Reed, which happened to be 1519. When Montezuma heard that Cortés had landed, according to Mexica sources, he "put his hand to his mouth" and stared off into space: "It was as if he were conquered by despair." Thereafter, as Cortés moved closer, Montezuma attempted to bribe him to keep away, rather than moving swiftly to strike at the invader. But then how does one strike at a god?

Montezuma greeted Cortés as Quetzalcóatl, but after Cortés seized him, imprisoned him, and made him a puppet ruler, he knew the extent to which he had been blinded.

Montezuma died in June 1520 during the chaos of Cortés's attempt to escape Tenochtitlán, possibly at the hands of his own people who, feeling he had betrayed them, are said to have hurled stones and spears at him when he appeared on a balcony; other sources, however, say that the Spaniards murdered him. Whatever the truth, Montezuma, a man in the grip of a malign prophecy, had long since lost control of his fate.

CORTÉS AND MONTEZUMA, DEPICTED BY GALLO GALLINA (1796–1874).

The Encounter between Hernando Cortes (1485–1547) and Montezuma II (1466–1520), from "Le Costume Ancien et Moderne," Volume I, plate 63, by Jules Ferrario, published c.1820s–30s (color engraving), Gallina, Gallo (1796–1874) / Private Collection / The Stapleton Collection / The Bridgeman Art Library International

BLOODY HUMAN SACRIFICES WERE ROUTINE

The creation myth of the Mexica, as revised by the royal counselor Tlacaelel foretold that eventually the sun would go dark—"that there shall be famine / And that we all shall perish," as a Nahuatl poem put it. In order to forestall this as long as possible, Tlacaelel claimed, the sun needed chalchihuatl, or life-energy, which could be provided only by spilling blood in offering to the fearsome god of war Huitzilopochtli, who would in turn take it to the sun.

So, at dawn every day, a captive—often drugged with hallucinogenics—was led up the steps of one of the main temples of Tenochtitlán. Four lesser priests held the

person by the arms and legs over a stone block, while the chief priest of the temple tore out the victim's heart with a flint or obsidian blade. The still-beating heart would then be held up to the sun, while the priest chanted a prayer that explained how this "precious cactus fruit" might keep the dark away for another twenty-four hours. The heart was then ritually burned, the head cut off, the torso fed to the dogs, and the limbs ritually eaten, with maize and chili. The blood of the victims was also used as a kind of purifying liquid, sprinkled around the city to ward off evil spirits.

The Spaniards were mightily offended by this practice and by the grotesque precincts of these temples, which were occupied by black-robed priests who often wore the flayed skins of their victims and had hair matted with blood, and, according to Bernal Díaz, "smelled like dead dogs." All this was one more justification for their conquest. Yet more than one historian has noted that Europeans at this time, while they did not engage in human sacrifice, were liberal in their use of capital punishment to remedy even minor crimes, and bodies rotting on gallows were on display in almost every European capital.

THE CHRONICLER OF NEW SPAIN

The most immediate and compelling contemporary account of the conquest of Mexico comes from a conquistador who accompanied Cortés: Bernal Díaz del Castillo, author of A True History of the Conquest of New Spain.

Born in 1492, the year Columbus discovered the Americas, Díaz was, like many of Cortés's conquistadors, from a family that offered him little in the way of an inheritance. He went to Cuba in 1514 to make his fortune and took part in an expedition that discovered the Yucatán coast. When the chance to go with Cortés to find the fabled empire of the Mexica presented itself, Díaz jumped at it, aiming, as he wrote with characteristic bluntness, to "serve God and his Majesty, to give light to those who were in the darkness [the pagan Mexica], and to grow rich, as all men desire to do."

Díaz saw action in more than one hundred battles and skirmishes, and was with Cortés every step of the way. His descriptions—of the swarming Mexica armies, horrible human sacrifices, and the siege and fall of Tenochtitlán—although sometimes long-winded, are generally thought to be accurate, and he writes with the relish and flair of a born storyteller.

After the fall of Mexico, Díaz received a pension from the Spanish crown and lived in Guatemala, where he worked as a municipal official. He did not write his True History until the early 1550s, when a chaplain of the Cortés family, who was not on the expedition to Mexico, wrote a memoir that glorified Cortés at the expense of the other conquistadors. Díaz's book remedied that: his Cortés, while undoubtedly charismatic, is an untrustworthy, even duplicitous, leader.

Díaz died in 1584, but his manuscript did not appear in print until 1632, considerably altered by an editor. Indeed, the book as he wrote it did not see the light of day until the early twentieth century.

12

THE THIRTY YEARS' WAR

1618–48

A THREE-DECADE-LONG CONFLICT, SPARKED BY RELIGIOUS
DIFFERENCES THAT EMBROILED MOST OF THE CONTINENT'S MAJOR
POWERS IN A DEVASTATING STRUGGLE FOR TERRITORY AND POWER

A WAR OF RELIGIONS—AND NATIONAL INTERESTS—
THAT PRESAGED THE HORROR OF MODERN WAR

Within ten years of Martin Luther's nailing of the Ninety-five Theses to the door
of All Saints Church in Wittenberg, the act that began the Reformation, the first
Protestant university had been founded in Germany. Within twenty years, King
Henry VIII of England had declared himself head of the Church of England.
Within half a century, Lutheranism and other Protestant sects such as Calvinism
had firmly established themselves throughout northern Europe. Naturally, the
staunchly Catholic Holy Roman Empire was not happy about this, and sporadic but vicious sectarian warfare broke out in Germany, Poland, Austria, and
Czechoslovakia between the empire and the forces of the Schmalkaldic League, an
alliance of Lutheran princes.

The Peace of Augsburg, signed in 1555, ended this fighting and allowed German
princes to decide whether their states should be Catholic or Lutheran. But, like many
treaties, Augsburg laid the seeds for more violence. Calvinists, Anabaptists, and
other growing Protestant sects had not been recognized; and the Catholic Counter-
Reformation was gathering strength. At the same time, individual nations were pushing to assert their interests, and religion provided a pretext for action.

The war can be divided into four phases. The first, the Bohemian Revolt (1618–
25), began with the so-called Defenestration of Prague, when a group of Protestant
nobles in that city expressed their opposition to the Hapsburg imposition of a
Catholic king by throwing three Catholic officials out of a window. After they then
elected their own Protestant monarch, the forces of the Holy Roman Empire invaded
Bohemia and crushed the Protestant army at the battle of White Mountain. The
Bohemian nobility was, as one historian has put it, "literally decapitated" and its
lands given to Catholic German princes. At this point, Spain, seeking to reestab-
lish itself as a preeminent power, opportunistically entered the conflict alongside the

Hapsburgs, forming what became known as the Catholic League, and helped install the Catholic Duke Maximilian of Bavaria as the new King of Bohemia.

These Catholic successes alarmed the King of Denmark, Christian IV, a Lutheran, who saw them as a threat to his nation's security. He began the second phase of the war, the so-called Danish Intervention (1625–29), by invading Germany. But Christian's campaign ended with disastrous defeats at the battle of Dessau Bridge in 1626, at the hands of the charismatic General Albrecht von Wallenstein, and at the battle of Lutter in 1626 against General Johann Tserclaes Graf von Tilly. In 1629, a triumphant Ferdinand II issued the highly controversial Edict of Restitution, which ordered Protestants to part with all Catholic land that had been under Protestant control since the Peace of Augsburg. Wallenstein objected to this—he had numerous Protestants in his army and owned a great deal of former Catholic land himself—and was dismissed by the emperor.

Then the Protestant Swedish king, Gustav II Adolf, or Gustavus Adolphus, with one eye on obtaining more land on the Baltic, launched another anti-Catholic campaign, the so-called Swedish Intervention (1630–35). Gustavus had perhaps the best army of any of the warring powers and was himself a brilliant military leader. With the aid of France and the Netherlands, he destroyed the forces of General Tilly at the pivotal Battle of Breitenfeld and moved deep into Germany. But in November of 1632, during a Swedish triumph over an Imperial army under a reinstated Wallenstein, Gustavus was killed. Although the Peace of Prague of 1635 left Sweden with gains, it also left the power of the Hapsburgs intact—much to the dismay of France.

Under its de facto head of state, Cardinal de Richelieu, France had for some time sought a reason to join forces with the Protestants. The fact that France, an ostensibly Catholic country wanted to fight on the Protestant side points out the complexity of the conflict and that it was ultimately as much about nation-building as religion. For France's main objective was to check the power of the Austrians. Richelieu saw his opportunity when Spanish forces stationed in Luxembourg invaded a small electorate that had allied itself with France. France then declared war, beginning the last phase of the conflict, the French Intervention (1636–48). France attacked the Spanish army in Luxembourg and pushed deep into southern Germany, while its Dutch allies took the war to the New World, disrupting Spanish treasure ships coming from the Caribbean and Mexico. But the Imperial forces steadily pushed France back and penetrated almost as far as Paris, before being defeated at the battle of Compiègne in 1636.

Widespread fighting continued until the death of Cardinal Richelieu in 1642. In 1643, Louis XIII died and his five-year-old son, Louis XIV, ascended the throne. Cardinal Mazarin, chief minister of France, began to reach out to Imperial leaders to secure peace. Still, fighting continued. After the bloody battle of Freiburg in 1644, the French occupied Alsace. This, coupled with the Swedish victory at the battle of Jankov in 1645 and the French triumph over Imperial forces at the second battle of Nordlingen in the same year spelled the death knell for Imperial forces. By this time, the conflict had taken a terrible toll on mainland Europe, Germany in particular. Warfare had ravaged great tracts of land, destroyed entire communities, and terrorized civilian populations.

In 1648, the Peace of Westphalia—also quite aptly known as the Peace of Exhaustion—concluded the war. Sweden received territory in northern Germany; France received the Alsace-Lorraine region (leading to conflict with the Germans for centuries to come); the Netherlands gained its independence from Spain; and the Holy Roman Empire granted equal recognition to Catholics, Lutherans, and Calvinists. The power of the Hapsburgs and the Holy Roman Empire waned dramatically as the princes of German territories were granted the right to almost complete sovereignty, save for a restriction not to wage war against the empire.

NEW TACTICS AND A NEW FORMATION ROB A MIGHTY ARMY OF INVINCIBILITY
The Battle of Breitenfeld, 1631

On Wednesday, September 17, 1631, two armies were about to clash over sloping, cultivated fields just outside the village of Breitenfeld, some 4 miles (6 km) from the outskirts of Leipzig, Germany. Although it was only nine o'clock in the morning, the day was fiercely hot, one in a string of very hot days that had left the tilled earth covered with a layer of loose soil. Gusty winds blew dust down the slight incline into the faces of twenty-three thousand Swedish soldiers commanded by the King of Sweden, Gustavus Adolphus, and about seventeen thousand Saxon troops led by John George I, Elector of Saxony, and General Hans Georg von Arnim. Gustavus Adolphus later commented that the Saxon cavalry, wearing their colorful coats and scarves and sitting astride beautiful horses, formed a "cheerful and beautiful company."

The Swedish troops at the center of the line, not quite so beautiful in their practical brown coats, coughed, wrapped their faces in rags, and waited. Looking up the slope ahead of them, the Protestant forces could see the massed troops belonging to the Imperial General Johann Tserclaes Graf von Tilly, thirty-one thousand men in all, commanded by Tilly and his brave but impetuous second-in-command, Count Gottfried Heinrich Pappenheim.

Not all the Swedish and Saxon troops were even in position when Tilly's cannons opened up, sending iron balls arcing into the Protestant lines.

Changing Fortunes

These cannonballs were the first shots in a battle that would turn around the desperate fortunes of the Protestant Union. The war had been going on for thirteen years, and the Protestants had suffered defeat after defeat at the hands of the Hapsburg and Catholic League forces. But in the spring of 1630, the Swedish king, Gustavus Adolphus, had invaded northern Germany, quickly overrunning Pomerania and capturing the all-important mouth of the River Oder, before moving deep into German territory. Now, the Lion of the North, as Gustavus was known, was poised to save the Protestant cause.

What's more, the Imperial forces were in disarray. Their brilliant leader, Albrecht von Wallenstein, had been dismissed by Holy Roman Emperor Frederick II and replaced with Tilly, a veteran but not exceptional warrior, and at the age of seventy-two probably well past his prime (his subordinate, the fiery Count Pappenheim, thought him almost senile). Unable to provision his army—which von Wallenstein had refused to feed from the ample stocks of food in his territory of Friedland—Tilly perhaps unwisely took the advice of Pappenheim to besiege the Protestant city of Magdeburg. This resulted in an appalling slaughter that became a rallying point for Protestants—after it the United Provinces of the Netherlands had pledged support to Gustavus, as had John George I of Saxony.

A YEAR AFTER BREITENFELD, AT THE BATTLE OF LÜTZEN, DEPICTED HERE BY JACQUES COURTOIS (1621–76), THE SWEDES WOULD TRIUMPH OVER THE HOLY ROMAN EMPIRE ONCE MORE—BUT ALSO LOSE THEIR LEADER.

The Battle of Lutzen in 1632, Courtois, Jacques (Le Bourguignon) (1621–76) / Palazzo Pitti, Florence, Italy / The Bridgeman Art Library International

Tilly had used John's defection as an excuse to invade Saxony, and by September 14, 1631, he had stormed and taken the town of Leipzig. Knowing that Swedish and Saxon forces were now advancing on him, Tilly, far from a supply base, prudently decided to defend himself within the fortified walls of Leipzig. But, here, once again, his subordinate Pappenheim had betrayed him. On September 17, he had left camp with a large reconnaissance force and engaged the Swedish forces moving on Leipzig. He then sent back word to Tilly that he was surrounded, could not return, and needed to be reinforced. Tilly bowed his head and loudly cried, "That fellow will rob me of my honor and reputation." However, he had little choice but to bring his forces into line to join Pappenheim and face the Swedes and Saxons.

An Artillery Duel

Shortly after the Imperial artillery opened up, the Swedes returned fire, and for the next five hours the battle was a duel of artillery and musketry. The Imperials got the worst of it. Although Tilly's forces outnumbered the Swedes and Saxons, they were lined up in traditional, large block-like infantry formations some fifty ranks deep, flanked by cavalry, with their artillery at the rear. The Swedes, on the other hand, adopting an innovative approach developed by Gustavus, were arrayed in wide, shallow formations only five or six men deep. Swedish artillery was able to do serious damage to the thick ranks of the Imperials, while the Imperial fire took a much lesser toll on the thinner, more spread out Swedish ranks. Furthermore, the Swedish musketeers, who had drilled incessantly, poured three times as much lead into the Imperial lines as their foes could return.

Finally, at about two o'clock, the stalemate was broken. Pappenheim, on the Imperial left flank, led a charge in a wide circle around the arc of the Swedish fire, aiming for the rear. The Swedes' turned to meet this charge, but Tilly took advantage of the Swedish distraction to attack the Elector John George's Saxons in a vicious, all-out assault. The Saxons—mainly green, untried troops—had withstood hours of gunnery, but could not withstand this: their line of beautifully dressed cavalry and infantry broke and fled, led by John George himself, who did not stop his horse until he was 15 miles (24 km) away.

With the Saxons gone, the Swedes stood alone as the Imperial forces closed in on both sides. The day was so dusty, the air so thick with smoke, that survivors of the battle told of not being able to see more than four steps in front of them. Gustavus and his officers were everywhere on the battlefield, rallying their forces. Swedes later remembered their king galloping up in a frenzy, shouting orders, sweat pouring off his face, yelling madly for water to soothe his parched throat—and then, before it could be delivered to him, riding off to another potential weak spot in the Swedish lines.

Despite the fact that they were outnumbered and threatened on both sides, the Swedes held. In part, this was due to Gustavus's flexible formations, which could quickly turn and face wherever they needed to in this fluid and confusing combat, and partly it was due to the incredible rate of fire his disciplined musketeers could maintain.

Gradually, the Imperials were pushed back up the slope. And then, around four in the afternoon, the wind shifted back in the direction of the Imperial lines, blowing the dust into their faces. Observing this, Gustavus took his cavalry reserves—about a thousand men in all—and led them in an all-out charge. This separated the Imperial infantry from the cavalry and broke the enemy once and for all. The Imperial troops went streaming back toward Leipzig; they were pursued and slaughtered by Swedish horsemen.

Tilly, wounded in three places, fled the battlefield. Pappenheim carried on a valiant rearguard action against the Swedes—at one point personally fighting off fourteen Swedish cavalrymen bent on capturing him—and managed to bring four intact regiments back to Leipzig. (The Imperials would be forced to abandon the city the next day.)

By seven o'clock, the battle was over. Seven thousand of Tilly's men lay dead on the parched fields outside Breitenfeld. Nine thousand were captured, and an untold number wounded. And a further horror was visited upon those Imperial soldiers who straggled across the countryside, lost in the chaos of war: Saxon peasants set upon them, butchering them by the hundreds in revenge for their pillaging of the country.

A SEVENTEENTH-CENTURY GERMAN ENGRAVING OF GUSTAVUS.

Portrait of Gustavus Adolphus II, King of Sweden (1594–1632) (engraving) (b/w photo), German School, (17th century) / Private Collection / The Bridgeman Art Library International

"How Merry Our Brothers Are!"

Around Swedish campfires that night there arose a clamor of bells—scores of the offering bells Gustavus's infantry had taken from the priests of the Imperial army. This caused the Swedish King to laugh: "How merry our brothers are," he exclaimed.

While there would be many more battles left to come, the Swedish victory at Breitenfeld—which would turn out to be the largest set-piece battle of the war—was hugely encouraging for Protestant forces. For while it was not a decisive victory, it was the point at which the Hapsburgs and the Imperial forces lost their aura of invincibility.

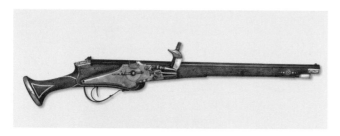

GUSTAVUS ADOLPHUS: THE LION OF THE NORTH AND FATHER OF MODERN WARFARE

Well over 6 feet (1.8 m) tall, with tawny hair and beard, and broadly muscled, Gustavus Adolphus, King of Sweden, was a big man in every way. He could speak ten languages and he could, and did, sit in a saddle for fifteen hours, shouting orders as he campaigned at the head of his superb Swedish army.

The son of King Charles IX, Gustavus was born in Stockholm in 1594. He developed an aptitude for military matters early—by the time he was sixteen he commanded a Swedish force that turned back Danish invaders at East Gotland. At seventeen, he became king. Sweden was then embroiled in territorial wars with Poland, Russia, and Denmark. Gustavus, fighting almost nonstop from 1613 to 1629, beat all his adversaries, acquiring vast tracts of land for the growing Swedish Empire and cutting off Russia's access to the Baltic.

Gustavus also fashioned his army into the best-trained force in Europe, taking what were essentially ragtag units and organizing them into well-drilled companies. He paid and fed them well, which helped limit the kinds of atrocities that were widespread during the war—it was recognized that the Swedes were generally not as bad as the soldiers of nearly every other country. His creation of what was among the first standing armies in Europe has gained him a lofty reputation in military history, with some even dubbing him the "Father of Modern Warfare."

At the time, Gustavus's conquests gained him the nickname of "the Lion of the North"; his renown was heightened by his intervention in the Thirty Years' War in 1630 and a string of victories, including his triumph at the pivotal battle of Breitenfeld. But disaster struck in November of 1632, when he was met at Lützen in Saxony with the Imperial army under the command of Wallenstein. There, during a pitched battle, Gustavus led a cavalry charge into a bank of fog and was seen no more. After Swedish forces triumphed, they went to look for their great king and discovered him, dead and stripped naked, under a pile of bodies.

The Lion of the North was brought home and buried with great honors. He had been such a strong stabilizing force in Sweden that even after his untimely death the country proceeded in an orderly fashion, with his young daughter Christina assuming the throne, advised by Gustavus's veteran ministers. Gustavus's example also inspired a series of brilliant Swedish warrior kings, in particular King Charles XI and his son, King Charles XII.

AN AGE OF INNOVATION WHEN THE FACE OF TACTICS AND WEAPONRY BEGAN TO CHANGE

The sprawling battles of the Thirty Years' War saw numerous breakthroughs in military tactics, many of them spawned by King Gustavus Adolphus of Sweden.

One of Gustavus's main contributions was to improve the infantry formation first developed by the Dutch leader Maurice of Nassau, son of William the Silent. Maurice's idea had been to abandon the centuries-old formation of infantrymen armed with pikes standing in ranks fifty deep, which he realized could be devastated by modern artillery, and spread them over a wider front so that bombardments had less impact and their musket fire was spread over a wider area. Gustavus refined this tactic and trained his infantry to fire rapid, devastating salvos.

Gustavus also pioneered the use of light cannons (those weighing 600 pounds [272 kg] or less), which could be pulled by one horse or six men, and had standard calibers so that ammunition could be more easily matched to the guns. Moreover, he required that this "field artillery" travel as part of the cavalry and infantry units rather than as a separate artillery unit; it was thus that he was able to provide supporting fire quickly when needed. Today, this concept is known as "combined arms" and is one of the linchpins of modern warfare.

The advent of the flintlock also put paid to another tactic of the period, the caracole. This was a cavalry charge in which the horsemen brandished wheel-lock pistols and rode right up to their enemy (sometimes close enough to touch them, for wheel-locks were inaccurate at all but very close range) before discharging their weapons and riding away. Flintlocks, with their faster rate of fire and longer range, could decimate such a charge. After the Thirty Years' War, cavalry would once again charge the way they used to. Instead of making themselves stationary targets while trying to fire pistols at close range, they took their chances against volley fire, riding with cold steel in hand, hoping the massed momentum of their horses and the sheer terror of their glittering swords would put enemy infantry to flight.

THE HORRORS OF TOTAL WAR ARE INTRODUCED TO EUROPE

Bertolt Brecht's great play Mother Courage and Her Children depicts the carnage of the Thirty Years' War, but was also meant to reflect the horrors being perpetrated in Poland after the German invasion of 1939. In other words, it captures in a universal

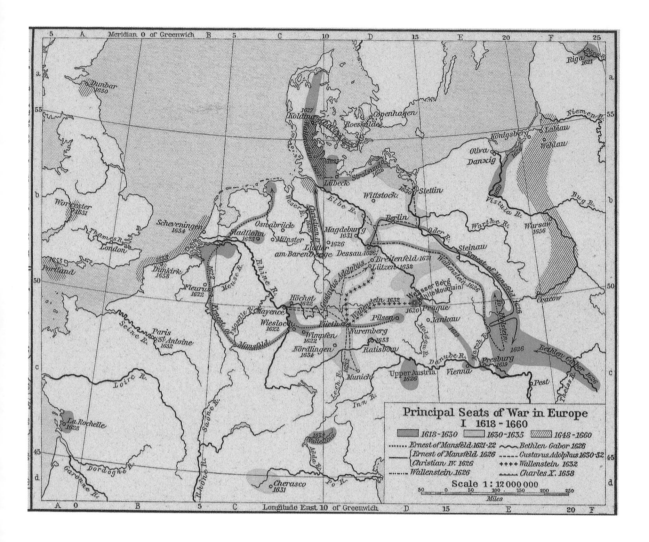

Principal Seats of War in Europe
I   1618 - 1660

| 1618-1630 | 1630-1635 | 1648-1660 |

Ernest of Mansfeld 1621-22 ....   Bethlen Gabor 1626
Ernest of Mansfeld 1626 ....   Gustavus Adolphus 1630-32
Christian IV. 1626 ....   ++++ Wallenstein 1632
Wallenstein 1626 ....   Charles X. 1658

Scale 1 : 12 000 000
Miles

THE TURNING POINT BATTLE OF BREITENFELD IN 1631 DURING THE THIRTY YEARS' WAR IS SHOWN ON THE MAP. THOUGH NOT A DECISIVE WIN, THE SWEDISH VICTORY AT THE BATTLE WAS HUGELY ENCOURAGING TO THE PROTESTANT FORCES AND WAS THE POINT AT WHICH THE HAPSBURGS AND IMPERIAL FORCES LOST THEIR AURA OF INVINCIBILITY.

fashion the agony of a civilian population at the mercy of warring armies during what seems like an endless cycle of violence.

The violence inflicted on both urban and rural populations from 1618 to 1648 was as horrible as any inflicted by modern warfare. Partly this was because of the makeup of the armies. Both sides used mercenaries who were poorly fed and paid and, therefore, resorted to living off the land, often besieging towns, many of them militarily unimportant, to rob them of food and wealth. During the 1631 sack of the Lutheran city of Magdeburg, on the Elbe River in Central Germany, General Graf von Tilly's Catholic League army butchered men, women, and children, most of whom had surrendered and were begging for their lives. The town was burned to the ground. Out of a population of 30,000, perhaps 5,000 survived—a census of the town taken in the 1640s revealed only 2,400 inhabitants.

The carnage in rural areas was often even worse. Roving bands of mercenary soldiers would approach poor and isolated farmsteads, take what little cash and ready food supplies a farmer might have, and then burn his home and crops. As a result, a fierce hatred developed between peasants and soldiers.

An example of this was recorded by a village constable in January of 1634, in the village of Linden, in modern-day Bavaria, Germany. Twenty Swedish soldiers rode into Linden and demanded food and wine. When it was not immediately forthcoming, they broke into one of the village's thirteen huts, raped the farmers wife and stole everything the family had. The next day, the villagers ambushed the soldiers, stripping them of their clothes and horses. The soldiers then returned with the village constable, who arrested the villagers and made a report to the Swedish commander. No one knows what happened next, but shortly thereafter the village of Linden is described ominously in German records as "uninhabited." Not until 1690 did it have enough of a population to register again on a census.

In combination with famine and disease (including an outbreak of bubonic plague in 1634), the Thirty Years' War is thought to have accounted for between four and seven million deaths by 1648. Such was the popular revulsion against the behavior of mercenary armies that the war helped bring about the creation of standing armies, which were generally much better disciplined.

13

THE SEVEN YEARS' WAR

1756–63

A WORLDWIDE CONFLICT THAT SAW EUROPE'S STRONGEST NATIONS
ENGAGED IN A POWER STRUGGLE ON THE CONTINENT, WHILE FRANCE
AND ENGLAND BATTLED OVER NORTH AMERICA

A WAR THAT SPREAD ACROSS CONTINENTS AND MADE ENGLAND A WORLD POWER

The Seven Years' War had its origins in a peace accord that satisfied no one: the Treaty of Aix-la-Chapelle, which ended the War of Austrian Succession of 1740–48. This war had been fought because Charles VI, the Austrian Holy Roman Emperor, lacking male heirs, had appointed his daughter, Maria Theresa, as empress, despite a tradition that dictated that only males could rule the empire. When Maria Theresa inherited the throne in 1740, King Frederick the Great of Prussia, along with other states whose royal families wanted a piece of the Austrian throne, used this breach of tradition as an excuse to invade a region of Austria called Silesia. Britain and the Netherlands, concerned about Frederick's increased military might, came into the war on the side of Austria. After the Treaty of Aix-la-Chapelle allowed the Prussians to keep Silesia, Maria Theresa almost immediately began plotting to get the region back and in 1756 formed a secret alliance against Prussia with Austria's former enemies, France and Russia.

When Frederick the Great discovered this, he decided his only chance of survival was a preemptive attack and invaded Saxony, a small eastern German state allied with Austria. He was supported by Great Britain, which, although formerly an ally of Austria, sought to protect the electorate of Hanover in Germany, the original seat of Britain's ruling house. In Europe, where the ensuing conflict was mainly a struggle between Austria and Prussia, Britain's involvement would be limited to financial backing for Frederick, crucial naval support, and a small ground force. But the outbreak of the Seven Years' War brought to a head ongoing British tussles with France in overseas colonies, especially in North America, where the two nations would fight all-out for control of that continent, a struggle that would come to be known as the French and Indian War.

Frederick's invasion brought an initial triumph against the Saxons and Austrians at the battle of Lobositz (now Lovosice in the Czech Republic) in October of 1756. He pushed on into Bohemia but was stopped by the Austrians at the battle of Kolín (also now in the Czech Republic) in June of 1757. The British suffered a serious setback in July when a combined Hanoverian-Hessian-German force was defeated by France and forced to sign the Convention of Klosterzeven, which allowed for the occupation of Hanover by the French. However, Britain's King George II soon repudiated the accord, relieved the duke of his command, and replaced him with Prince Ferdinand of Brunswick, a highly regarded Prussian soldier, who would henceforth command the Anglo-German forces.

In November, Frederick won a major victory over a French-Austrian force at Rossbach, Saxony, and in December he defeated an Austrian army at the battle of Leuthen in Silesia. Another great Prussian triumph against Austrian and French forces ensued in July 1758 at Krefeld (now in western Germany), and in August, near Brandenburg, Germany, Frederick defeated a larger Russian force at the bloody battle of Zorndorf.

THE DEATH OF 32-YEAR-OLD BRITISH GENERAL JAMES WOLFE DURING THE BATTLE AGAINST FRENCH FORCES IN QUEBEC IS SHOWN IN THIS FAMOUS OIL ON PANEL PAINTING BY AMERICAN ARTIST BENJAMIN WEST. WEST DEPICTS WOLFE IN THE POSE OF CHRIST REMOVED FROM THE CROSS.

The Death of General Wolfe (1727–59) on 13th September 1759, c.1770 (oil on copper panel), West, Benjamin (1738–1820) (after) / National Army Museum, London / The Bridgeman Art Library International

In North America meanwhile, where conflict centered on the St. Lawrence and Ohio rivers, the war had begun with a string of victories for the French, including the capture of Fort William Henry at the south end of Lake George in 1757 (the battle culminating in a notorious massacre of prisoners by French Indian forces, which subsequently became a rallying point for British colonists) and Fort Carillon (later called Fort Ticonderoga) in July of 1758. These defeats prompted Britain to pour funds into its colonial struggle. This, combined with a smallpox epidemic that devastated France's Indian allies in 1758, led to a startling series of British triumphs—at Louisbourg, Nova Scotia, in August of 1758, at Crown Point (now in New York state) in October, and at Fort Ticonderoga in June of 1759; the British and their Iroquois allies also managed to push the French back from the Ohio River valley. These triumphs culminated with the British capture of the last French stronghold of Quebec in September of 1759, which signaled the end of French control over North America, subsequently sealed by the loss of Montreal in 1760 and naval defeats in the West Indies in 1762.

The year 1759, indeed, would become for Britain the "Year of Victories," for in addition to the triumph at Quebec, it also saw the nation score two major naval victories over France at Lagos Bay, Portugal, and Quiberon Bay off the west coast of France. However,

1759 also saw the fortunes of Britain's ally Prussia take a turn for the worse. Frederick was defeated by an Austrian-Russian force at the battle of Kunersdorf, near Frankfurt, in August, and by Austria at the battle of Maxen, Saxony, in November, and the setbacks continued through 1760. Prussia might even have been completely destroyed had it not been for the withdrawal from the war of Russia in early 1762 following a change of leadership. As it was, Frederick was able to recover and win an important victory at Freiberg, Saxony, in October of 1762, driving the Austrians from Silesia.

The Russian withdrawal, and sheer exhaustion, encouraged all parties to seek peace. Under the Treaty of Paris of February 10, 1763, France was forced to cede all its North American territories to Britain, with the exception of New Orleans, St. Pierre and Miquelon, and the Caribbean islands of Guadeloupe and Martinique. The Treaty of Hubertusburg, signed five days later, essentially returned Europe to its prewar status quo, with Prussia still in control of Silesia and its standing in Europe greatly enhanced.

A NIGHTTIME RAID WINS THE BATTLE FOR THE CITY THAT CONTROLLED NORTH AMERICA
The Battle of Quebec, 1759

As the summer turned to fall in 1759, Quebec, the forbidding fortress on the rocky peninsula jutting out into the St. Lawrence River, was the proudest of the French fortresses in Canada and, together with the less strategically significant town of Montreal, further up the river, was the nation's last great stronghold in North America. The grand fortress of Louisbourg on the Atlantic coast at Cape Breton had fallen to British guns in the summer of 1758, which had opened the way for a British amphibian advance up the St. Lawrence River to the very doorstep of Quebec. For the British, Quebec would be a glorious prize, for it controlled the watery highway that led straight to the heart of the continent and its lucrative fur trade. Whoever controlled Quebec controlled North America.

The British fleet arrived on the river outside the city in June of 1759. It was forty-nine ships strong and carried 8,500 hardened British soldiers (among its officers was one James Cook, future explorer of the Pacific). At the behest of Major General James Wolfe, the commanding officer, the soldiers disembarked at the Ile d'Orléans, just downstream from the city. Wolfe then set about establishing a battery, with which he began a steady bombardment of Quebec, which sat 350 feet (106 m) above the river, behind high walls. On July 12, Wolfe also attempted a frontal assault on the entrenched French force dug in 6 miles (10 km) south of Quebec, but this was repulsed with more than four hundred British casualties.

The bombardment continued unabated, but Quebec remained impervious to Wolfe's attacks. Long-distance cannonade might make life miserable for the Quebecois, but it could not batter down the walls of the city.

James Wolfe is one of the most fascinating military figures in British history. At the time of the battle for Quebec he was thirty-two years old and an up-and-coming star of the British military, favored by Secretary of State William Pitt himself. Wolfe had cut his teeth fighting Jacobite rebels in Scotland, and had distinguished himself at the siege of Louisbourg by finding a way into the previously unapproachable fortress.

Wolfe was an odd duck: tall, gangling, red-haired, nearly skeletal in appearance, cold, and imperious. There was something about him, as the historian John Keegan has written, that "set teeth on edge." He was also sickly, given to bouts of consumption, prone to painful kidney stones, and probably weakened by being bled by his physicians. By the time he arrived at Quebec, Wolfe was apparently convinced that he would die very soon, a fact that had a powerful bearing on the events that were to come.

Unable initially to find a way into Quebec, Wolfe had to settle on what he called "War of the Worst Shape … Skirmishing Cruelty & Devastation." Throughout July and August, his troops spread around the beautiful pastoral countryside outside Quebec, filled with farmhouses, churches, and windmills, and turned it into a smoking wasteland. Estimates at the time counted 1,400 farmsteads destroyed. No one knows how many lives were lost. Wolfe's aim was to draw the French forces out of Quebec to do battle. But the invitation was persistently refused by his opposite number, the Marquis Louis-Joseph de Montcalm.

Fifteen years older than Wolfe, Montcalm was a professional, aristocratic soldier who had gone to war at the age of fifteen. He had been wounded several times in the War of Austrian Succession and had so far served with distinction in the Seven Years' War, scoring a string of successes against the British in the early years of the conflict. His troops numbered about twelve thousand, scraped together from everywhere in Canada, though many of them were untried militia (they even included a thirty-five-man unit from a local Jesuit seminary). With this force, Montcalm had managed to fortify not only Quebec, but also the heights upriver of the city, in case the British fleet managed to slip by the city's defenses. Most of the men manning the heights were militia, so Montcalm had also reinforced them with one thousand regular soldiers led by a top aide, Louis-Antoine de Bougainville (the second future Pacific explorer present at the battle).

Much as he tried, the depressed and feverish Wolfe could find no way around these defenses. He convened a meeting of his three brigadiers, all of whom despised him—a feeling he returned. Their advice was simply to try to get past the city and cut off its lines of supply; it would starve to death in the coming winter. But Wolfe was not at all sure he, or his army, would survive the coming winter either.

A Path to Victory

A way out of Wolfe's dilemma was provided by a colorful character named Robert Stobo. A captain in the British colonial forces, Stobo had been captured by the French as early as 1755 and held prisoner in Quebec. After the arrival of Wolfe's force, he escaped and made his way to the British encampment on the Ile d'Orléans. There, he told Wolfe of a narrow footpath that led up the cliff to Quebec from a place called L'Anse au Foulon (Fuller's Cove), upriver of the city. According to Stobo, the French knew of the footpath, but, confident that an army would never get up it, had stationed only a small force at its end.

The next day, Wolfe went out into the St. Lawrence in a small boat, disguised as an ordinary soldier, and spent hours studying the pathway through a telescope. By the time he came back, he had made a daring plan: to send a column of British troops up the path, have them overwhelm the French forces there, and establish a foothold. Behind them would come the rest of his army, ready to do battle.

There is some evidence that Wolfe, who intended to lead the attack, believed that it would fail and that he would die on the cliffs above L'Anse au Foulon. Because, as he surmised, he was dying anyway, this would be a way out of his predicament: he could cover himself with glory, even if he could not successfully besiege Quebec. On September 12, the night of the attack, he gave his will, personal papers, and a picture of his fiancée to a friend, and then dressed in a brand new uniform.

But the evening went far better than the death-obsessed Wolfe expected. He and his force of about five thousand men floated noiselessly down the St. Lawrence under the noses of the French. Wolfe climbed the cliff with a detachment of two hundred Royal Marines, drove off the French garrison with no trouble, and, at 4 a.m. on September 13, found himself alive. Not only that, but thousands more British troops then climbed the cliff path and were soon gathering around him. So, a little after dawn, Wolfe marched his five thousand men 2 miles (3.2 km) through light rain squalls to the Plains of Abraham, a wide, flat, open area west of the city, and set up his army in a broad formation across the Grand Allée, the main road into town.

Montcalm, who had been up most of the night supervising defenses on another part of the French lines, rode up around 7 a.m. to see the British arrayed before him. He could not believe his eyes and said to an aide, "I see them where they have no business to be." One of his men later recalled that Montcalm looked "as if he saw his fate upon him."

Montcalm now had a decision to make. The British wanted to do battle and had taken their enemy by surprise. However, time was not on their side: Bougainville's force, stationed upriver, would certainly have heard the gunfire by now and be racing back to attack the British at the rear. All Montcalm had to do was sit tight inside the walls of Quebec.

But instead, he almost instantly ordered his troops outside to attack the British. Why he did this is uncertain: Wolfe was now in a position to set up siege guns, and it may be that Montcalm feared that Quebec could not withstand such a bombardment. Whatever his rationale, it was certainly a terrible mistake.

"A Perfect Volley"

As the French regular infantry lined up outside Quebec, French Indians and militia hiding in the woods on either side of the plains poured merciless sniper fire into the British lines. In response, Wolfe ordered his troops to lie down—an unusual order for a commander of that time to give his infantry, but one that made a good deal of sense. Wolfe, however, did not lie down but walked long the lines like a man who did not have a care in the world, as bullets zipped by his head.

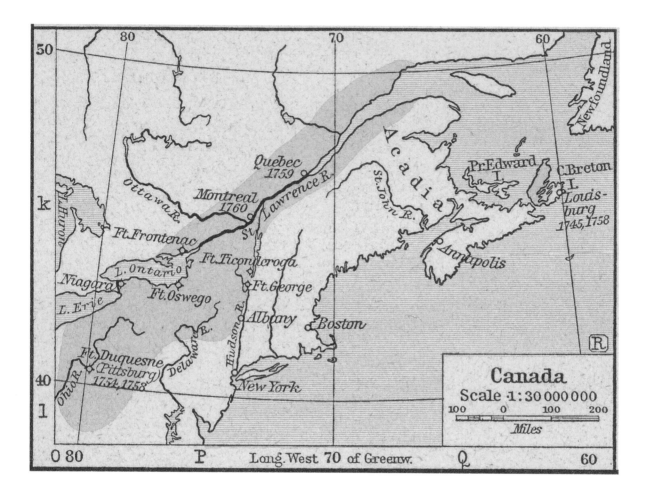

THE SEVEN YEARS' WAR WAS A WORLDWIDE CONFLICT, WHICH, IN NORTH AMERICA, CENTERED ON THE ST. LAWRENCE AND OHIO RIVERS IN THE NORTHEASTERN REGIONS OF PRESENT-DAY CANADA AND THE UNITED STATES, SHOWN IN THE MAP. THE BATTLE OF QUEBEC IN 1759 WOULD EVENTUALLY RESULT IN THE LOSS OF THE WHOLE OF NORTH AMERICA TO BRITAIN.

At about 10 a.m., the French infantry began advancing. Wolfe ordered his men to their feet, and a wall of red uniforms stretched across the plain, anchored on the left by Scottish Highlanders in their tartans—the troops Wolfe considered to be his strongest. The French, in their red waistcoats and white surcoats, charged toward the British, cheering and shouting, but soon lost unit cohesion. When they reached a point about 130 yards (120 m) from the British line, many of them opened fire; but they were at the far end of musket range, and their balls did little damage to the British soldiers.

Still, however, the French kept advancing, and the British soldiers knelt and prepared themselves. Wolfe had ordered them to load double shots in their guns and, as a sergeant later recalled, "not to fire a Shot until the enemy should be within Forty yards of the point of our bayonet." Legend has it that a single volley—a single "perfect volley," as one British officer called it—was fired at the enemy by every man in the British line; certainly, there were no more than three. In any event, the effect of thousands of musket balls fired at 40 yards (37 m) was devastating. Many French soldiers were literally blown apart. And those who still had their limbs turned and began to run almost immediately. At this, the Highlanders unsheathed their claymores—traditional Scottish broadswords carried by soldiers and officers alike—and attacked. This, however, exposed the Highlanders to fire from the Indians and militia in the woods, and they took heavy casualties, which in turn allowed Quebec's defenders to retreat within the city walls.

Around this time, on the right side of the British line, Wolfe was mortally wounded by flanking fire. He had already been wounded once, in the wrist—a nasty gash from a skimming bullet, which he had nonchalantly bound up in a handkerchief. But as the French turned to run, he was hit directly in the chest by a bullet. He died soon after, as he had predicted he would, but not without knowing that his men had the enemy on the run. His heroic death was subsequently memorialized in art and literature, particularly in a famous oil painting by Benjamin West, The Death of General Wolfe (c. 1771), which depicts the British commander in the pose of Christ removed from the cross.

Ironically, shortly after Wolfe died, Bougainville at last appeared with his men on the Grand Allée, but the British rallied to set up a defensive line and drive him off. Had he appeared but an hour before, the fate of Quebec—and North America—might have been very different.

As the French forces retreated, Montcalm, too, was mortally wounded, hit by grapeshot from a British cannon. He was transported into the city by several soldiers, who kept him upright on the horse he insisted on riding. He died the next morning and was buried in a shell crater in the garden of an Ursuline convent. His death, too, would soon be mythologized by artists and writers.

As Montcalm died, the French still controlled Quebec, and there was still a large force of militia and Indians outside it, as well as Bougainville's army. However, French morale had been shattered, and, with rations running low, the city surrendered on September 18. The French would make an attempt to retake it the following year, but that would fail, and the fall of Quebec would result in the loss of the whole of North America to Britain.

PRUSSIA'S ENLIGHTENED TACTICIAN DRILLED HIS COUNTRY'S ARMY INTO GREATNESS

To his army, King Frederick II of Prussia was "Old Fritz," a misanthropic, grim-faced man who had taught them to fear him and their officers more than they feared the enemy. And yet, the soldiers respected him, too. For it was his conception of Prussian military might that had by the mid-eighteenth century made the country one of Europe's great powers.

Frederick was born in 1712. As a young man, he was more interested in the arts than in military affairs and feuded constantly with his father, King Frederick William I. Yet, on assuming the throne in 1740, he quickly perceived that Prussia faced a dilemma. A small state made up of disconnected principalities and surrounded by bigger, more prosperous countries—Frederick called it "a mollusk without a shell"—it either had to accept being swallowed up by its neighbors or try to expand and thereby preserve itself.

Frederick knew that, given his country's population base, he could raise an army of no more than 150,000. It followed, therefore, that his army had to be in quality what it could be not in quantity. So he focused on rigorous training and discipline. As his small army could not engage in protracted and bloody conflicts, Frederick made sure it was highly maneuverable. He drilled it incessantly in cadenced marching—not seen since the days of the Romans—whereby the men marched to the rhythm of call-and-response chants; this kept them in step, in turn making it easier for them to move from columns into lines of battle. He also trained his soldiers to fire more shots per minute from their muskets than any other army, and his cavalry to strike harder and faster than any cavalry corps it faced.

Maria Theresa's controversial accession as Holy Roman Empress gave Frederick the perfect opportunity to test his military machine and at the same time begin the expansion of Prussia that he felt was necessary for its survival. And in the ensuing conflict his army proved itself again and again, repeatedly defeating larger French and Austrian forces. But it was eventually overwhelmed and depleted almost by half at Kunersdorf in 1759—a defeat so devastating that Frederick nearly abdicated.

Despite this, at the war's end Prussia remained intact and had grown immensely in stature. Frederick lived out the rest of his reign corresponding with the philosopher Voltaire and ruling Prussia as an enlightened despot. As time passed, however, he became eccentric and solitary, wandering the streets of Berlin either alone or in the company of his beloved greyhounds. He died at the age of seventy-four in 1786.

THE BIRTH OF THE GREATEST NAVY IN THE WORLD

The British Royal Navy outclassed every other fleet in the Seven Years' War and was a key reason for the British victory. As an island nation, Great Britain had a much better established navy than France at the start of the conflict, and this turned out to be the most effective way for it to offset the massive French population advantage (there were twenty-five million people in France, as opposed to seven million in Britain).

The British opened the war with a tonnage of 277,000 tons (250,000 tonnes) and ended it with about 375,000 tons (340,000 tonnes); the French would boast, at best, 162,000 tons (147,000 tonnes). The British were also adept at capturing French and, later, Spanish ships, which they added to their fleet, along with the ships being constantly built—the British added sixty-nine new or refurbished vessels to their fleet during the course of the war; the French added only six. The French were further hampered by a disagreement in high circles of government about how to divide naval resources between land and sea.

The British employed their naval superiority in three ways: to capture and destroy French trading vessels heading from India and North America to Europe, to blockade the French fleet in its own home waters, and to attack the French fleet wherever they found it. In 1759, at the battles of Lagos Bay, Portugal, and Quiberon Bay, on the French west coast, the British registered victories so complete that, as one historian has written, they simply "swept the French off the ocean."

The unblemished British naval triumph in the Seven Years' War opened the door to the global voyages of the likes of Captain James Cook, which would in turn bring the nation immense wealth from trade during the late eighteenth and nineteenth centuries.

THE WEAPON THAT TURNED BATTLEFIELDS INTO SLAUGHTERHOUSES

The flintlock musket was the main weapon of the Seven Years' War for all armies involved. Introduced at the beginning of the eighteenth century, the flintlock was not accurate beyond 50 yards (46 m), but it allowed, for the first time, for massed and rapid firepower (a trained musketeer could fire three rounds a minute).

In turn, the widespread use of the flintlock changed the way armies maneuvered and arrayed themselves. Extended front lines just two men deep, which allowed for massed firing, became the norm—at the battle of Leuthen, the Austrian lines were 4.5 miles (7.2 km) wide. Each battalion along the line was flanked by two or three artillery pieces, which provided additional firepower but also marked a dividing line between battalions. The soldiers were split into small groups, each of which fired a volley in turn, from the center of the line out to the wings. After three volleys, the soldiers would fire at will.

At close range, the heavy musket ball could do horrible damage, which made the battlefields of the Seven Years' War, as the historian Frank McLynn has written, "scenes of frightful carnage … with men running around without eyes or noses or other extremities." The so-called "perfect volley" fired by the British at Quebec, which sent about three thousand musket balls into the French at close range, was a commanding officer's dream, but it turned the battlefield into an abattoir.

14

THE AMERICAN REVOLUTION

1775–83

THE REBELLION OF NORTH AMERICAN COLONISTS AGAINST THE
BRITISH GOVERNMENT, WHICH CREATED THE UNITED STATES AND
EXPORTED IDEAS OF FREEDOM AND EQUALITY AROUND THE WORLD

IN ONE OF THE MOST SUCCESSFUL REVOLUTIONS IN THE HISTORY OF THE WORLD, AMERICA THREW OFF BRITISH RULE AND BECAME INDEPENDENT

After the end of the Seven Years' War, the British government attempted to recoup some of the massive financial costs of its victory by raising taxes on its North American colonists; between 1764 and 1767, the British Parliament passed the Sugar, Stamp, and Townshend acts, all placing heavy tariffs or direct taxes on American goods. This gave rise to a good deal of dissatisfaction among the colonists, and a desire for additional rights. Initially, most colonists did not seek independence from Britain, but simply the same rights that British citizens had, in particular the right to govern themselves through their own legislative assemblies. But attitudes began to harden after incidents such as the Boston Massacre in 1770, in which British troops fired on Americans protesting the British military occupation of Boston, killing three, and the Boston Tea Party in 1773, in which American rebels tossed tea overboard from British ships in Boston Harbor to protest the favorable treatment given to British tea merchants. The first Continental Congress, a meeting of the leaders of twelve of the thirteen colonies, took place in September 1774. Colonial militia groups known as Minutemen began to form outside of Boston and caches of arms and powder were hidden in farms and cellars.

In April of 1775, the shooting war began. British troops sent by General Thomas Gage to seize one such arms cache clashed with Minutemen in Lexington and Concord, who had been alerted by rebels Paul Revere and William Dawes. Heavy casualties resulted on both sides. In May, a group of rebels under Vermont militia leader Ethan Allen and Connecticut militia captain Benedict Arnold seized the key British Lake Champlain strongholds of Ticonderoga and Crown Point. In June, rebels battled British troops at Bunker Hill near Boston, inflicting more losses, though they were ultimately forced to relinquish the hill.

In the meantime, the second Continental Congress had met and named George Washington commander in chief of the Continental army. Americans, fired up by the fighting in Massachusetts and the rhetoric of rebel leaders such as Tom Paine and John Adams and his cousin Samuel, flocked to join the army. Even so, there was still a clear divide in America between two groups; Tories, or Loyalists, who sympathized with the British and King George III—whose policies toward the American rebels were, at this point, harsh and uncompromising—and those American colonists who now increasingly sought independence.

AN OIL PAINTING OF THE FIRST ENGAGEMENT BETWEEN BRITISH AND AMERICAN TROOPS IN 1775

A View of the Taking of Quebec, September 13th 1759 (color engraving), English School, (18th century) / Private Collection / The Bridgeman Art Library International

In the fall of 1775, the American rebels invaded Canada in an attempt to open a two-front war that would drain British resources. However, a force of colonial fighters under Benedict Arnold, now a colonel, was defeated outside Quebec and forced to retreat back into the American colonies. In June of 1776, the British, having withdrawn from Boston, landed thirty-two thousand troops, the largest army seen to date on the North American continent, in New York. Under General William Howe, this force sought to cut off the northern colonies—which King George and his ministers considered to be the more troublesome—from the southern ones.

Although he moved slowly, Howe was able to defeat American forces under George Washington at the battles of Brooklyn, Long Island, White Plains, and Morristown, driving Washington's force south through New Jersey and across the Delaware River into Pennsylvania. However, another prong of the British attack—British troops under General Guy Carleton moving south from Canada to attack New York in the west via Lake Champlain and Lake George—was halted in October when General Benedict Arnold challenged it with a hastily built American fleet near Valcour Island on Lake Champlain. Although the Americans were ultimately defeated, they delayed Carlton long enough that he was forced to turn back to winter in Canada.

On July 4, 1776, the Continental Congress issued the Declaration of Independence, calling for the severing of all ties from Great Britain. And the year ended on a high note for the rebels with George Washington's successful surprise attack against British and Hessian troops at Trenton the day after Christmas, which began with his famous night crossing of the frozen Delaware River. This gave the rebels a huge psychological boost because it showed that they could win against the seemingly unbeatable forces of Howe.

The year 1777 was a pivotal one. The British once again tried to split the American colonies in half by sending forces under General John Burgoyne south from Canada in the summer to meet with General Howe, who was to move up the Hudson River from Albany, New York. But Howe, tempted by the prize of capturing the rebel capital of Philadelphia, instead moved south, seizing that city in September; Burgoyne, after initial successes, found himself isolated and was ultimately defeated at the battle of Saratoga in October.

The French entered the war on the American side the following year, and the British retreated from Philadelphia to New York, with George Washington's army shadowing them. The action now shifted to the southern colonies. In 1780, British forces under Sir Henry Clinton captured Charleston, South Carolina, the south's biggest port; in August of that year, General Lord Cornwallis defeated the forces of General Horatio Gates at Camden and began a campaign to subdue the south. But twin rebel victories—at King's Mountain in October and in November at the battle of Cowpens—severely hurt the British.

Harried by both the Americans and the French under the Marquis de Lafayette, Cornwallis retreated to Yorktown, Virginia, in October of 1782. Hemmed in by a Franco-American force led by George Washington on land, and by a French fleet at sea, he was forced to surrender on October 19, ending the last major battle of the conflict. Under the Treaty of Paris of 1783, Great Britain recognized American independence.

THE BATTLE THAT KEPT THE AMERICANS FROM LOSING THE WAR—AND MADE A HERO OUT OF BENEDICT ARNOLD
The Battle of Saratoga, 1777

British commander "Gentleman Johnny" Burgoyne—so called not only because he was good to his soldiers, but because he "bestowed so much time on his toilet that he looked more like a man of fashion than a warrior"—marched through the American wilderness south of Lake Champlain in the late summer of 1777 as if he were going on an excursion. Long supply trains carried featherbed mattresses, heavy chests full of clothing, and fine foods. Officers' wives came along on the trip, as well as camp followers for the soldiers. The forces included 4,000 British regulars, 500 artillery men (lugging 130 brass guns), a loyalist militia of 500 Americans and Canadians, 3,000 German mercenaries or Hessians, and 400 Indians, whose tattooed faces (not to mention the scalps dangling from their belts) frightened the ladies.

Burgoyne, who had begun his march south from Canada in the spring, was relaxed and confident, as he had a low opinion of the American soldiers opposing him, agreeing with a former British commander, James Wolfe, who thought American colonial fighters "the most contemptible cowardly dogs you can conceive." Despite the American stand at Bunker Hill and the brave victory of George Washington and his men at the battle of Trenton, Burgoyne was sure he could sweep aside the Americans, link up with General William Howe at Albany, who would be moving up the Hudson to meet him from New York, and cut the colonies in half, severing New England and New York from the south.

In July, Burgoyne recaptured Fort Ticonderoga with such ease that when King George III heard about it, perhaps a month later, he went skipping into the queen's bedroom, clapping his hands and shouting with glee, "I beat them! Beat all the Americans!" But it wasn't going to be quite that simple.

A Series of Mistakes

After his quick victory at Ticonderoga, Burgoyne made a number of mistakes. He needed to reach the Hudson River, to sail down to Albany, but he chose to take his army 23 miles (37 km) overland from Lake Champlain, rather than continuing by boat down Lake George and then portaging only 10 miles (16 km) to the river. His troops became mired in the wilderness and were repeatedly ambushed by the Americans, with the result that they covered an average of just 1 mile (1.6 km) a day—it took them twenty-three days to reach the Hudson.

Another mistake was not keeping his Indians in check. Just before the army reached the Hudson, some of these warriors murdered a young woman named Miss Jane McCrea, who was engaged to marry a Tory officer in Burgoyne's militia. The uproar at this quickly spread through the entire region—both Tories and patriots alike blamed Burgoyne for the outrage, and volunteers poured into the American camps farther down the Hudson.

And on August 3, when he finally reached the Hudson, Burgoyne received shocking news: General Howe was not going to link up with him in Albany, but was in fact on his way to besiege Philadelphia. There had been some leeway in Howe's orders, he expected Burgoyne to succeed without a problem, and he wanted to cover himself with glory before the younger officer got it all. He had left seven thousand men in New York under Sir Henry Clinton, but this force had not even started up the river.

To make matters even worse, Burgoyne's trip from Lake Champlain had cost him badly needed supplies; a raiding expedition sent to Bennington, Vermont, had been bloodily repulsed; and another British column moving through the Mohawk Valley had been blocked and was already retreating to Canada. Under the circumstances, it might have been wiser for Burgoyne to do the same, but he had dreams of glory. So he crossed the Hudson to its left bank, and continued south to meet the Americans about 9 miles (14.5 km) south of the settlement that would later became known as Saratoga, and which would give its name to the ensuing engagements.

On the left side of the Hudson, an American force of about seven thousand men—with more new recruits pouring in daily—was entrenched at a bluff called Bemis Heights, which rose sharply from almost at the river's edge to a height of more than 100 feet (30 m). The commander of the Americans was General Horatio Gates, a poor, defensive-minded soldier who nonetheless had two brilliant subordinates: General Benedict Arnold and General Daniel Morgan. Gates's position on Bemis Heights was quite strong, but he had failed to fortify two higher ridges behind him. On the morning of September 19, as "the sun burned off the mist and melted a light frost into dew," Burgoyne sent about four thousand men, divided into three columns, to attempt to capture this ground.

A PLAN OF THE SITE OF THE BATTLE OF SARATOGA, FLANKED BY ILLUSTRATIONS OF THE FARMHOUSE THAT SERVED AS THE REBEL COMMAND POST.

They never got there. Although General Gates had wanted to stay behind his fortifications and await the British, Arnold urged him to meet Burgoyne's forces in front of the Continental lines, in the woods, where the British would be unable to unleash their

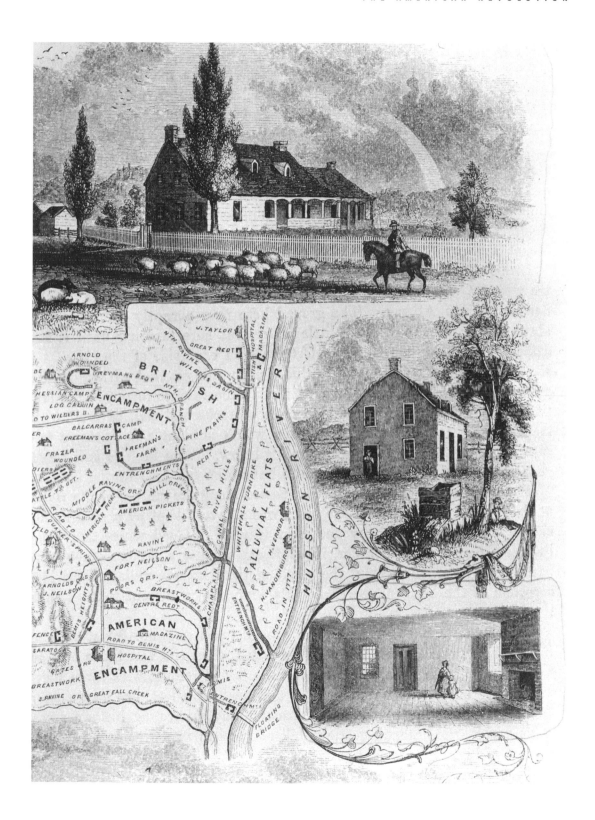

devastating volley fire. With some reluctance, Gates agreed. As the British columns entered a 350-yard (320-m)-wide clearing known as Freeman's Farm, Gates ordered Daniel Morgan's riflemen to take up positions in the woods. These men, dead shots with their long rifles, climbed into trees or hid in the underbrush, communicating to each other by turkey calls. Then they began to pick off the British officers—they called them "kingbirds" for the white underbellies beneath their red coats—one by one.

Soon after, the American lines charged. A fierce struggle raged for three hours, with each side taking turns at pushing the other back, the battle fluctuating "like the waves of a stormy sea," as one observer wrote. In charge of the left flank, Arnold dashed forward in a frantic charge, trying to break down the British right, and was only forced to withdraw under a savage flank attack by five hundred Hessians.

Eventually, the Americans withdrew, leaving the battlefield to Burgoyne, but it was a costly victory for the British. They had lost more than 600 men, killed, wounded, or taken prisoner, compared to about 380 casualties for the Americans. The dead lay "as thick as I ever saw rock heaps lay in a field," as one American soldier described it to his family. The British had won, but as an officer in Burgoyne's staff put it, "no very great advantage, honor excepted, was gained by the day."

Battle for Bemis Heights

For the next three weeks, both sides strengthened their positions on Bemis Heights. Burgoyne was waiting for word that Sir Henry Clinton was moving north to meet him, but although Clinton had begun to move north up the Hudson on October 5, he had failed, despite numerous attempts, to get word through to Burgoyne. In any event, he stopped well short of Albany, moving too cautiously for fear of attack, and assuming, as had Howe, that Burgoyne could easily beat the Continentals.

Gates, in the meantime, welcomed thousands of new recruits into his lines, men who had poured in from all over New York, Vermont, and Connecticut. The Americans were having their problems, too, however. Arnold, always prickly when it came to matters of honor, had become enraged at Gates for not mentioning his part in the battle at Freeman's Farm in dispatches to Congress; indeed, he had become so insubordinate that Gates ordered him confined to his tent and chose another officer to command the American right wing.

On October 7, Burgoyne, growing more desperate, decided to take a chance and sent a column of about 1,700 men on a reconnaissance in force, under General Simon Fraser, toward the American right flank, seeking a breakthrough. The Americans reacted almost immediately, with Daniel Morgan's men sharpshooting at the enemy and killing Fraser.

Meanwhile, Arnold, confined to camp, was like a caged lion, desperate to get into a fight. One observer wrote, "He rode about the camp betraying great agitation and wrath, and he ... was observed to drink freely." Finally, against orders, he rushed into the battle.

Arnold's arrival changed the course of the wavering encounter. He first help rally the forces of the American general Ebenezer Learned, leading them in a charge that drove the British back to their redoubts. A soldier later described how Arnold led from the front, "He was a bloody fellow ... It was 'Come on, boys!' Twasn't 'Go, boys!'"

BENEDICT ARNOLD'S BELATED ENTRY INTO THE FRAY AT BEMIS HEIGHTS TIPPED THE BALANCE TOWARD AN AMERICAN VICTORY.

Then, joining Learned's men with those of Daniel Morgan, Arnold, fighting in a frenzy, led another charge directly at British positions. At this point he was seriously wounded in the leg; yet he still urged his men on to take the British fortifications, which they did.

When darkness fell on the battlefield, the Americans were in a commanding position. The British had lost 600 men, the Americans about 130. There was nothing for Burgoyne to do but withdraw, which he did, to what is now Saratoga. The next day he surrendered his entire force to Horatio Gates. He and his officers were paroled back to England. His men were sent to a prison camp.

"Up to the Stars"

The news of Burgoyne's defeat, John Adams wrote a friend, "lifted us up to the stars," particularly after the loss of Philadelphia to the British. Indeed, the battle of Saratoga would have far-reaching consequences. Not only was it an extraordinary morale boost for the Americans, but it also encouraged France to come into the war, in February of 1778, which helped the patriot cause immeasurably. One negative effect, however, was its impact on Benedict Arnold. Gates's treatment of him and the general's subsequent attempts to rob him of any credit for his courageous work that day undoubtedly pushed Arnold farther toward the act of treason that would make his name infamous in U.S. history.

GEORGE WASHINGTON: AN INDISPENSABLE LEADER

When the British sharpshooter Patrick Ferguson had George Washington in his sights but decided against shooting him, it is no exaggeration to say that the course of American history was changed. For Washington was the one person without whom the American rebels could not have succeeded.

CORNWALLIS SURRENDERS AT YORKTOWN, OCTOBER 19, 1781.

Washington was born into a genteel Virginia family in 1732, and given a strong education in mathematics and the classics. For a profession, he took up surveying. He became a militia major and in 1753 was sent by the Governor of Virginia to warn the French against further encroachment on land in the Ohio valley. He was then made a lieutenant colonel in the newly created Virginia Regiment, but suffered a disastrous defeat when he was overwhelmed by the French in an all-day battle at Fort Necessity, in southwestern Pennsylvania. He redeemed himself in the French and Indian War, before getting married and returning to civilian life as a planter and politician. Soon he became the leader of a group of colonists who opposed British rule, and a delegate to both the First and Second Continental Congresses. In 1775, he was named commander in chief of the Continental army.

At 6 feet 2 inches (188 cm) tall—taller, as the diminutive John Adams said acerbically, than everyone else in the room—Washington was the perfect choice. He wasn't always successful in battle—in fact, he was soundly beaten by the British during most of 1776.

In fact, some members of Congress sought to replace him. But although he was sometimes despairing in private, in public he was a tower of strength, and he was able to draw on deep reserves of stubbornness and stamina. His famous crossing of the Delaware to launch a surprise attack on Hessian forces at Trenton on December 26, 1776, helped turn the war around, and his brilliant maneuvering alongside the French at Yorktown effectively ended it. Moreover, Washington's integrity was unquestioned. Following his rapid rise in stature over the course of the war, he could have become king; but although he railed against Congress for not giving him enough men and supplies, he always deferred to civilian authority.

A reluctant first president after the war ("My movement to the chair of government will be accompanied by feelings not unlike those of a culprit who is going to his place of execution," he told a friend), he nonetheless served his country ably for two terms and died at the age of sixty-seven in 1799.

THE BRITISH ARMY IN NORTH AMERICA: LESSONS NOT LEARNED, AT GREAT COST

Lessons learned by the British during the French and Indian War about exploiting natural ground cover were not carried through to the American Revolution, where, in the main, British forces stuck with the rigid formations used on European battlefields: lines of men blasting away at each other from 50 to 75 yards (45 to 70 m), supported by cannons.

At Saratoga, Burgoyne was harried by Morgan's riflemen and outflanked by the Continentals' clever use of cover. In the south, Colonel Banastre Tarleton was defeated by General Daniel Morgan at Cowpens because Morgan was able to use British preconceptions about the inferiority of American forces against them: Morgan knew that the British assumed the Americans would run away, so he told his advance guard to pretend to run and had another force lie in wait for the pursuing Britons—a trap that soundly defeated Tarleton.

British soldiers carried the famous Brown Bess musket, a .75-caliber flintlock, which may have been named for the brown varnish applied to its barrel to keep it from rusting, and were far more expert with the bayonet than the Americans ever became.

About thirty thousand of the troops the British used against the Americans in the war were German mercenaries, mainly men from the region of Hesse-Kassel and consequently known as Hessians. They were feared and hated by the Americans for their supposed brutality and because of the fact that they were mercenaries—Americans considered the use of such paid fighters on the part of King George unfair. However, after the war many Hessians settled in the United States.

THE LONG RIFLE: DEADLIEST WEAPON OF THE REVOLUTIONARY WAR

Most of the fighting in the American Revolution was done with muskets, whose range was short and whose efficiency depended on the number of shots produced by repeated volley fire. But another kind of firearm was also used by the Americans, especially by backwoodsmen from Kentucky and Pennsylvania: the so-called long rifle.

Usually made by German gunsmiths in Pennsylvania, the long rifle had a barrel over 4 feet (1.2 m) long, which was usually inlaid with intricate silver engravings. Grooves on the inside of the barrel, known as "riflings" and carved by hand, were what gave the gun its incredible accuracy. While a musket might be accurate at up to 75 yards (70 m), a trained long rifleman could hit his mark at 500 yards (460 m), and there are reported instances of General Daniel Morgan's men making killing shots from 1,000 yards (900 m).

Long rifles had their drawbacks, however. They were slower to load because the lead balls they shot had to be tightly fit into the rifling on the inside of the barrel, which sometimes meant ramming them home with a mallet. And the narrow circumference of the barrel could not firmly fit a bayonet ring, so that riflemen could not make a bayonet charge or withstand one.

But as a sniper's weapon, they were extraordinarily effective. During the battle of Saratoga Daniel Morgan gathered his finest marksmen and pointed out the British general Simon Fraser, who was rallying his men. "Do you see that gallant officer mounted on a charger?" Morgan said. "That is General Fraser—I respect and honor him, but it is necessary that he should die." The long riflemen raised their weapons and in a moment Fraser fell, mortally wounded.

WASHINGTON LED COURAGEOUSLY, AND LED BY EXAMPLE.

George Washington at Dorchester Heights, Massachusetts (colour litho), Leutze, Emanuel Gottlieb (1816–68) (after) / Private Collection / Peter Newark American Pictures / The Bridgeman Art Library

15

THE FRENCH REVOLUTIONARY WARS

1792–1802

THIS DECADE-LONG CONFLICT RESHAPED FRANCE AFTER THE REVOLUTION AND SET THE STAGE FOR THE TITANIC EUROPEAN POWER STRUGGLES OF THE NINETEENTH CENTURY.

WARS OF LIBERTY THAT OVERTHREW THE OLD ORDER IN FRANCE AND TRANSFORMED ALL OF EUROPE

In 1789, the history of France changed forever. Burdened with the largest population in Western Europe, a faltering economy, and heavy taxation, the country saw huge masses of unemployed drift toward urban areas, where radicals stirred unrest over the repressive and unresponsive regime of King Louis XVI.

Encouraged by the successful American Revolution, the French revolted, creating a national legislative body. In September 1791, Louis was forced to approve a new constitution for France; a year later, the monarchy was abolished. In January 1793, Louis XVI was beheaded. (His queen, Marie Antoinette, followed him to the guillotine in October.)

Other European countries, notably Great Britain, Austria, and Prussia, were concerned about developments in France. In August 1791, the Holy Roman Emperor Leopold II (brother of Marie Antoinette) and King Frederick William II of Prussia issued the Declaration of Pillnitz, in which they threatened unspecified consequences should anything happen to Louis XVI and Marie. The Pillnitz Declaration was, in the main, posturing, because almost no one felt that the Bourbon Dynasty could be restored, but in a France divided by food shortages and full of rumors of enemies, it was taken seriously.

French politicians, in the form of the National Convention, the new ruling body of France, also saw this as an opportunity to push France's borders back out to their traditional outlines, which meant heading north into the Austrian Netherlands (modern-day Belgium and Luxembourg) and west to the Rhine. In April 1792, France declared war on Austria and invaded Belgium. Alarmed, Britain, Austria, Spain, Prussia, Russia, and Holland formed what is known as the First Coalition. The disorganized French troops were easily driven back, and a mainly Prussian invasion force supported by Austrian infantry and French royalist émigrés now headed into France.

The situation seemed dire for the new Republic, but the Prussians were stopped near the Belgian village of Valmy in September 1792 by a newly-inspired French army.

After the Prussians withdrew, the French embarked on a string of military successes that saw Revolutionary armies push south into Italy, west into Germany as far as Frankfurt, and finally north into Belgium, where the French won a victory over the Austrians at the Battle of Jemappes in November, thus occupying the whole country.

In January 1793, the execution of Louis XVI galvanized much of Europe, and the Coalition attacked with renewed energy. The allies at first pushed back the French on all fronts, regaining almost everything they had lost the previous year, but with mass conscriptions, the French were able to field a huge, motivated army by the fall of 1793. In 1794, the revolutionaries won key victories, driving the Prussians across the Rhine and winning the Battle of Fleurus, which gained them back the Austrian Netherlands.

The French continued on to occupy the Dutch Netherlands, the Rhineland, and parts of Italy (the latter victories due to the successes of the charismatic young leader Napoleon Bonaparte). With Holland conquered, Spain and Prussia sued for peace in 1795. The First Coalition phase of the French Revolutionary Wars then ended in 1797 when Austria signed the Treaty of Campo Formio in October, recognizing France's territorial gains.

However, Great Britain, alone among the Coalition powers, remained in the war, depending particularly on her powerful navy, which kept France blockaded. In part to threaten British interests in India, Napoleon attacked Egypt, destroying Mamluk forces at the Battle of the Pyramids in July 1798. However, the following month the great British admiral Horatio Nelson demolished the French fleet at Aboukir in the Battle of the Nile, thus ending Napoleon's hopes of conquering the country.

Inspired by this victory, and as other French forces struck farther south into Italy, capturing the Papal States, the Second Coalition of allied powers was formed, consisting of Russia, Britain, Austria, Portugal, Britain, and the Ottoman Empire. Russian and Austrian forces won pivotal victories in northern Italy early in 1799, but dissension between the Austrians and Russians, and growing unrest in Poland forced Russia to withdraw from the war.

The French under Napoleon (who, in a coup d'état, had become First Consul of France) defeated the Austrians at the Battle of Marengo in June 1800 and reoccupied northern Italy. The Austrians made a separate peace with France in February 1801, in the Treaty of Lunéville.

A combined British and Ottoman force finally defeated the French Army of the Orient in Egypt in September of that year. But, war-weary and fighting almost alone, the British finally signed the Treaty of Amiens in March 1802, thus ending the French Revolutionary Wars. Peace would be short-lived, however, because a newly crowned Emperor Napoleon Bonaparte would soon pit his will and army against all of Europe.

A RAGGED BAND OF CITIZEN SOLDIERS HELD OFF THE MOST POWERFUL ARMY IN EUROPE, SAVING THE REVOLUTION
The Battle of Valmy: September 20, 1792

A mist hugged the ground, not the light mist of spring and summer, but a thick, low mist of autumn, one that clung to the bushes and trees like lamb's wool. In the night the mist had drifted over the high plain occupied by the French, collecting in the ravines and low places, making visibility impossible. Almost no one in this ragtag Revolutionary army of some 36,000 had been able to sleep; because campfires were not allowed, the soldiers huddled together for warmth and strength.

In the dark distance, they could hear the gathering Prussian army, the hooves of crack cavalry, the thunderous tread of the formidable infantry, and the creaking supply caissons. There were 30,000 Prussians out in the Argonne Forest, in what is now modern-day Belgium, accompanied by a contingent of light Austrian troops and a regiment of Frenchmen who had remained loyal to King Louis XVI and sought to restore him to his throne.

The French soldiers on the ridge near the little village of Valmy knew that the way to Paris, one hundred miles distant, lay open to this formidable Coalition force—that in fact, the Prussians lay between them and their own homes. In the morning, the Prussians intended to crush this threat in their rear, just the way they had crushed the French armies all that fateful summer of 1792.

Then they would march on to Paris and deal, once and for all, with the Revolution.

Five months earlier, on April 20, after much debate, the French National Assembly declared war against Austria and, soon after, Prussia. This was partly in response to the Declaration of Pillnitz, which threatened the stability of the new French Republic, and partly because many radical French thinkers thought that now was the time to spread the word of the Revolution—and also to regain territory lost in previous wars, particularly the Austrian Netherlands (modern-day Belgium).

"This war will be the last war," declared Foreign Minister Charles François Dumouriez, meaning that after this conflict, Europe would understand the power of Revolutionary France's new way of life. The next month, Dumouriez, appointed general in charge of the French Revolutionary Army, sent troops to invade Belgium.

Dumouriez and other French politicians were soon to discover they had little cause for optimism. The French army had lost more than half of its officers as defectors to the Austrians and Prussians. The levée en masse of the next year was not yet in place, and so Dumouriez and his generals had to be content with a rabble of volunteers in an army that was also rife with spies for Dumouriez's political enemies back in Paris. It was, to say the least, an impossible army, poorly trained and rife with divisions.

Going up against the well-trained cadres of the Austrians and Prussians, whose skills had been honed in the Seven Years' War, the results were predictable. The first French corps, consisting of about 1,000 soldiers, crossed the frontier into Belgium in June, encountered a far smaller Austrian force at the city of Tournai, and immediately fled in panic, crying "We've been betrayed!" They didn't stop running until they were back in Lille, where they murdered their own general, whom they, in their panic, thought had betrayed them to the Austrians.

Similar scenes were played out elsewhere along France's northern border that summer—10,000 cavalry troops beat a hasty retreat after exchanging a volley with a far inferior Austrian force in Belgium, while another French division turned tail when a rumor spread through the ranks that their powder was defective. In Paris, the politicians blamed the generals in the field, old-line royalists such as the famous Marquis de Lafayette. In fact, the National Assembly declared him a traitor, and he was forced to flee for his life to Liège, where he was taken prisoner by the Austrians.

Observing all this from along the Rhine, General Karl Wilhelm Ferdinand, Duke of Brunswick and commander of the Prussian Army, saw that rapid disintegration of French forces had opened up a glorious opportunity. With his well-trained army, he could strike right at the heart of France, heading southeast. Nothing lay in his way but three poorly maintained fortresses at Sedan, Longwy, and Verdun, and two small armies. One of these was commanded by a journeyman commander named General François Kellerman; the other had been leaderless since Lafayette fled.

Promenade to Paris

The pickings seemed so easy to the Prussian army that its officers gaily talked about a "promenade to Paris," a walkover of the obviously cowardly rabble who made up the French Revolutionary Army. The Prussian invasion, launched in late July, was seen as such an excursion that sightseers went along with the army, including young German poet Johann Wolfgang von Goethe, who was impressed by the discipline of the Prussian regulars, although he confessed himself dismayed by some of the French aristocrats who had joined up to fight against their former fellow citizens and who put on insufferable airs.

At first, the Prussians simply rolled over the French, much as the German panzers would make mincemeat of French defenses in 1940. Fortress Longwy was lost on August 21; Verdun fell September 2.

"Moving majestically forward, with leisurely deliberation," as historian Edward Creasy wrote, the massive Prussian column placed itself between the two French armies and was preparing to destroy each in turn before striking at Paris, when General Dumouriez arrived from Paris to take control of the leaderless forces. Seeing that, as he later wrote, "France was within a hairsbreadth of destruction," he was able to gather the scattered and demoralized troops of Lafayette's former army and make a brilliant stand in the Argonne Forest, that dense swath of Belgium woodland and rocky hills that was also the scene for so much fighting in the Second World War. Forcing the Duke of Brunswick's columns ever farther south, he pushed them directly against the forces of François Kellerman, who were situated on that high plateau near Valmy, waiting in the fog.

Vive la Nation!

The French Revolutionary army, at this stage in the war, was not yet the citizen-soldiery it would become, but almost literally citizens. There were cooks, artists, shoemakers, tanners, farmers, writers, politicians, men from every walk of life. And not just men, either. The Revolution had become known for its women fighters, the most famous being Reine Chapuy, Rose Bouillon, Catherine Pocheta, and the young Fernig sisters. These men and women did not have uniforms, and their weaponry ran from standard issue French muskets to fowling guns, spears, pikes, and swords.

But they had several advantages the advancing Prussians knew little about. To begin with, their subalterns—the army's class of noncommissioned officers—had not fled with the royalist officers and were there to provide backbone for these raw soldiers. True, the army had performed poorly during the summer, but at Valmy that morning the noncoms moved quietly among the army, steadying the soldiers as the fog lifted and the white uniforms of the Prussians came into view.

Another French advantage was its artillery corps, forty cannon strong. The Duke of Brunswick outgunned the Revolutionary army by some fourteen pieces, but the French cannons were de Gribeauval 12-pounders with accurate sights and the ability to elevate and fire rapidly.

And—the final and decisive French advantage of the day—they were led by General François Kellerman, already fifty-seven years old, who had fought in the Seven Years' War. An object of some suspicion by radical French politicians because of his long association with the royal army, he had thus far escaped the purges that had befallen more prominent officers, mostly because of his journeyman status.

He wasn't considered a brilliant general, simply one who followed orders. That morning, however, he was inspired. Watching the Prussian cavalry move out from the main body of infantry to attempt to envelop his lines, seeing the nervousness among his troops,

whom cavalry frightened particularly, he rode his horse through the French lines shouting "Vive le nation!" "Vive la nation" over and over again. Gradually, the French soldiers took up the chant, so that the cry could be heard by the approaching Prussians.

But of course patriotic cries meant little to the Duke of Brunswick, who simply pushed his artillery to within 1,300 yards of French defenses and opened fire with a deafening roar.

A Kind of Blood-Red Tint

Brunswick and other Coalition officers expected the French to run at the first sound of the guns, to be chased down by the cavalry and slaughtered. After all, these soldiers had not made a stand since the war began. But the unexpected happened: With an answering roar, the French artillery opened up, and the Battle of Valmy was on.

THE BATTLE OF VALMY WAS ONE OF THE MOST IMPORTANT CLASHES IN WORLD HISTORY. WITHOUT THE FRENCH VICTORY THERE WOULD HAVE BEEN NO SUCCESSFUL FRENCH REVOLUTION AND NO NAPOLEONIC WARS.

Battle of Valmy, 20th September 1792, 1835 (oil on canvas) (detail of left hand side), Mauzaisse, Jean Baptiste (1784-1844) / Louvre, Paris, France / The Bridgeman Art Library

French soldiers rammed home shot after shot, sweating even on the cool day, and watched with cheers as they struck home among the massed Prussian troops. And Prussian cannonballs did their work among the French, although because of the wet ground—which caused the round shot to stick in the mud, rather than bounce murderously through the ranks—there were fewer casualties on both sides than otherwise might have been expected.

Valmy has been called one of the strangest great battles in the history of the world. It was essentially a battle fought by cannonade, which went on for hours. Goethe himself, riding through the shelling with a young man's foolish curiosity, compared the sound of the thousands of shots fired to "the humming of tops, the gurgling of water, and the whistling of birds." As the cannonade continued, Goethe claimed that he began to see the world around him as if through "a kind of blood-red tint"—an observation that might seem fanciful, but that has been repeated by other soldiers caught in intense artillery fire.

Finally, early in the afternoon, Brunswick decided to attack, but his men immediately met a killing field of accurate cannon fire and withdrew. At this point, thinking that the Prussian fire was growing less intense, Kellerman personally led a charge against the enemy. Racing through the smoke of battle out onto an open part of the plateau, the column he led was devastated by a hidden Prussian battery; Kellerman's horse was shot out from under him, and he had to be carried back to French lines by his own men. When this happened, the Prussians massed for attack, thinking the French were finally going to break, but Kellerman, now on foot, called out to his soldiers that this was the chance they had been waiting for—to let the enemy come close and then give them the bayonet.

More cheers of "Vive le nation" rang across the woods, and the advancing Prussians hesitated. They would have to charge up the hill, against a French army that seemed, for the first time, fearless and invigorated. The Duke of Brunswick paused—one of the most significant pauses in history—and decided slaughtering his fine army simply wasn't worth it.

A New Era

The casualties that day—300 French soldiers, perhaps 200 Prussians and Austrians—were insignificant in the larger scheme of things, but the victory at Valmy could not have been more momentous. That night, the weary French troops, many of whom had not even fired a shot or seen a Prussian up close, realized that the Prussians were no longer on the offensive. Indeed, after waiting ten days, the Duke of Brunswick brought his army back across the Rhine, deciding to fight another day.

There would be many other days and many other battles in the next twenty years of combat between France and the rest of Europe, but the French army proved it could defend the new liberty of its society. The day after the battle, the French Assembly declared France a Republic; four months later, King Louis XVI was executed.

A line can be drawn from the Battle of Valmy all the way to the Battle of Waterloo because without the victory at Valmy there would have been no French Revolutionary conflict, no Napoleonic Wars.

The importance of some events in history takes a while to set in, but not that of Valmy. The participants knew right away that something crucial had happened. The night of the battle, the French cheered and danced around their campfires, while there was gloom in the Prussian camp. Goethe, finding himself sitting around a campfire with Prussian officers, most of whom stared in sullen silence at the crackling flames, told them: "From this place and from this day forth commences a new era in the world's history, and you can all say that you were present at its birth."

He was right, but it is doubtful the Prussians found much comfort in this.

THE YOUNG NAPOLEON: A BRILLIANT LEADER ARISES TO SAVE THE FRENCH

Although he was later to spell the end of the French Revolution when he assumed the mantle of emperor in 1804, Napoleon Bonaparte personified the egalitarian spirit of the early days of the Republic. Born in 1769 to a poor Corsican family, he did not even speak French until he was nine years old and had arrived at the Royal Military School near Troyes, to be trained as an artillery officer. Short of stature, passionate, given to fits of near-epileptic intensity when he did not get his way, Napoleon was, as one of his teachers would write: "capricious, haughty and frightfully egotistical … [yet] proud, ambitious and aspiring to everything."

Bonaparte was brilliantly talented, but it was the Revolution that made him, because this eccentric Corsican would never have risen in the ranks of the royal French army. But with thousands of officers defecting, he found his chance. Known as a fervid supporter of the Republican cause, he was assigned as a captain of artillery to the siege of the southern port city of Toulon in September 1793. Royalist forces, aided by the Spanish, held the city while the British navy patrolled threateningly offshore. The twenty-four-year-old Napoleon seized the moment, finding the perfect positions to mount his artillery, forcing the British ships to withdraw. He was then wounded with a bayonet in the thigh while leading the assault that liberated the city. Within eight weeks, he was promoted to brigadier general, and his meteoric rise began.

In 1794, Bonaparte served in Italy as chief of staff to the French army there, lost this position after Maximilien de Robespierre and his Committee of Public Safety were purged, but landed on his feet politically again due to connections with those who formed the First Directory. Always having the knack of being in the right place at the right time, Napoleon found himself, in October 1795, in charge of an artillery battery facing a mob of counter-revolutionaries and royalists on the streets of Paris. He gave the order to fire canister point blank into the crowd, killing 1,400 of them.

It was the English writer Thomas Carlyle, not Bonaparte, who coined the famously insouciant line where Napoleon claimed to have given the mob "a whiff of grapeshot." What Napoleon actually wrote to one of his brothers was equally as cool-headed: "The enemy attacked us in the Tuilleries. We killed a great many of them … As usual, I did not receive a scratch. I could not be happier."

Shortly thereafter, Napoleon was given command of the French army in Italy. It was here he engineered the lightning strikes that were to make his reputation. Napoleon believed that an army should always be on the attack and that its only goal was to completely destroy the enemy. Within three weeks, he had swept aside the Piedmontese army, captured Milan and Naples, and turned his attention to Austria.

He won the battle of Rivoli on January 14, 1797; of Tagliamento on March 16; and of Arcola on November 15–17. These were not easy victories—fought over mountainous terrain, against a better-armed and trained enemy—but Napoleon triumphed. Napoleon himself led from the front—at Arcola he famously grabbed a banner and charged at the head of his men across a bridge, saving the day for the French.

Having nearly single-handedly forced the Austrians to the Treaty of Campo Formio, Napoleon returned to Paris in triumph. When he again left France at the head of the Army of the Orient in 1798—set on invading Egypt—the intimations of greatness that were always inside the young Corsican had come to the fore. One observer noted that "all bowed before the glory of his victories and the haughtiness of his demeanor. He was no longer the general of a triumphant Republic, but a conqueror on his own account...."

THE FRENCH CITIZEN-SOLDIER: A TOUGH AND MOTIVATED VOLUNTEER FIGHTER

"From this moment on until such time as all enemies have been driven from the soil of the Republic, all Frenchmen are in permanent requisition for the services of the armies. The young men shall fight; the married men shall forge arms and transport provisions; the women shall make tents and clothes and serve in the hospitals; the children shall turn linen into lint; the old men shall take to the squares in order to rouse the courage of the warriors..."

This passionate declaration, issued by the Committee of Public Safety on August 23, 1793, constituted one of the most important moments of the French Revolutionary Wars. For the first time, as the military philosopher Clausewitz later put it, there was "participation of the people in this great affair of state."

At the beginning of the Revolutionary Wars, more than half the army's officers, loyal to the king, had defected to the enemy, and the trustworthiness of those left behind was suspect. The army itself was ill-disciplined and poorly supplied. But, declaring that "the fatherland was in danger," the Committee conscripted all males between eighteen and twenty-five in what was called a levée en masse; appropriated as well were all material resources.

From every corner of France came not only willing men and women, but weapons, clothes, food, ammunition, and livestock. A year later, the French army had swollen to some 750,000 people, soldiers who were fairly well armed and trained. While it can't be said that such conscription was universally popular, the French achieved a great deal of success with their levy for a number of reasons. The typical draftee can be likened to a motivated volunteer fighter of the American Revolution at the time, often supplying his own arms and animals, leaving behind a family that supported him, and bringing with him men from his neighborhood or village. The very size of the levée overwhelmed the armies of the First Coalition, who had previously been on the verge of victory.

These raw recruits were trained under the auspices of Lazare Carnot, who had been a captain of engineers, but now became a kind of human resources manager for the French, whipping this huge mass of soldiers into shape, using the small corps of young and aggressive noncommissioned officers, and officers who arose from the ranks. It was a glorious time for any French fighter with intelligence, drive, and bravery, who was willing, as Carnot urged, "to give battle on a large scale and pursue the enemy until he is destroyed." One such upstart from the ranks, a captain named Napoleon, was to shape this levée en masse into the most formidable fighting force of its era.

THE FERNIG SISTERS—"VERY CAPABLE OF KILLING"

The French Revolution destroyed the monarchy that had ruled France for centuries, and it loosened people's ideas about the role of women in war. Just as numerous women took part in the violence of the Revolution and its aftermath (Maximilien de Robespierre had a body-guard made up entirely of women, in part to protect him from another woman, a royalist, who was trying to assassinate him), there were brave women fighters in the French army.

Chief among these were the Fernig sisters—Félicité, twenty-two, and Théophile, seventeen. Born in Flanders, they had been raised outdoors by their huntsman father and were sharpshooters and excellent archers. When the Revolutionary Wars broke out, they fought with local militia against the Austrians, blackening their faces, wearing men's clothing, and using their knowledge of the countryside to set up night ambushes. Their exploits became known, and they were introduced to General Charles François Dumouriez, who was so impressed by Fernig sisters that he gave them horses and uni-forms. The sisters fought at Valmy and Jemappes; at the latter battle, Félicité killed two Austrians who were about to bayonet a young Belgian officer to death. Both women, as a French review board later wrote, "were very capable of killing their men."

When Dumouriez ran afoul of the radical French government and defected in 1794, the loyal Fernig sisters defected with him. Although a monument now stands to them at the site of the battle of Jemappes, the French revolutionary government at the time never forgave them, and they remained outcasts for the rest of their lives.

FRENCH HEROINES FÉLICITÉ AND THÉOPHILE FERNIG, PICTURED ABOVE, WERE ONLY A COUPLE OF THE WOMEN WHO FOUGHT WITH THE FRENCH ARMY AGAINST AUSTRIA.

The French Heroines, Félicité and Théo-phile de Fernig in 1792, from "Le Petit Journal", 27th August 1894 (coloured engraving), Lix, Frédéric (1830–97) / Private Collection, Archives Charmet / The Bridgeman Art Library

16

THE NAPOLEONIC WARS

1803–1815

AFTER BARELY A PAUSE, EUROPE PLUNGES BACK INTO WAR, WITH
FRANCE'S REVOLUTIONARY IDEALS NOW SUBSUMED BY NAPOLEON
BONAPARTE'S CONQUERING AMBITIONS.

NAPOLEON TAKES ON EUROPE TO QUENCH HIS INSATIABLE THIRST FOR CONQUEST

After Napoleon Bonaparte was named First Consul of France and then emperor in 1804, what had been the French Revolutionary Wars evolved into a contest pitting Napoleon's own personal drive to conquer Europe against Europe's attempts to stop him.

Following the Treaty of Amiens (1802), the French continued to seize territory, including parts of Piedmont, Italy; Switzerland; and the Netherlands, angering the British, who in turn refused to turn over Malta as mandated by the treaty and instead declared war in 1803. Napoleon's plan to invade England foundered because of the might of the British Royal Navy. France's fleet was mainly destroyed by Admiral Horatio Nelson at the Battle of Trafalgar, off Spain, in 1805. But Europe belonged to Napoleon's superb Grand Army. Napoleon executed a series of stunning victories, defeating Austrian armies at Ulm, Austerlitz , and Jena after the first of what would be five Napoleonic War Coalitions was formed against him.

As the British navy blockaded France and seized French territory in the West Indies, Napoleon invaded Spain and Portugal; set up relatives as puppet kings in Spain, Italy, and the Netherlands; and defeated Coalition army after Coalition army. In 1808, he took a French army to Spain and forced the evacuation of the British army without even having to fight a major battle. The following year, however, he suffered his first defeat of the war, at the hands of the Austrians at Aspern-Essling. He won the next battle (at Wagram, in July) but only at the near-Pyrrhic cost of 34,000 French casualties.

Despite mass conscription—France had a population of 27 million at the time, compared to 11 million for the British, making it easier to recruit—Napoleon's Grand Army was gradually running out of men to replenish its ranks. Although Napoleon owned all of Western Europe by 1810, he foolishly decided to invade Russia in 1812, with famously disastrous results.

By December of that year Napoleon, faced with unrest at home, was forced to abandon his army, which suffered perhaps 400,000 casualties in the campaign. Despite the fact that he was able to raise a large army to fight the following year, his aura of invincibility was shattered and newly confident Coalition forces closed in for the kill: General Arthur Wellesley, Lord Wellington won stunning victories in Portugal and Spain and entered France, while Napoleon lost the largest battle of the war at Leipzig in October 1813.

A defeated Napoleon abdicated in April 1814 and was sent into exile on the island of Elba, Italy, but, resentful of his enforced captivity, escaped in early 1815, raised an army, and marched on Paris, where he forced the newly installed King Louis XVIII to flee. The Seventh, and last, Coalition of the Napoleonic Wars was formed, and the Duke of Wellington, with a little aid from Marshall Blücher and the Prussians, destroyed Europe's nemesis once and for all at the Battle of Waterloo. Napoleon was forced once again into exile—this time to the far-flung South Atlantic island of St. Helena—where he died in 1822.

The effect of the Napoleonic Wars was widespread. A reactionary climate ensued, with the Bourbon Dynasty placed back on the throne of France, although, ironically, Napoleon's carefully scripted appeals to the nationalism of the French people had their effect on the countries that had been enemies of the French. Independence movements began in Russia, Germany, and elsewhere, including South America (after the collapse of Spain as an empire) and Greece. These nationalist movements ultimately succeeded and altered the balance of power in Europe, and the world, by the twentieth century.

THE INVASION THAT DEVASTATED NAPOLEON'S GRAND ARMEE
The Invasion of Russia: 1812

For a year or so, beginning in 1810, those around the Emperor Napoleon had found him possessed of an unnatural lassitude. The dramatic, contradictory, impossible-to-predict little man who shook his fists and threatened and yelled when things did not go his way had been replaced by a relatively easygoing and now rather overweight new father of a young son by his marriage to Marie-Louise, Archduchess of Austria, the woman he had divorced his first wife, Josephine, to marry. Napoleon doted on his son. Upon his birth, he picked the boy up and "in a fever of joy" presented him to his courtiers, proclaiming, "Now begins the finest period of my reign."

By late 1811, though, people were beginning to wonder. Napoleon had not gone back to Spain to take command, despite the fact that the bloody war there had turned against the French. Was the great Napoleon tired of war and—some dared to hope—ready to see peace in Europe?

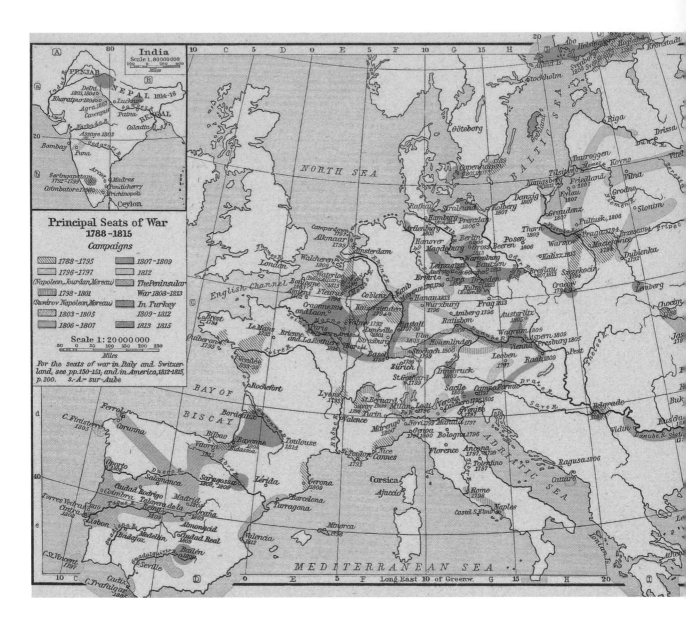

These were fond hopes indeed. Napoleon, always moody, had merely been tired of the protracted Spanish war and was waiting for a new world to conquer. And he found one. In 1812, Napoleon shook off his ennui and became as energized as anyone had ever seen him—traveling to inspect French fortifications, giving orders for new corps to be formed, and demanding that large munitions dumps be built in Poland and Germany. For those who knew Napoleon well, this manic phase meant he was going to war, a war that could only be with Russia.

"How Do You Expect To Be Able To Stop Me?"

Russia under Tsar Alexander I had been a reluctant ally of Napoleon's ever since the two countries had made peace five years earlier at Tilsit in 1807 following Napoleon's victory over a major Russian army at the Battle of Friedland in June of that year. But friendship with Napoleon was well-nigh impossible for Alexander. Napoleon's Continental System, which refused to allow barter with Great Britain, hurt Russia's trade badly. In the meantime, French encroachment in Poland, eastern Germany, and the Balkans threatened Russia's security.

In 1811, Tsar Alexander refused to comply with the Continental System and began making peace overtures to other neighbors, such as Sweden and the Ottoman Empire. When Napoleon realized this, he knew that war would surely follow. And, typically, he decided to strike first. The manic phase that many of his advisors saw in 1812 was a Napoleon in the almost-ecstatic grip of preparing for the largest invasion the world had ever known since the Mongol hordes traveled the other way in the fourteenth century. Napoleon had assembled 190,000 horses, wagons that could carry 7,000 tons of supplies daily, and an immense force of 614,000 men, compared to perhaps 220,000 Russian soldiers. He told his subordinates, "The aim of all my moves will be to concentrate an army of 400,000 men at a single point," break through Russian defenses, capture Moscow, and force Alexander in Saint Petersburg to sue for peace.

On June 24, 1812, Napoleon, at the head of a personal command group of 225,000 French soldiers, crossed the River Nieman and headed into Russian Poland. When Alexander I heard of this, he wrote a dispatch to Napoleon that began: "Monsieur mon frère, I learned yesterday that, in spite of the loyalty I have demonstrated in maintaining my engagements with Your Majesty, [your] troops have crossed the Russian border."

THE PRINCIPAL SEATS OF WAR IN EUROPE DURING 1788–1815 ARE DEPICTED IN THIS 1920S MAP. NAPOLEON'S INSATIABLE QUEST FOR CONQUEST WOULD TAKE HIM TO RUSSIA IN 1812, INSET ON RIGHT, WHERE RUSSIAN TROOPS, THE UNPREDICTABLE RUSSIAN WEATHER, STARVATION, AND WEARINESS WOULD DECIMATE HIS GRAND ARMEE.

Alexander went on to beg Napoleon to reconsider his invasion. To which Napoleon replied: "I have undertaken great preparations, and my forces are three times greater than yours … How do you expect to be able to stop me?"

Dead Horses

The answer to that question was almost immediately clear as Napoleon advanced into the vast plains of Russia. The Russian army did not try to stop him, but in fact retreated before him—as it had done against the Swedes in the Great Northern War, as it would do 140 years later against the Germans in World War II. Although Napoleon should have foreseen this, he did not, and he found himself robbed of the quick battle and victory he desired.

The farther into Russia Napoleon went, the farther the Russians retreated from the prongs of his mighty army groups, and gradually weariness and hunger began to tell on Napoleon's men. Their supply lines stretched for hundreds of miles and were easily broken up by Cossack cavalry. The Grand Army also began to feel the toll of the unpredictable Russian weather. Torrential rains would fall, creating thigh-deep mud, only to be followed by days of blazing sun that would bake deep ruts into the rudimentary roads being used.

Horses were the first to go, their intestines literally bursting open from eating green corn or thatch pulled from peasants' roofs. For many soldiers in the Grand Army, the memory of that period was of the stench of tens of thousands of dying horses and clouds of dust arising from the endless plains. Soon, the men themselves began to die, from dysentery, typhus, starvation, or simply exhaustion. When, on July 28, Napoleon finally crossed the Vilna River and entered the city of Vitebsk, hoping to catch the army of the Russian General Mikhail Barclay de Tolly, he found that Barclay had once again withdrawn with his forces. Napoleon raged to his advisors: "Alexander can see perfectly well how incompetent his generals are, and as a result he is losing his country."

But in fact, Alexander's generals were winning the war for him. Napoleon began to send peace overtures to the Tsar—written in a tone far removed from his arrogant message at the beginning of the campaign— but Alexander simply did not reply. In the meantime, the Russian retreat continued all throughout August, and now September had arrived.

Battle at Borodino

On September 7, Napoleon finally caught with the army of General Mikhail Kutuzov, who had replaced Barclay, near the little town of Borodino, some seventy-five miles southwest of Moscow. Kutuzov had approximately 106,000 men entrenched in strong positions among the hills and steep bluffs of the area, and Napoleon's commander, Marshal Louis-Nicolas Davout, recommended a flanking action to their left. Once he got past the formidable Russian guns, he told Napoleon that he could swing around and fall upon the enemy's flanks. But Napoleon—foreshadowing what would happen three years later at Waterloo—ordered a frontal attack. This was the move of an exhausted (and possibly sick) commander, because even though the French still outnumbered the Russians, they had lost thousands of men since invading and were hundreds of miles from home.

Even so, at the Emperor's command, the attack began, with Napoleon sending 100,000 of his troops straight at the lines held by Marshal Peter Bagration, one of the ablest Russian commanders. "The huge Russian redoubt belched out a veritable hell against our center," one French onlooker wrote. Many of Napoleon's faithful soldiers simply disappeared, blown to smithereens. But after hours of fighting, which included a massive bombardment by 300 guns, the Russians, with heavy losses, including the life of General Peter Bagration, were forced to withdraw. However, Napoleon refused to allow his Old Guard reserve of troops to follow up on the victory, and the Russian army lived to fight another day.

It was a French victory, but a Pyrrhic one, with Napoleon's losses totaling an incredible 40,000 dead and wounded. The Russians lost 50,000, but, close to home, could replenish these losses. Now, even the Emperor's confidence seemed to be shaken. "These Russians let themselves be killed as if they were not men, but mere machines," he told an advisor, unable to grasp the patriotism of his opponents.

The Eerie Silence of Moscow

Still, the way now lay open to Moscow, which Napoleon entered at the head of his army on September 15. He had expected a triumphal procession through a humbled and captive city population; instead, as one historian has written, "there was no life to be seen anywhere, not a face in a window, not a child in a garden, not a horse, carriage, or wagon in the streets."

The Russians had completely evacuated Moscow, leaving the beautiful city, with its 1,200 steeples, towers, clocks, and cupolas—"more Asiatic than European in appearance," wrote one French officer—completely deserted. Nonplussed, Napoleon made his way to the Kremlin, where all that could be heard was the chiming of clocks. That night, as the army dug in around Moscow, the fires began, first in the Chinese quarter, but then spreading rapidly throughout the city.

It soon became apparent that the Russians had left behind a hidden team of arsonists, whose job it was to set fire to Moscow. Napoleon, forced to flee the city for three days while the flames raged, simply could not believe that the Russians would destroy their own beautiful capital city to deny it to the French. He wrote a note to Tsar Alexander in Saint Petersburg that shows just how out of touch with reality the Emperor was becoming. "I waged war on Your Majesty without personal animosity," Napoleon wrote. "The fine, beautiful city of Moscow no longer exists because [your commanders] have burned it. A letter of capitulation from you before or after the battle [of Borodino] could have stopped my march."

Alexander did not reply. Instead, as the Russian fall set in, he ordered his commanders to close in and encircle French troops in the burned city of Moscow.

The Death March

Napoleon's commanders expected him to evacuate Moscow. It was the only move left open to him if he wanted to save his army, but he refused, instead claiming that "I could hardly be better suited than where I am now, in Moscow, to sit out the winter."

Perhaps Napoleon was fooled by the unusually warm fall weather because October had come by now and the temperatures were practically balmy. But rumors began to spread among the French, not for the first time, that the Emperor had lost his mind. He spent most of his time holed up within the walls of the Kremlin, eating alone,

[handwritten marginalia:] (XX) WhEN NApoleoN ENTERED moscow, he FoUND THAT moscow HAD BEEN BURNED DOWN, HE DECIDED TO STAY IN mOSCoW

keeping his own counsel. When Napoleon saw his staff officers, he seemed to be obsessed with the Tsar: "Alexander will never have had a better opportunity for a favorable peace than he does here!" he shouted one night, and people who heard him thought he had indeed lost his mind.

But Napoleon was a great survivor, and he had a survivor's instinct. Even while all of his protesting was going on, he was secretly planning to evacuate the Russian capital, although it was in part to deal with the news, which arrived from Paris, that Wellington's British army was making advances in Spain. At noon on October 19, Napoleon rode out of the gates of Moscow, heading southwest, at the head of a long column of soldiers bearing booty from the city, including statues, paintings, and Persian carpets. He had attacked Russia with 612,000 troops, 450,000 of them active combat soldiers. He now left with 102,000 men. Out of his original 1,300 pieces of artillery, he now had 533. He left about 15,000 wounded behind, as well as a rear guard detachment of 7,000 men who had orders to blow up the Kremlin, a task that was only haphazardly attempted before these men, too, retreated, leaving the grand palace intact.

The retreat back to France has fallen into legend. The first severe frost came late in October, and the first snow fell on November 4. By December, temperatures had dropped to -29°F (-34°C). Forced by Russian armies to use the same route they had

IN THE RETREAT FROM MOSCOW, A BAND OF MEN UNDER MARSHAL MICHEL NEY BECAME SEPARATED FROM THE MAIN ARMY AND OPEN TO ATTACK. THEY WERE PART OF THE FEW WHO SURVIVED A CONCENTRATED ATTACK FROM THE RUSSIANS.

taken coming into Moscow, the Grand Army found nothing but scorched earth and corpses in their path. The Russians harried them with partisan actions by Cossack cavalrymen, who isolated and slaughtered straggling units. Men froze and died standing up. Hunting packs of wolves set upon the soldiers, and some French troops, too weak to defend themselves, were torn apart limb from limb. A soldier remembered the state of the troops years later: "Many of them walked, leaning on sticks, their beards and hair a mass of ice …The men who fell imploring help, I fear, were not listened to."

Napoleon, having heard of an attempted coup d'état in Paris by General Claude-Francois de Malet, abandoned his troops at the village of Smorgoni, in Lithuania. With a 200-man guard, he raced for Paris on sleigh and carriage, at last arriving late one night in December, "passing at full gallop beneath the half-finished Arc de Triomphe," to arrive at his palace around midnight, much to the consternation of a sleepy guard who answered the Emperor's imperious knocking while still dressed in his nightshirt.

Although troops continued to stagger and die in the frozen wastes to the east, the campaign to conquer Russia was over. Of 612,000 French soldiers and their allies, 400,000 had died, and 100,000 had been taken prisoner. Even as Napoleon planned to rise again to destroy the Coalition armies and Russia—and he did raise an army of 300,000 men the next year—a decisive turning point had been reached in the Napoleonic Wars. Never again would Napoleon be seen as invincible. From this point on, it was only a matter of time before the Coalition forces, filled with renewed hope, would destroy the Emperor of France, once and for all.

ARTHUR WELLESLEY, DUKE OF WELLINGTON, THE GREAT SOLDIER WHO DEFEATED NAPOLEON

Arthur Wesley—the family would only later change the spelling to Wellesley, a more aristocratic name that also could not be mistaken for John Wesley, a firebrand preacher of the same name—was born to Anglo-Irish nobility in County Meath, Ireland, in 1769. His parents were, as one of his brothers later put it, "frivolous and careless personages" who paid little attention to young Arthur, merely sending him off to good public schools and forgetting about him. But the famous story is that when Wellesley turned eighteen, his mother happened to spot him one night in London, across a crowded theater: "I do believe there is my ugly boy, Arthur," she exclaimed. "What can I do with him?"

The answer was to buy him a commission in the British army. After Wellesley saw short service in Ireland, he went off to India in 1796. Once in that country, Wellesley—who was indeed a bit of an "ugly boy," tall and ungainly, with such a hooked nose that his troops would later call him "Beaky"—distinguished himself in the battles against local Indian potentates in the province of Mysore and returned home, in 1803, as a major general and a knight companion of the Order of the Bath.

In 1809, Wellesley was appointed commander in chief of British forces fighting the Peninsular War and first saw action against Napoleon's armies (although not Napoleon, who had already left Spain to fight the Austrians). There his genius as a commander came to the fore. He was primarily a defensive specialist—one reason why Napoleon despised him—who liked nothing better than to find a well-protected position, anchor his flanks against a river or some high point of land, place his troops on the rear slope of a hill or ridge, and let the enemy give battle, if they might.

These tactics—as well as the judicious use of bold strikes—won Wellesley Portugal and Spain and allowed him to invade France, thus helping bring an end to Napoleon's reign in 1814. When Napoleon escaped from Elba the following year, it was the now Duke of Wellington who commanded the Allied army that faced him in Belgium,

at Waterloo. Here was the defensive specialist facing off against the offensive genius. Here were two commanders who despised each other—Wellington would later say that "Bonaparte's whole life, civil, political, military, was a fraud"—commanding in a battle that was to determine the fate of Europe.

Although Wellington was to call Waterloo "the nearest run thing," the tired Napoleon he faced was not the Napoleon of old, and Wellington's defensive strategies carried the day. While Napoleon died an early death, Wellington went on to become prime minister of Britain, one of the figures who would shape postwar Europe.

Every bit as arrogant as Napoleon, in his own way—he once said, "I began to feel that the finger of Providence was upon me"—he never allowed his ego to interfere with common sense, and thus finally won out against the brilliant, passionate, but ultimately intemperate Napoleon.

THE PENINSULAR WAR: THE DIRTY GUERILLA WAR THAT FRANCE WAS UNABLE TO STOP

Francisco de Goya's famous painting Execution of the Defenders of Madrid, 3 May, 1808, captures all of the terror, blood, and passion of the Peninsular War: Surrounded by bodies, facing a French firing squad, the Spanish man at the center of the painting, wearing the white shirt of the martyr, stretches his arms wide as if to ask Why? before the bullets tear into his body.

In the space of little more than a decade, the French, once revolutionaries who had thrown off a tyrannical yoke, were now a force of repression. And nowhere was the repression felt more than in the Iberian Peninsula, during what became known as the Peninsular War.

The Peninsular War began in 1807 when Napoleon decided to attack Portugal for refusing to go along with his Continental System, moving thousands of troops into Spain under the pretext of supporting this invasion. Napoleon then duped the "half-wit" Spanish monarch Charles IV into abdicating and put his own brother Joseph on the throne. The Spanish people rose in rebellion in Madrid on May 2, 1808, a rebellion brutally put down by Napoleon's chief commander, Marshal Joachim Murat. Hundreds of Spanish were rounded up and executed at various locations around the city, a massacre commemorated in de Goya's famous paintings, including The Riot Against the Mameluke Mercenaries, The Second of May 1808.

Such bloody reprisals created a national resentment against the French, and an uprising in both Spain and Portugal followed, backed by Britain, which landed an expeditionary force in August 1808 led by Lieutenant General Sir Arthur Wellesley, at which point a see-saw battle for Portugal and Spain began. Wellesley drove the French army under Napoleon's General Jean Junot out of Portugal. Wellesley left, but then Napoleon himself returned to the Peninsula at the head of 200,000 veteran French troops and pushed the British army out of Portugal in early 1809, very nearly destroying it.

Wellesley returned that summer (after Napoleon left to fight elsewhere in Europe) and began the long, hard, slogging campaign to oust the French from the Iberian Peninsula. The campaign was ferocious, with hundreds of thousands of dead and a high toll of civilian casualties. The word "guerilla" was coined for the actions of Spanish irregular fighters against the French, because the Spanish called the Peninsular War Guerra de Guerrillas, or "the war of the little wars."

The Spanish guerillas, passionate about their country, outraged by atrocities against citizen populations (including nuns, monks, and priests) struck French troops hard in hit-and-run attacks. When Wellesley was finally successful in driving the French out of Portugal and Spain, it was in good measure due to the fact that the Spanish guerillas

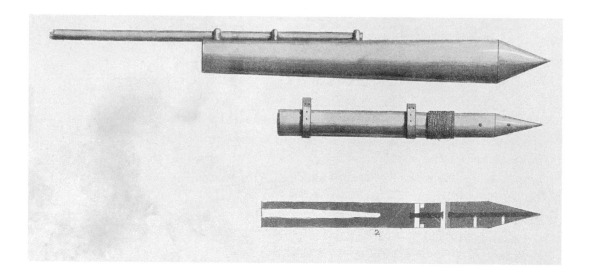

had sowed terror within the ranks of the French army there. Ironically, it would be the example of the Spanish guerilla fighters in the Peninsula that would later encourage other guerillas to rise up against Spanish rule in South America.

THE CONGREVE ROCKET: INACCURATE, BUT A POWERFUL WEAPON OF TERROR

Bombardments during the Napoleonic Wars were terrifying enough, especially if you were a soldier standing on an open field watching the sky in front of you fill with arching black dots that would, in a matter of seconds, turn into cannonballs, any single one of which could disembowel you and ten of your comrades. But the rocket developed by Sir William Congreve and first used against the French during the Napoleonic Wars was a very different type of missile indeed.

Congreve, son of the controller of the British Royal Armory, had been impressed by the way certain Indian princes used rockets (themselves borrowed from the Chinese) in the Mysore Wars fought in India in the late eighteenth century. And so Congreve set out to develop one that could be adapted to European warfare. He came up with what became known as the Congreve Rocket, a sturdy iron tube filled with explosions and capped with a conical nose, the whole thing weighing perhaps 30 pounds (13.5 kg). The tubes were set in metal baseplates, filled with black powder, and attached to wooden guide poles. A fuse was then lit that set off a propellant mixture. The rockets took off in a burst of flame and actually had a range of 2 miles (3 km) or so.

The Congreve rocket was not an accurate weapon, but the shrieking sound it made as it hurtled through the air, especially in conjunction with other types of artillery, was enough to set the hardiest veteran to flight. The British used it quite effectively after it became operational in 1804. Boulogne, France, was bombarded by Congreves in 1806 and suffered a fire that burned acres of the city and caused severe casualties, and Copenhagen and Danzig both suffered serious destruction from hundreds of rockets launched by British artillerists. Purists such as the Duke of Wellington disliked this weapon ("I do not want to set fire to any town," he once said of the Congreves), but rockets had a powerful effect.

Congreve rockets were used by the British until the 1850s, when more sophisticated rocketry became available, but they had a second life as a distress signal for ships at sea, a life that lasted into the early twentieth century.

17

THE TAIPING REBELLION

1851–1864

THIS CIVIL WAR IN MID–NINETEENTH CENTURY CHINA KILLED MORE PEOPLE THAN ANY OTHER WAR IN HISTORY EXCEPT WORLD WAR II AND INSPIRED MAO ZEDONG'S REBELLION A CENTURY LATER.

AN EPOCHAL CHINESE REBELLION DRIVEN BY A DELUSIONAL LEADER THAT COST MILLIONS THEIR LIVES

By the 1830s, the Qing Dynasty had been ruling China for 200 years, since the Manchu conquest of the country in the seventeenth century. The Imperial Court in Beijing was sophisticated and cultivated, the tentacles of its massive bureaucracy spreading out over the countryside, but most Chinese peasants and workers lived in abject poverty. After China's humiliating defeat by Great Britain in the First Opium War in 1842, even these downtrodden people began to see the Qing rulers as corrupt and weak. When the Yellow and Yangtze rivers overflowed their banks in the 1840s, causing widespread flooding and years of starvation, the country was ripe for rebellion.

The source of the Taiping Rebellion was a highly unlikely one—a deluded failed clerk named Hong Xiuquan. Born a Hakka outsider in the southern Chinese province of Guangdong, Hong failed his civil service exam twice. Perhaps unhinged by this humiliation and influenced by the Christian missionaries who were then preaching in the country, Hong developed the delusion that he was the second son of God, Jesus Christ's younger brother—his Chinese son. In 1844, expelled by the Confucian authorities of his village, Hong set off to preach that the word of his Taiping Tianguo, or "Heavenly Kingdom of Great Peace."

As Hong wandered his poor and mountainous province, his message became more political. He had been sent by God to destroy the "demon devils" who ruled China, as well as to create a new way of life, a "Human Fellowship" in which men and women would be equal, and wealth would be shared.

Peasants gradually began to flock to Hong, and by 1850 he had gathered an army of 40,000 near Thistle Mountain in Guangxi Province. Finally alarmed, the Qing rulers sent an army to attack Hong there, but his highly trained and regimented cadre beat them handily in January 1851. After this victory, more peasants joined Hong until his army was hundreds of thousands strong.

Marching down from the Guangxi mountains, Hong and his men swept northeast through the Yangtze River Valley with the city of Nanjing and the port of Shanghai as their targets. They defeated Qing forces at Yong'an and Quanzhou and finally captured Nanjing with an army 500,000 strong in March 1853. Renaming Nanjing his "Heavenly Capital," Hong now recruited a standing army of more than 1,000,000 men and women.

The Taipings held Nanjing for eleven years, but were unable to capitalize on their victory, mainly because of Hong Xiuquan's increasing mysticism, licentiousness, and paranoia. As Taiping and Qing forces fought a series of fierce battles over central China, disease and starvation swept the country, causing untold suffering. After failing in a bid to seize Shanghai, the Taiping forces were driven back, thanks in part to the efforts of Charles "Chinese" Gordon, the charismatic British commander of the so-called "Ever-Victorious Army," who used modern tactics and massed firepower to defeat the Taipings in battle after battle. In May 1864, the Taipings were besieged in their capital city of Nanjing by Imperial troops. Hong Xiuquan died of illness (or possibly suicide) on June 1 and the city fell a month later.

The Qing Dynasty was saved, but it was fatefully weakened. Compromised by the aid it had enlisted from foreign governments, it would fall for good in 1911. In the meantime, an estimated 20 to 40 million people died, making the Taiping Rebellion the most costly war in world history, with the exception of World War II. And within Hong's madness lay the seeds that would become Mao Zedong's successful revolution of the mid-twentieth century.

MODERN FIREPOWER AND MASSED TACTICS DESTROY THE REBELLIONS TAIPINGS

The Siege of Nanjing: October 1863–July 1864

Slowly but surely, the Taiping forces were being driven back. General Li Xiucheng, commander of the rebel army that had tried and failed to take Shanghai in 1862, saw

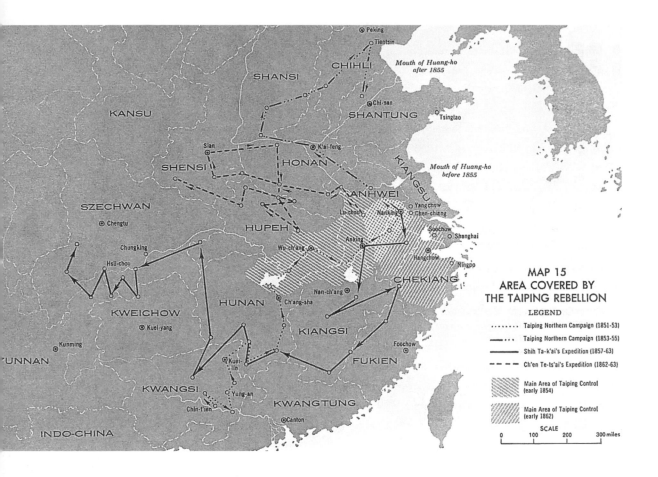

MAP 15
AREA COVERED BY
THE TAIPING REBELLION

LEGEND

········· Taiping Northern Campaign (1851-53)
─── ··· Taiping Northern Campaign (1853-55)
───── Shih Ta-k'ai's Expedition (1857-63)
─ ─ ─ ─ Ch'en Te-ts'ai's Expedition (1862-63)

▨ Main Area of Taiping Control (early 1854)
▨ Main Area of Taiping Control (early 1862)

SCALE
0   100   200   300 miles

THIS MAP DETAILS THE SETTING
OF THE TAIPING REBELLION.

From The Taiping Rebellion
by Franz Michael

the net inexorably closing around the Heavenly Capital of Nanjing as 80,000 Qing troops, backed by foreign mercenaries and transported by shallow draft steamships owned by the French and British, took Taiping town after town, always promising mercy if the Taipings surrendered—and then slaughtering them—men, women, and children—in orgies of stabbing, shooting, and beheading.

The Qing commander, General Zeng Guoquan, was the ninth brother of Qing strategist Zeng Guofan, who had planned this attack on the vital city of Nanjing and was known with terror in the Taiping army as "General Number 9." A squat, scarred man, he gave no quarter and expected none. In October, his troops finally appeared and began to form a perimeter around Nanjing. They built a moat 10 miles (16 km) long around its southern perimeter, beginning at the Yangtze River, effectively forcing any relief for the city to come from a direction interdicted by massive amounts of Qing troops.

THE TAIPING REBELLION 179

In mid-December, Zeng sent his men in their first assault against Nanjing's massive walls. They tunneled under them, filled the tunnels with gunpowder, and blew it up, causing sections of wall to crumble. But Taiping forces, fighting valiantly, pushed the Qings back and repaired the damage.

At this point, Li Xiucheng screwed up his courage and went to see Hong Xiuquan, Heavenly Ruler, to tell him some bad news.

"Why Should I Fear the Demon Zeng?"

Men had been beheaded merely for sneezing in this man's presence, and Li was nervous as he entered the Heavenly Palace, guarded by a cadre of foreign mercenaries, and found Hong surrounded by concubines, a pale, dangerous wraith of a man.

Bowing before Hong, Li told him that their only hope for survival was to flee. "The supply routes are cut and the gates are blocked," he told Hong, who listened impassively. "The morale of the people is not steady. The capital cannot be defended. We should give up the city and go elsewhere."

Hong stared at him and gave a chilling answer: "I have received the sacred command of God, the sacred command of the Heavenly Brother Jesus, to come down into the world to become the only true Sovereign of the myriad countries under Heaven … Why should I fear the demon Zeng?"

Li still believed that Hong was, in fact, the son of God, but he knew that this answer sealed his fate and the fate of the thousands of men, women, and children within the city's walls. Hong was out of touch with reality, unfit to command an army, and had been for some time. When the city had been captured and renamed the Heavenly Capital some eleven years before, Hong had been at the peak of his powers and had entered Nanjing in triumph, wearing yellow robes and yellow shoes, the Chinese imperial colors. But since then, Hong had steadily deteriorated.

While Hong's armies fought fruitless battles against Qing forces—battles that sapped strength and morale without achieving clear goals—he remained in Nanjing. Although issuing puritanical edicts to his people, he spent most of his time with his eighty-eight-concubine harem, within a palace protected by Irish and British mercenaries, who were a status symbol for Hong. Hong devoted a great deal of time to mystical poetry and writing down directions for the 2,000 women devoted to cleaning the palace, cooking for him, and bathing and dressing him.

It was no wonder that the reality of the situation outside the walls of Nanjing—what one historian has called "the bloody horror" of raging civil war—made no impact on the Son of Heaven.

Fierce Underground Fighting

As 1864 began, Li Xiucheng attempted to stockpile what grain he could, sortiing outside the city walls to try to capture supplies, but with little luck. By February, the last grain supplies outside the city were captured by Zeng's troops, making the town reliant upon only the rapidly dwindling rice in the granaries inside Nanjing. The corruption of Hong's relatives, whom he placed in a position of power, and who demanded large bribes for grain, caused starvation among the city's ordinary people beginning in early spring.

Well and truly trapped, General Li Xiucheng watched as the Qings captured every hill, circumvallated the city with a twin line of trenches and breastworks 300 yards (275 m) apart, and placed small forts every quarter to a half a mile (400 to 800 m), 120 in all, each manned by a Qing garrison. As people begin to starve, the Qings sent word to the city that anyone who deserted to the Qing side would be fed and treated well. People risked death to slip out of Nanjing, but when they got to Qing lines, many were executed. According to Charles Gordon, a British observer to the siege now that he had disbanded his Ever-Victorious Army, the escaping women were put in stockades where "the country people … take as wives any who so desired."

The Qings began to build their mines, tunneling ever closer to the city walls, while Taiping forces dug countertunnels. A savage underground war broke out in the flatland near the city's walls, with Taiping forces breaking into enemy tunnels and either filling them with water or human waste or fighting hand-to-hand battles, sword and spears flashing in dark caves and recesses. One Qing tactic was to let the Taipings into their tunnels, then blow in noxious smoke with bellows, causing the rebels to die gasping and choking.

Manna

By the spring of 1864, the Qing forces had moved their breastworks to within 100 yards (91 m) of the city. The defenders, low on ammunition, could do little about this but watch. Li finally went to see Hong again, telling him: "There is no food in the whole city, and many men and women are dying. I request a directive as to what should be done to put the people's mind at ease."

Hong, still surrounded by his women and his writing instruments, but in yellow robes that had become dirty and tattered, answered him as loftily as he had before. Taking his cue from the biblical book of Exodus, in which God provided food from heaven for the escaping Israelites, he told Li Xiucheng: "Everyone in the city should eat manna. That will keep them alive."

Then he ordered: "Bring some here and after preparing it I shall partake of some first."

There was dead silence in the room. Li and Hong's women and courtiers could not begin to respond to such a strange order. Impatiently, Hong got down off his throne and went into the palace's central courtyard, where he collected weeds, lumped them into a ball, then handed them to Li, telling him: "Everyone should eat accordingly and everyone will have enough to eat."

As Li stared at him, the Son of Heaven put a small tangle of weeds into his mouth and began to chew them.

Over the next month, as the battles under and outside the city's walls became fiercer and fiercer, Hong, on his diet of weeds, grew weaker and weaker. Some historians have suggested that the weeds were poisonous, others that he was simply starving to death, still others that he may have committed suicide. In any event, the Son of Heaven died on June 1, a day after the palace issued a decree to the haggard and starving population of Nanjing that Hong had decided to visit heaven and request of God and Jesus that they send an heavenly army down to smite the forces of General Number 9.

Li watched as Hong was buried on the palace grounds, without a coffin. After all, because he was coming back soon, why would he need one?

"Because I Did Not Understand"

At exactly noon on July 19, Zeng Guoquan gave a signal, and a huge explosion top- pled a massive section of walls along the eastern side of Nanjing. Fire and smoke belched into the air as Qing forces poured into the breach. The Taipings could stop them only briefly, then turned and ran.

The battle was no longer a battle, but a slaughter. The Qings rampaged through the city, raping and murdering, while members of Hong's family sought ways to escape. Usually, burdened down by the loot they had stolen from treasuries, they were caught and executed. Hong's son and heir, the Young Monarch, managed to make his way out of the city disguised as a Qing soldier, but he was caught in the following weeks and executed.

But aside from Hong's corrupt family, none of the Taipings left in the city surren- dered. A slaughter of epic proportions took place, with Qing forces killing an estimated 80,000 to 100,000 men, women, and children while General Number 9 and his officers cantered their horses through streets literally flowing with blood. Although Taiping armies existed outside the city, the back of the rebellion was broken, and the war was soon to be over.

And what of General Li? After fighting all day, he found his way to a hilltop palace within Nanjing where he fell asleep. He was robbed during the night. The next morning, a Qing patrol captured him, and he was taken to Qing headquarters, where he gave his confession, which included recounting his conversations with the Son of Heaven. He told his captors that, with Hong gone, the Taiping rebellion was over. He begged them fruitlessly for mercy, not for himself, but for the many whose screams still echoed through the city. Then, as if awakening from a nightmare into a newer, darker nightmare, he mused as to why he never tried to stop Hong: "It is really because I did not understand. If I had understood…."

His sentence trailed off, and his confession ended there. That night, he was taken to a small courtyard in the Son of Heaven's former palace and beheaded.

HONG XIUQUAN: THE SECOND SON OF GOD AND CAUSE OF A VIOLENT WHIRLWIND OF REVOLUTION

Hong Huoxiu was born in the Guangdong Province in China in 1814. His family were peasant farmers and ethnic Hakkas—people who had emigrated to China centuries before, but who spoke a different dialect. Other Chinese looked down upon the Hakkas and refused to intermarry with them. Growing into an intelligent and quick-witted young man, Hong passed a test in his village to become an imperial clerk and then was sent to the city of Guangzhou in 1836 to take the Confucian state exam.

To Hong's mortification—and that of his entire family and village—the twenty-two year old failed the exam. The next year, he failed again. The second failure left him prostrate with shame and literally delirious. While in such a heightened state, he dreamed that he was the son of the Christian God he had heard about and that his father had tasked him with ridding China of the "demons" who were repressing its people. His new name, God told him, would be Hong Xiuquan, which means "Son of Heaven."

When Hong awoke, he insisted on being called by this name, but seven years would pass before he began his rebellion. In the meantime, he married and twice more failed to pass the civil service exam. Finally, at the urging of his friend Li Jingfang, Hong dusted off and read a tract that he had been given by a Christian missionary while in Guangzhou. Under the influence of these words, Hong decided that his dream meant that he was the second son of God—the younger brother of Jesus Christ.

Forming a small group of loyal followers who armed themselves with 20-foot (6 m) swords—to fight off demons—Hong left the village under pressure from Confucian authorities, found his way to the mountainous province of Guangxi, and slowly gathered an army of Hakka peasants. These men and women, believing that he would rid them of their Manchu oppressors, pooled their possessions, trained with rigorous discipline, and believed in Hong's Taiping Tianguo, or "Heavenly Kingdom of Great Peace."

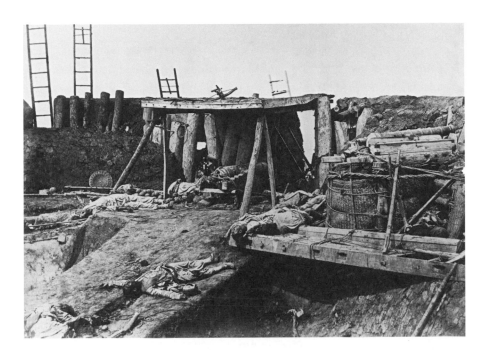

By 1851, swollen to some 40,000 strong, the Taipings, as they became known, destroyed an army that the alarmed Qing rulers of the country had sent to defeat them. After this victory, Hong sent his army sweeping across China, heading for Nanjing. The Taiping Army would reach an almost unimaginable 1,000,000 soldiers and capture Nanjing, but their leader became increasingly unstable, extremely puritanical, and megalomaniacal.

Outside Nanjing, uncontrollable civil war swept through the countryside. Inside, Hong, paranoid and hidden, appointed his thirteen-year-old son as chief administrator, stated that he was seeing ghosts, and claimed that he was possessed by the spirit of a biblical prophet. As the Imperial army besieged Nanjing in the spring of 1864, Hong's people turned to him, begging for food. He told them: "Everyone in the city should eat manna. That will keep them alive." He himself began to eat weeds and, on June 1, died. There were rumors that Hong committed suicide, but he almost certainly perished of starvation and disease.

PICTURED: DEAD BODIES LYING IN THE TAKU FORTS DURING THE TAIPING UPRISING. AN ESTIMATED 20–40 MILLION SOLDIERS AND CIVILIANS DIED IN COMBAT, OF STARVATION, AND FROM DISEASE.

Getty Images

TOLL OF WAR: WHEN MILLIONS DIED, DEATH BECAME PART OF THE LANDSCAPE

At first, most of the western world knew nothing of the carnage of the Taiping Rebellion, but by the early 1860s, reports began to drift out. These were carried mainly by letters written by foreign army officers or missionaries, or by journalists visiting the country.

These reports describe death on a scale that dwarfed even the killing going on in the battlefields of the American Civil War, which was considered mayhem of a new and modern type. Missionaries wrote of trying to pole their skiffs down the Yangtze River but finding the going slow because of the thousands of corpses that bumped monotonously against their hulls. One army officer wrote of stacks of dead on a recent battlefield, literally "walls 10 feet (3 m) high" around which the officer had to walk. Older battlefields saw "human bones bleaching among cannonballs."

In villages hit by endemic disease and starvation, "the houses are in ruins; streets filled with filth; human bodies are left to decay in open places or thrown into pools and cisterns, there to rot," an English missionary wrote. One American journalist saw a New Year's celebration occurring, firecrackers and streamers among piled dead, as if the dead were now simply part of the landscape.

Travelers near Shanghai and Nanjing, principal areas of fighting, found most houses destroyed; people slept on mats in the open, or in ruins. Children starved to death. Young men were forced by Taiping or Qing forces into military service, and young women were abducted and sold into concubinage. Only the elderly remained, "with countenances showing their suffering and despair," according to the American journalist. Massive groups of refugees wandered the countryside, caught between the warring armies, and forced their way into Shanghai, which had not fallen to the Taipings. Shanghai was home to a sizeable contingent of foreigners, who soon saw their dogs disappearing, one by one, food for starving Chinese.

FREDERICK TOWNSEND WARD: THE AMERICAN WHO CREATED THE EVER-VICTORIOUS ARMY

Frederick Townsend Ward, the man who created and trained the Ever-Victorious Army, wasn't destined to be as famous as Charles Gordon, who led it to its greatest victories, but without Ward the Qing Imperial Court would have had a hard time in winning its war against the Taipings.

Ward, an American born in Salem, Massachusetts, in 1831, was a freebooter or filibuster—a U.S. military adventurer who sought to overthrow foreign countries, or at least, profit from fighting in their wars as a mercenary. Darkly handsome, reckless, and adventurous, Ward sailed to China numerous times aboard clipper ships, fought with the filibuster William Walker's forces during the latter's invasion of Mexico in 1853, managed to find his way to the Crimean War battlefields a few years later, and finally ended up in China by about 1860, working as a trader for a family business.

But soon the Chinese "Pirate Suppression Bureau" gave Ward command of an armed steamboat called "Confucius," with which Ward did an admirable job of

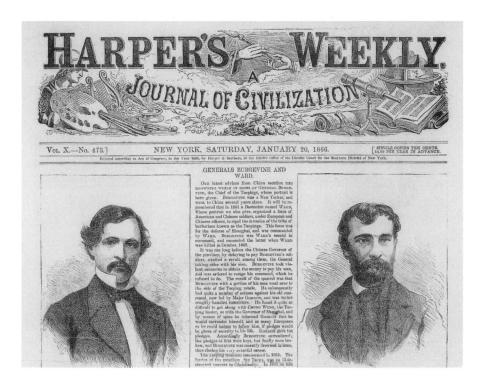

protecting convoys on the Yangtze River from Taiping pirates. Thereafter, Chinese functionaries in Shanghai allowed him to control a small group of foreign mercenaries armed with modern Colt pistols and rifles, arms that far outclassed the outmoded muskets of the Taipings. Ward led this "Shanghai Foreign Arms Corps" in a successful assault on a Taiping fortified town in 1860. Although Ward was badly wounded in a subsequent action, he returned to action and began recruiting Chinese as soldiers—with the difference that he trained them in western tactics.

In 1862, the Ever-Victorious Army, numbering perhaps 1,500 men, was ready to take the field. Under a banner inscribed with Ward's name rendered in Chinese, Ward led them in a series of actions against Taiping forces far larger than his. Due to Ward's unit's superior tactics and weaponry, they were victorious. Ward's forces growing to 5,000 men, he attacked the fortified town of Cixi in September of 1862, but he was mortally wounded near its walls. After Ward's death, command of his army would pass to Charles Gordon, who would become far more famous. But it was Ward who had finally discovered the key to beating the Taipings.

AMERICAN FREDERICK TOWNSEND WARD BEGAN TO TRAIN CHINESE FORCES IN WESTERN TACTICS AND WON A SERIES OF VICTORIES. THE DASHING WARD WOULD GO DOWN IN OBSCURITY, HOWEVER, AFTER BEING MORTALLY WOUNDED IN 1862.

18

THE U.S. CIVIL WAR

1861–1865

AN EVENT THAT INDELIBLY ALTERED U.S. HISTORY, THE CIVIL WAR
COST 600,000 LIVES AND TURNED THE COUNTRY FROM A COLLECTION
OF STATES INTO A NATION, YET LEFT LINGERING SCARS

FOUR BLOODY YEARS OF WAR TO SAVE THE UNION TURNED AMERICA INTO A NATION

The inciting event of the U.S. Civil War was the election, in November 1860, of Abraham Lincoln as president. Lincoln was an avowed anti-slavery Republican, which spelled trouble to the United States' Southern states. For years, the Southern states had been locked in what they saw as a life-and-death struggle with their counterparts in the North over the morality and legality of slavery. There were some 4,000,000 slaves in the South at the beginning of the Civil War, and they were needed to grow the cotton and tobacco crops that were the engines driving the Southern economy.

Every time a new western state was added to the Union, the South wanted it to be a slave-holding state, while the North wanted it to be free. The more populous, industrialized Northern states were better represented in the House of Representatives, where representation depended on population. The South, afraid that the North would gain enough power to abolish slavery, sought to have new states become slave states to at least keep the balance of power in the U.S. Senate.

But the election of Lincoln made this a hopeless cause, because he had made it known during his campaign that he would vigorously oppose any additional slave states. Within several months, eleven states, beginning with South Carolina, had seceded and formed the Confederate States of America, whose president was Jefferson Davis and whose leading general would become Robert E. Lee.

The first shot of the Civil War was fired on April 12, 1861, when a Confederate mortar lobbed a shell at Fort Sumter, the Union fort in the harbor of Charleston, South Carolina. Within a few days, Sumter was forced to surrender, and the North and South were at war.

At the very beginning, it appeared the North held the advantage. There were twenty-two Union states versus eleven Confederate ones. The North was far more populous, having 22 million people to the 9 million belonging to the South (of which 4 million were slaves). Also, the North possessed far more heavy industry than the South.

Yet the advantage was not all on the Union side. Most of the regular army officers of the United States, West Point graduates who had seen action in the Mexican War, opted for the Southern side. Northern generals tended to be political appointees. The South early on had a conscription system, while the North, for the first two years of the war, depended on a volunteer army. More important, the South did not need to invade and conquer Northern territory to win the war. It needed simply to hold its own and win enough major victories to convince the North to sue for peace and allow the Confederacy to secede and become a separate nation.

At the start of the war, Lincoln immediately blockaded Southern ports, the first step in the "Anaconda Plan" to squeeze the Confederacy into submission, which entailed opening up the Mississippi River to Union forces and capturing the South's capital city of Richmond, Virginia. At first, the Confederate army under Robert E. Lee was successful in the eastern theater of operations, beating the Union at the Battle of Bull Run (also known as the First Battle of Manassas for the town near where it was fought) in Virginia in July 1861.

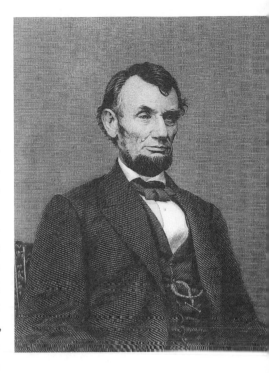

In the beginning of 1862, however, a relatively unknown Union major general named Ulysses S. Grant captured Fort Henry and Fort Donelson on the Tennessee River, severely crippling the Confederates in the western theater of operations. In the spring of that year, Lincoln's new commander of the Army of the Potomac, General George McClellan, launched his campaign on the Virginia peninsula to capture Richmond, but, moving far too slowly and hampered by Stonewall Jackson's campaign in the Shenandoah Valley, he was badly beaten by Confederate forces in the Seven Days' Battles and forced back toward Washington.

In the meantime, Grant fought the Confederates to a draw in the bloody Battle of Shiloh, Tennessee. That battle convinced both sides that this war would be unlike any other to date. The only bright lights for the Union were Admiral David Farragut's capture of New Orleans in the spring and the fact that George McClellan was able to stem Lee's advance north at the battle known as Antietam by the North (for a stream in the middle of the battlefield) and Sharpsburg by the South (for a nearby village) in September 1862.

However, McClellan did not follow up on his victory, and Lincoln relieved him of command. In the next twelve months, Lincoln would appoint five different generals head of the Army of the Potomac, seeking to find a man aggressive enough to beat Lee. At the end of December 1862, the Union Army under General Ambrose Burnside

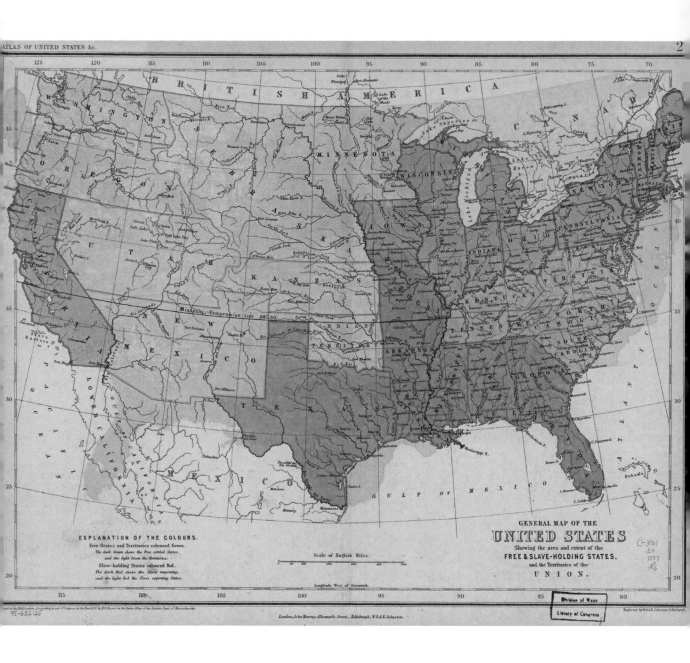

THIS NINETEENTH CENTURY
MAP DEPICTS THE SLAVE-
HOLDING STATES IN THE SOUTH
AND THE FREE STATES OF THE
NORTH.

Library of Congress, Geography and
Map Division

suffered a disastrous defeat at Fredericksburg, Virginia. His successor, General Joseph Hooker, was decisively defeated by Lee at Chancellorsville, Virginia, in May 1863, although Stonewall Jackson was killed, which was a severe blow to the South.

Lincoln appointed General George Gordon Meade as his new commander in chief. Meade at last was able to decisively defeat Lee at the pivotal Battle of Gettysburg, Pennsylvania, in July. At the same time, General Ulysses S. Grant, now commander of

Union forces in the west, was able to capture the pivotal Confederate fortress of Vicksburg, on the Mississippi. Grant's further destruction of Confederate forces at Chattanooga, Tennessee, meant that the Confederates were now being driven into a corner.

The year 1864 saw Lincoln appoint Grant as commander of all Union forces. The Union's manpower was increased due to conscription, and its massive industrial might provided endless munitions and supplies. Grant now waged a vicious war of attrition against a South weakened by irreplaceable manpower shortages and the Union's effective blockade. As Grant advanced on Virginia, major battles were fought in May and June in Wilderness, Spotsylvania Courthouse, and Cold Harbor, and by June 1864, Union soldiers were besieging Petersburg, near Richmond.

In the meantime, General William Tecumseh Sherman, now commander of Union forces in the west, had been sent to attack the major rail terminus and supply city of Atlanta, Georgia. He achieved this goal in September, and then he marched famously through the South to the coast at Savannah, Georgia, leaving a trail of death and destruction 300 miles (485 km) long and 60 miles (95 km) wide.

In March 1865, Lee's army was defeated at Petersburg, and Richmond fell soon after. Lee surrendered his army to Grant at Appomattox Court House in Virginia on April 9. The last major Confederate force, that of General Joseph E. Johnston, surrendered to Sherman near Durham, North Carolina, on April 18.

But Lincoln had been assassinated by Southern firebrand John Wilkes Booth in Washington, D.C., on April 14, leaving the war-torn country with an uncertain future. After a Reconstruction period that was more corrupt and vindictive than healing, the South would take at least a century to fully rejoin the Union. Scars of the war, especially in terms of racism and a Southern sense of "apartness," still remain today.

OVER THREE DAYS IN JULY, THE SOUTH WAS STOPPED COLD— AND A PENSYLVANIA VILLAGE WAS IMMORTALIZED
The Battle of Gettysburg: July 1863

In June 1863, the finest soldiers on the North American continent—or so they considered themselves—began pouring into the lush and peaceful fields of south-central Pennsylvania. They were the Army of Northern Virginia, 75,000-Confederates strong, and they had marched west and north from Virginia, through Maryland, to find themselves in the rich heartland of their enemies.

Their general, Robert E. Lee, had forbidden plundering, but these soldiers were hungry, and they needed supplies. So they took what they could—food, clothing, horses, and even money that they "requisitioned" from banks and stores—leaving Confederate IOUs in their wake. When one farm woman complained after her livestock was stolen, General James Longstreet politely told her: "Yes, madam, it's very sad, very sad, and this sort of thing has been going on in Virginia more than two years, very sad."

Looking back, many Confederate soldiers saw this pleasant month of June—seemingly endless days of fine, balmy weather and rich Yankee buttermilk—as a dreamlike idyll. In fact, the rebel soldiers under one of Lee's division commanders, A.P. Hill, felt supremely confident as they approached a small crossroads town called Gettysburg. They had destroyed the Federals at Fredericksburg, Virginia, the previous December and outfought them at Chancellorsville, Virginia, just a month before. Now they were heading north to bring the war to the hated enemy and win independence for the Southern states.

But first they would stop at Gettysburg. There was a shoe factory there, and one thing A.P. Hill's men needed was good shoe leather.

"Those People"

War is inextricable from politics, and as Lee accompanied his men north that late spring, he had powerful political goals in mind. Lee so wanted to impress the Northern peace party, the Copperheads, with his good intentions that he ordered his soldiers not to hurt civilians or plunder their belongings.

More important, Lee wanted to destroy the Army of the Potomac under Joseph Hooker, whom he had beaten handily at Chancellorsville. Hooker was now belatedly following the Army of Northern Virginia as it headed into Union territory. Once Lee had beaten the Army of the Potomac, he was sure that foreign countries such as Great Britain and France would recognize the Confederacy and that Washington would sue for peace.

These were fine political goals, but a great general like Lee allowed himself to forget that the shedding of blood to gain political ends is an unpredictable matter. Lee may have been convinced of his army's invincibility and that "those people"—as Lee called the Yankee soldiers—would turn tail and run, as they had before. But Lee's force was not without its weaknesses. His boldest and most aggressive commander, Stonewall Jackson, had been killed by friendly fire in May at Chancellorsville after essentially winning that battle for Lee. And Lee's eyes and ears, the cavalry of Jeb Stuart, were not with him. Stuart had exploited Lee's order to go on a wild end run around Hooker's entire Union Army.

Thus, as Lee marched north, he did not know where the Army of the Potomac was, quite, nor did he know that, on June 28, Lincoln had replaced Hooker with General George Gordon Meade, a Union officer who had worked his way up through the ranks by excelling at combat. Meade was determined to stop Lee and—with his own cavalry—found out quickly that the Confederates had entered Pennsylvania.

Meade aggressively moved his 90,000-man army north from Maryland, where it was stationed, to confront the Confederates.

Lee had split his forces to achieve his objectives in Pennsylvania, which included capturing the state capital of Harrisburg and blowing up key railroad bridges. But when Lee finally got word of Meade's men approaching, he sent orders for all of his commanders to bring their forces to Gettysburg. This was not because Lee wanted to fight a battle there, but simply because the town was the nexus of numerous highways.

The Battle Begins

But when A.P Hill's men arrived in Gettysburg on the morning of July 1, they did not care about this grander strategy. They wanted shoes, and they figured they would get them before the rest of the Confederate army showed up. But instead of the few Union militiamen they had been expecting, they found two brigades of Union cavalry under John Buford, who had ridden into town the previous day ahead of Federal forces. Buford is recognized as one of the Union heroes of the battle, men who, acting independently,

THE BATTLE OF ANTIETAM, FOUGHT TO A BLOODY DRAW, STEMMED LEE'S ADVANCE NORTHWARD, BUT COST 22,000 KILLED ON BOTH SIDES.

The Battle of Antietam, 1862 (colour litho), Thulstrup, Thure de (1848-1930) / Private Collection, Peter Newark Military Pictures / The Bridgeman Art Library

saw opportunities and seized them. He realized that the hills and ridges proximate to Gettysburg were important defensive points, and he was determined to hold them.

And so Buford dismounted his men and stationed them on the high ground northwest of Gettysburg. When A.P. Hill's men showed up, Buford's men made a fight of it, holding them off for two hours until a Union infantry corps showed up to reinforce them. What had been a hot skirmish began to turn into a real battle, as couriers were sent by both sides for more and more troops.

By the afternoon of July 1, 24,000 Confederates fought 19,000 Yankees along the ridges northwest of town. Lee realized that he had the enemy outnumbered and might be able to break their lines. He launched a Confederate attack that turned the Yankee right flank and finally forced their line to crumble. Union forces fled back through the town of Gettysburg to Cemetery Hill, to the south.

However, the battle was far from over. Lee knew that the Army of the Potomac was almost certainly moving quickly to Gettysburg. He needed to gain the high ground of Cemetery Ridge before the enemy could dig in there in strength. Late on the afternoon of July 1, Lee ordered General Richard Ewell, commander of Second

Corps and the man who had replaced Stonewall Jackson, to attack Cemetery Hill "if practicable." It was therefore a discretionary order, and Ewell decided the enemy was already too well dug-in and thus declined. Although Ewell was a capable commander, he lacked Jackson's acumen and bulldog aggressiveness. But had Ewell attacked that afternoon, he would almost certainly have broken the Union lines.

"The Enemy Is There"

That night, Meade and the rest of the Union forces had shown up and built a line of defensive breastworks several miles long. The Union line extended across Cemetery Hill and Cemetery Ridge, all the way to a hill called Little Round Top.

On the morning of July 2, Longstreet and Lee surveyed these defenses and had their first, but not last, dispute of the battle. Longstreet felt that the Union line was now too strong to attack. He wanted Lee to flank the Yankees to the south and take up defensive positions. This would put the whole Army of Northern Virginia between Washington, D.C., and Gettysburg, something that would certainly make the Yankees leave their own defensive positions and attack. Once they did, the Confederates would cut them to pieces.

Lee would have none of this. He thought going on the defensive would make his troops lose their supreme confidence, their almost palpable desire to attack the enemy. Lee pointed at Cemetery Ridge and said to Longstreet, "The enemy is there, and I am going to attack him there."

Longstreet replied, "If he is there, it will be because he is anxious that we should attack him; a good reason, in my judgment, for not doing so."

But Lee dismissed this and ordered Longstreet to attack. Smarting under the rebuff, Longstreet took almost the entire day to prepare his forces, so the attack did not kick off until 4 p.m. Longstreet sent his 15,000 hardened soldiers screaming their rebel yell straight at the Union lines. The fighting was fierce, in places that have become famous in U.S. history—the Peach Orchard, the Wheat Field, and a tumble of huge rocks known to the local townspeople as the Devil's Den.

Despite the lateness of the attack, the Confederates found extraordinary opportunity. Inexplicably, the Union had neglected to occupy Little Round Top, the hill that anchored the south flank of their line. If Longstreet's men could reach it, they would be able to fire down on the Yankees and send a flanking force into the Union rear.

The rebels realized this and raced for the hill. At the same time, a Union engineering officer named General Gouverneur K. Warren saw the problem, too. Galloping pell-mell to the nearest Union brigade, he convinced its officers to send men storming up the other side of Little Round Top. They got to the summit just before the Confederates, and a pitched battle ensued. For more than two hours, on the slopes of a hill covered with rocks and trees and cut with ravines, an Alabaman regiment and a Maine regiment fought and struggled bitterly.

Leading the Maine regiment was another one of Gettysburg's Union heroes, Colonel Joshua L. Chamberlain, who was a former professor of rhetoric at Bowdoin College. As twilight lengthened, Chamberlain found that a third of his men were casualties and that the rest were rapidly running out of ammunition. Down the hill, through the drifting smoke and hoarse cries of the wounded littering the slope, Chamberlain could see the Alabamians preparing for another charge.

And so Chamberlain made one of the most important decisions of the war: He shouted for his men to fix bayonets and charge. Racing in a frenzy down the hill, the Mainers took the Confederates by surprise, shattered their charge, and forced most of them to surrender. Little Round Top was saved because Union soldiers had acted most unlike the Union soldiers the Confederates had come to know: They had refused to yield.

"The Hopeless Slaughter"

The Confederate assaults on the Union line on July 2 were poorly coordinated, and they had failed to make a significant dent in the enemy. Late that evening, as both sides were licking their wounds (18,000 Confederates and Yankees had died or been wounded that day), Lee called a conference of his officers. Much to their surprise, Lee told them that it was his intention, to attack the center of Meade's lines the next day. Lee was convinced that the Union commander had weakened his center to make his flanks strong enough to face the Confederate attacks.

The other Confederate officers, particularly Longstreet, did not see the logic in this, and they protested, to little avail. Lee—perhaps weakened by a bout of diarrhea he was suffering or lacking intelligence that might have been provided by Jeb Stuart (whose troopers had only just joined the Confederate camp, wretchedly tired from their long ride)—was determined to push this battle to achieve his goals.

Once again, it was up to Longstreet to prepare this attack, and, once again, he dallied. "My heart was heavy," he later wrote, "I could see the desperate and hopeless nature of the charge and the hopeless slaughter it would cause." But at 1 p.m., Longstreet ordered the massed guns of the Confederates to open up in a huge bombardment of Union lines—the largest rebel bombardment of the war.

After two hours, what became known as Pickett's Charge, after General George Pickett, who commanded a Virginia division in the attack, began. Nine Confederate brigades participated—belonging to Pickett, General Isaac Trimble, and General James Johnston Pettigrew. The brigades arrayed themselves, flags flying, over a front 1 mile (1.5 km) long with three-quarters of a mile (1 km) of gently sloping fields before them. In the distance, the Yankees waited behind stone fences and barricades.

At Pickett's command, the rebels marched off. People present on both sides were awed by the beauty of the beginning of the charge, which seemed, as historian James M. McPherson put it, "a picture-book view of war." But the picture book view didn't last very long. The Confederate barrage hadn't significantly harmed the Yankee artillery. And as the Yankee artillery got within range, it opened up, shattering the perfect ranks of gray. Then, as the rebels ran screaming at the Yankee lines, the Union soldiers opened up from 200 yards (185 m) away. As Longstreet predicted, it was a slaughter, with men being blown apart where they stood. Union regiments raced out from their positions on the sides of the battlefield to flank the Confederates with fire. The rebels were caught in a killing zone in which it was difficult to even move without being hit.

THE AURA OF INVINCIBILITY OF THE ARMY OF NORTHERN VIRGINIA
WAS SHATTERED. THE UNION WAS GIVEN RENEWED HOPE.

Half an hour after the attack began, 200 Confederates, led by General Lewis Armistead, forced their way through Union lines. They were all killed within a few minutes. Armistead died with his hand on a Yankee cannon—the supposed "high water mark" of the Confederate effort in the Civil War. The soldiers who survived the attack streamed back toward Confederate lines. Of the 14,000 Confederates who charged, only 7,000 returned. Lee himself met with the soldiers who survived, telling them: "It is all my fault. It is I who have lost this fight."

Lee expected Meade to attack the next day, July 4, but the new general and his Union forces were worn out and chose to follow Lee's retreating men only desultorily. It was pouring rain as the Confederates retreated, carrying their wounded. Civil War soldiers noted that it often rained after a large battle, and they theorized it might be because the clouds were disturbed by the artillery fire.

They had lost 28,000 men killed, missing, or injured (Union losses were 23,000), but they had, in fact, lost a great deal more. The aura of invincibility of the Army of Northern Virginia was shattered. The Union (heartened also by Grant's great victory at Vicksburg on July 4) was given renewed hope.

Lee returned to Richmond, where he tendered his resignation to Jefferson Davis. "No one," he wrote, "is more aware than myself of my inability for the duties of my position." Davis refused to accept this, and Lee soldiered on. Lee performed brilliantly in the last two years of the war, but he would never again find himself with an undefeated army at his back, entering the territory of the enemy with victory within his grasp.

GENERAL ULYSSES S. GRANT: THE EVERYMAN HERO WHO CHANGED THE FORTUNES OF THE UNION

Ulysses S. Grant went through desperate journeys during the course of his life that would have daunted his namesake—the wandering hero of the Odyssey. Grant's Cyclops were whole Confederate armies, and his Siren was the seductive call of alcohol.

Grant was born in 1822 in a two-room cabin in Point Pleasant, Ohio, where his father ran a tannery. Grant's boyhood was mainly undistinguished except for his love of horses, and he was an excellent rider all his life. Nonetheless, he managed to secure an appointment to the U.S. Military Academy at West Point, from which he graduated, in the middle of his class, in 1843. He went on to serve bravely in the Mexican–American War of 1846–1848, which was a proving ground for many future Union and Confederate officers. During that war, Grant was promoted to captain.

But after the war, Grant became a journeyman officer, serving in desolate and depressing western outposts, at which point he began to drink heavily. Grant left the army in 1854 and—after working as a farmer and bill collector—brought his wife, Julia, and his growing family to Galena, Illinois, where he went to work in his family's leather goods shop as an assistant to his younger brother.

Grant—a short, gruff, and rather taciturn figure—served a kind of exile in Galena. He continued to drink (although how much is disputed) and probably suffered from some kind of clinical depression, finding himself, at the age of thirty-eight in 1860, working in the family store. But as the Civil War broke out, at a time when experienced Union officers were needed, Grant used a connection he had made with Illinois Congressman Elihu Washburne to become a brigadier general of the Twenty-First Illinois Regiment.

In February 1862, supported by gunboats, Grant set off on a campaign to capture the key Confederate Forts Henry and Donelson, which protected the Tennessee and Cumberland Rivers, major Confederate waterways. At a time when the Union was receiving little good news, Grant took the forts, and he became famous for telling Donelson's Confederate commander: "No terms except an unconditional and immediate surrender can be accepted."

Suddenly the U.S. in Grant's initials stood for "Unconditional Surrender." Grant, after besieging and taking Vicksburg, was on his way to becoming the premier Union general of the war. He was a fighting man at a time when the Union desperately needed these. He did not make a lot of friends with his gruffness, and tales of his drinking abounded, many of them apocryphal. It appears that Grant could go long periods of time without drinking, but when he did touch alcohol, he binged. Fortunately, his wife, Julia, and Chief of Staff John A. Rawlins were able to keep him away from alcohol most of the time.

Grant's other staunch supporter was President Abraham Lincoln. Lincoln may not have said (to those who complained about Grant's drinking): "Find out what whiskey he consumes; I want to send some to all my generals!" but he did proclaim: "What I want are generals who will fight battles and win victories … Grant has done this, and I propose to stand by him."

This was a wise move on Lincoln's part. After Grant was made commander in chief of all Union armies in early 1864, he attacked Robert E. Lee's dwindling army with vigor, sending William Tecumseh Sherman to take Atlanta while attacking with the Army of the Potomac into Virginia, cornering Lee, and forcing him to surrender in 1865. A grateful nation made Grant an enduring hero and twice elected him president, in 1868 and 1872. His administrations were not notably successful. Although Grant himself was an honest man, he was surrounded by scandals. But it is not an exaggeration to say that Grant was one of the most important military commanders in U.S. history.

GENERAL ROBERT E. LEE: A BRILLIANT GENERAL WHO STRUGGLED IN VAIN FOR THE CONFEDERACY

Despite the fact that Robert E. Lee was the losing general in a massive and destructive war effort fought, at least in part, to preserve the institution of slavery, Lee was (and still is) revered as a military genius and hero.

Unlike Grant, Lee's life before the war was one of unchecked successes. Born in Virginia in 1807, the son of Revolutionary War hero "Light-Horse Harry" Lee, Robert E. Lee graduated from West Point second in his class, received a commission to the Army Corps of Engineers, and fought heroically in the Mexican–American War, emerging with the rank of colonel and the admiration of his commander, General Winfield Scott, who called him "the very best soldier I have ever seen in the field."

After that war, Lee was appointed Superintendent of West Point, and then he served as a cavalry colonel in West Texas. Lee stayed in the regular army right up to Virginia's secession from the Union. (It was in this capacity that Lee and his chief lieutenant, Jeb Stuart, captured abolitionist John Brown at Harpers Ferry). When Virginia seceded, Lee resigned his commission, saying that he could not fight against the land of his birth.

Lee was soon named a full general of the Confederate army, and he served as a military advisor to Confederate President Jefferson Davis. Lee planned Stonewall Jackson's Shenandoah Valley campaign. Lee took over command of the Army of Northern Virginia in the spring of 1862 and repeatedly rebuffed the efforts of General

George McClellan to capture Richmond that summer.

In the fall, Lee's own invasion of Maryland was stopped at the fierce battle of Antietam—the single bloodiest day in U.S. history—where he suffered 10,000 casualties to McClellan's 12,000. But with an army of only 38,000 men, Lee managed to intimidate McClellan's Union force of some 75,000. The next year, Lee won his signal victory at Chancellorsville, where he divided his forces in front of Joseph Hooker's larger Union army and sent Jackson crashing into the northern right flank.

Some historians believe that Lee's momentous string of victories in 1862 and early 1863 had less to do with his tactical acumen than with the timidity of the Federal commanders he faced. But Lee certainly knew how to aggressively exploit the weaknesses of his opponents. Despite the fact that Lee had the demeanor of a southern gentleman, he was an iron-fisted commander who waged war hard.

After repulsing Ambrose Burnside at Fredericksburg, Virginia, Lee viewed the slaughtered Union dead who had charged the entrenched Confederate lines and remarked to General James Longstreet: "It is well that war is so terrible. We would grow too fond of it." But Lee himself would make the same mistake of attacking an entrenched enemy armed with modern rifles in July 1863 at Gettysburg, Pennsylvania, where he sent a massive infantry assault against the Union Army in what is called Pickett's Charge. The result was his defeat and the beginning of the end for the Confederacy.

Increasingly cornered by Grant, Lee fought a series of brilliant but costly rear-guard actions in 1864, before finally surrendering to Grant at Appomattox Court House in April 1865. Lee became president of Washington College (now Washington and Lee University) in Virginia, a state where he was held in reverence. By his demeanor and military successes, he had made the cause of the Confederacy seem a holy one, even though, in the end, he had failed to win the single victory needed to bring the North to its knees. Lee died in 1870 of heart failure. He had actually applied to have his citizenship restored by the Federal government, but the application was lost. It was found again in 1970 and granted posthumously.

ROBERT E. LEE IS STILL CONSIDERED ONE OF THE MOST REVERED MILITARY LEADERS OF THE SOUTH. HIS HUNGER FOR VICTORY OVER THE NORTH LED TO POOR JUDGMENT IN THE BATTLE OF GETTYSBURG. THE DEFEAT SERIOUSLY WOUNDED LEE'S SPIRIT. HE LATER SAID, "IT IS ALL MY FAULT. IT IS I WHO HAVE LOST THIS FIGHT."

ABRAHAM LINCOLN AND THE MOST FAMOUS SPEECH IN AMERICAN HISTORY

One of the greatest speeches ever given in U.S. history was also one of the most unnoticed at the time it was spoken.

The date was November 19, 1863. The place was the new Soldier's National Cemetery being dedicated outside the town of Gettysburg, Pennsylvania, where, four months earlier, thousands of young men of both the North and South had given their lives in a battle that had finally stopped the northward advance of Robert E. Lee's Army

of Virginia. The Confederate dead had been roughly tumbled into mass graves. The Union corpses had been dug up from the hasty graves prepared for them that summer, arduously identified by which states their units were from (if that was possible), and then reburied in wide semi-circles around a monument to their valor.

Abraham Lincoln arrived the night before to address the crowds at the dedication, but he was not the principal speaker. That honor had gone to the famous orator Edward Everett, who spoke for more than two hours. This was not a snub to Lincoln, as legend has it, but merely a reflection of the fact that, at the time, U.S. presidents had little involvement in state affairs. Lincoln rose to speak after Everett was through, however, and in just three minutes and 272 words focused his listeners on the purpose behind the horrible casualties such as the dead young men who surrounded them—that of creating a nation "of the people, by the people, for the people."

Although most of the attention at the time was focused on Everett, it was Lincoln who summed up the meaning of the solemn day in words that have run through history. In fact, Everett wrote the president the next day, saying: "I should be glad, if I could flatter myself, that I came as near to the central idea of the occasion in two hours, as you did in two minutes.

BLACK SOLDIERS: TO FIGHT FOR THE UNION MEANT RISKING EVERYTHING FOR FREEDOM

Abraham Lincoln issued the Emancipation Proclamation on New Year's Day, 1863, which freed all slaves and called for them to be enlisted in the Union Army and Navy.

This was easier said than done because a good deal of prejudice existed on the Union side toward blacks. Ironically, the Northern War Department called the conflict "a white man's war," and initially refused to accept blacks into the armed forces as soldiers. This was not solely due to racism. It was recognized that armed black men were the Confederates' worst nightmare and that they would fight all the harder against the Union should black soldiers be sent against them. However, abolitionists and more radical Republicans soon put enough pressure on the War Department, and the recruitment of black soldiers began.

The most famous black regiment was the 54th Massachusetts, led by a white man, son of a famous abolitionist family, Colonel Robert Gould Shaw. In July of 1864, the 54th attacked Fort Wagner, a Confederate fort that defended the entrance to Charleston Harbor. During this frontal assault, Shaw was killed, and the 54th lost nearly half its men. But the unit managed to hold the fort for an hour before retreating before a counterattack.

Northern newspapers compared this battle to Bunker Hill in its importance to the abolitionist movement, but Confederates were not moved. They refused to return Shaw's body to his family, saying "we have buried him with his niggers." There were numerous incidents during the war of Confederates bayoneting black soldiers who tried to surrender. But by war's end, 130,000 black soldiers and sailors were fighting for the Union—men whom, as Lincoln put it, had "staked their lives" for their country.

THE 54TH MASSACHUSETTS INFANTRY WAS THE MOST FAMOUS REGIMENT OF BLACK FIGHTERS. INITIALLY THERE WAS RESISTANCE ON THE PART OF THE WAR DEPARTMENT, WHICH BELIEVED THAT HAVING BLACK SOLDIERS FIGHT AGAINST THE CONFEDERATES WOULD ONLY ENRAGE THEM MORE AND CAUSE EVEN GREATER DESTRUCTION TO UNION FORCES. AFTER ENOUGH PRESSURE, HOWEVER, THEY FINALLY GAVE IN.

William J. Netson, 54th Massachusetts Infantry, c.1863 (tintype), American School, (19th century) / © Massachusetts Historical Society, Boston, MA, USA, / The Bridgeman Art Library

19

WORLD WAR I

1914–1918

A SERIES OF INTERLOCKING ALLIANCES PLACED EUROPE AT THE
EPICENTER OF A CONFLICT THAT COST 20 MILLION LIVES, DESTROYED
CENTURIES-OLD EMPIRES, AND SET THE STAGE FOR WORLD WAR II

"A TRAGIC AND UNNECESSARY CONFLICT" THAT DESTROYED THE OLD ORDER AND CHANGED THE COURSE OF THE TWENTIETH CENTURY

World War I was a historic clash that caused unprecedented bloodshed, mainly because of the joining of old world diplomacy and expectations with modern fire-power and mass armies.

As the twentieth century began, Germany's military and economic ascendancy since the Franco-Prussian War continued unabated. This rise was watched nervously by Russia, Great Britain, and France, which had formed an arrangement to go to each other's aid if attacked, known as the Triple Entente. In the meantime, Germany's ally, Austria-Hungary, grew increasingly concerned about nationalistic forces in the Balkans, to its south, especially in Serbia, which was Russia's ally.

Germany, Austria-Hungary, and Italy had formed the Triple Alliance, to defend each other in the event of war. All of these interlocking alliances were, in some ways, meant to encourage war. The countries involved each felt that they had something to gain by a limited conflict. France and Great Britain felt Germany could be contained, Austria-Hungary wanted to quash Baltic nationalism once and for all, and Germany wanted to increase its status in the world.

Thus, when Serbian nationalist Gavrilo Princip killed the heir to the Austro-Hungarian throne, Archduke Franz Ferdinand, on June 28, 1914, most of those concerned thought that a short war might not be the worst thing that would happen. This was because they were going by nineteenth-century standards of warfare. But the result was a twentieth-century war that historian John Keegan has called "a tragic and unnecessary conflict."

On July 28, 1914, Austria-Hungary declared war on Serbia. Shortly thereafter, Russia mobilized its forces for war against Germany, Germany declared war on Russia and France, and France declared war on Germany and Austria-Hungary. On August 4, Germany declared war on neutral Belgium and invaded as part of the right-flanking move, a giant wheeling movement to attack France from the northeast, which lay at the heart of the famous Schlieffen Plan to neutralize France in six weeks. As a result of this invasion, Great Britain declared war on Germany, and the sides coalesced.

The Central Powers—so-named because they were located between Russia and France—were Germany and Austria-Hungary, shortly to be joined by the Ottoman Empire (Turkey and the Middle East). The allies were France, Russia, and the United Kingdom, later to be joined Italy—which had balked at entering the war on the Central Power side—the United States, and numerous other smaller countries.

Almost every country involved in the conflict had a war plan at the ready. Germany, well aware of the problem of fighting a two-front war against Russia and France, sought to knock out France with the Schlieffen Plan, named after its originator, former German Chief of Staff Alfred von Schlieffen. The plan called for a blocking army to face the French in the west, while seven other German army groups swung northeast through Luxembourg and Belgium to smash down into France and capture Paris. But von Schlieffen's successor, General Helmuth von Moltke, fatally weakened the thrust by depleting the armies sweeping through Belgium to strengthen Germany's western defensive positions.

The French and British were able to blunt the German attack in the First Battle of the Marne in September, beginning a stalemate in France that would last for four years. However, in August, German forces had inflicted 150,000 casualties on the Russians at the Battle of Tannenberg, in East Prussia (near the modern-day Polish town of Olsztyn). This resulted in the almost complete destruction of the Russians in that area and kept them at bay for almost a year.

On the western front, a rapidly growing line of trenches, ultimately 470 miles (756 km) long, snaked from Switzerland to the North Sea, containing the armies of either side. A series of attritional battles were then fought. At the First Battle of Ypres (October–November 1914), the Germans lost 130,000 casualties, the British and French 108,000. The Second Battle of Ypres (April–May 1915) saw poisonous chlorine gas used by the Germans against French troops. From February to December 1916, the Battle of Verdun, in the Lorraine region of eastern France was fought, costing 1 million French, British, and German casualties. The Battle of the Somme, in northern France (July–November 1916) counted 57,000 British casualties on its first day alone—making it the bloodiest day in the history of warfare—while ultimately costing a combined total of 1,265,000 French, British, and German dead and wounded.

Old ways of making war, especially the frontal assault, had come head to head with modern weapons, such as the rapid-firing machine gun, the might of heavy artillery, poison gas, tanks, and air power. The commanders on both sides were discovering that the massive size of modern armies and the relatively small battlefield areas left almost no room to maneuver by attacking the enemy flanks.

Frontal assaults caused almost apocalyptically large casualty counts. Historian Dennis Showalter wrote that the killing came eventually to seem "mechanical," as if bodies were simply being fed to the engines of warfare. Digging deeper and deeper into the earth resulted in stalemate. When the allies attempted to break the stalemate by attacking the Turks in the Gallipoli Peninsula—hoping to gain a foothold in southeastern Europe and ultimately draw German troops away from the western front—it failed miserably.

The same stalemate happened on the eastern front as the Germans, Russians, and Austro-Hungarians fought each other along 900 miles (1,448 km) of trenches. However, with a larger territory within which to maneuver, the Germans outflanked the Russians in June 1915 and drove them out of Poland. Russia rebounded a year later with an offensive against Austria-Hungary, which successfully pushed the enemy back 50 miles (80 km) along a 250-mile (402 km) front. But the Russian army, plagued by poor morale, desertions, and a lack of supplies from the tottering tsarist government back home, was force to stop short of its goals.

Far from Europe, the Germans, French, and British fought over German possession in sub Saharan Africa, while the British prevailed over Turkey's possessions in the Middle East, ultimately bringing down the old Ottoman Empire. On the high seas, Great Britain had imposed a successful blockade in the North Sea to keep all shipping away from Germany. From May 1–June 31, 1916, the naval clash many had predicted between the great dreadnought class battleships of Great Britain and Germany took place at the Battle of Jutland. Both fleets fought to a draw, although the British were able to keep their supremacy in the North Sea.

By January 1917, the Germans had decided to resort to a policy of unrestricted U-boat warfare, sinking any ship of any country, merchantman or warship, that approached Great Britain's ports. It was thought that this policy would force Great Britain to sue for peace within five months. Instead, it helped bring the previously neutral United States into the war.

In 1915, the Germans had torpedoed the British ocean liner Lusitania, which carried on it 128 Americans. The United States had merely protested the incident. But the German announcement that it would began unrestricted submarine warfare, combined with the British interception and decoding of the Zimmerman Telegram (in which the German undersecretary of foreign affairs encouraged Mexico to declare war on the United States) caused the United States to declare war in April 1917. From the Allied point of view, it was just in time. British and French forces were exhausted by years of bloodshed, and the German blockade was taking its toll. The American Expeditionary Force of 500,000 men that arrived in France in June infused fresh strength into the British and French forces. The French in particular were exhausted, having lost hundreds of thousands of men in a failed spring offensive that had caused the troops to mutiny.

THE BRITISH LOST 60,000 CASUALTIES ON THE FIRST DAY OF THE BATTLE OF THE SOMME, MAKING IT THE BLOODIEST SINGLE DAY IN THE HISTORY OF THE BRITISH ARMY. HERE, GERMAN SOLDIERS FIGHT BACK FROM THEIR STRONG DEFENSIVE POSITIONS.

Getty Images

The Russian Revolution had caused the collapse of the Russian provisional government that October, and Austrian-German forces had defeated the Italians at the Battle of Caporetto, thus freeing Germans troops and resources for the western front. In the spring 1918, the Germans launched their massive, last-ditch Ludendorff Offensive, designed by Erich Ludendorff to force the British and French to the peace table before the Americans arrived in full force. However, the combined forces of the French, British, and, finally, the Americans were able to drive the Germans back.

In September, the allies launched the last major offensive of the war, fought mainly by U.S. forces in the Meuse-Argonne region of France. As they pushed the Germans farther and farther back, the Ottoman Empire sued for peace, as did Austria-Hungary. Fighting alone, the Germans finally agreed to an armistice as war-weary citizens revolted. Kaiser Wilhelm II abdicated on November 9, and an armistice was signed on November 11, 1918.

After World War I, the world felt enormous political changes. The Russian monarchy fell, the Ottoman Empire finally crumbled, and the Austro-Hungarian Empire was torn apart into numerous small states. The Treaty of Versailles, which ended the war, forced Germany to admit guilt for the war, give up 25,000 square miles (64,750 square kilometers) of territory, pay heavy reparations, and limit its army to 100,000 troops without heavy weapons, submarines, or airplanes. German anger over what it perceived as harsh conditions was a significant contributing factor to the beginning of World War II.

SOLDIERS RODE TO BATTLE IN TAXIS AND SAVED THE FRENCH FROM ANNIHILATION
The First Battle of Marne: 1914

On the last day of August 1914, the citizens of Paris heard a low buzzing noise that sounded irritatingly like a bee trapped behind glass in summer's waning heat. The noise grew louder and louder. When they looked up in the sky, they saw a German biplane overflying the city. The plane circled ever lower and lower, insolently ignoring the few rifle shots loosed at it by soldiers racing to the roofs of buildings. When the plane arrived over the huge square called the Invalides Esplanade, it dropped a message tied to an iron rod, waggled its wings, and flew off at a leisurely pace.

The message read: "The German army will arrive in three days."

Almost no one in Paris doubted this. Already, all over the French countryside, the forces of the French and the British Expeditionary Force (BEF) were reeling back from a German onslaught that had swung five armies down through Belgium like "a great hour hand in counterclockwise motion," as one historian put it. At the very tip of the hour hand was the German First Army, north and west of Paris, racing to capture the city with the Second Army on its left, northeast of the city.

As the Germans advanced, the roads around the capital filled with retreating soldiers, still in their bright red and blue uniforms. But now, as no less an eminence than French Commander in Chief General Joseph Joffre noticed while inspecting his troops, the "red trousers had faded to the color of pale brick, coats were ragged and torn, shoes caked with mud, eyes cavernous in faces dulled by exhaustion …Twenty days of campaigning seemed to have aged the soldiers as many years."

"It Is the Thirty-Fifth Day!"

To be closer to the progress of the new war, Kaiser Wilhelm II had shifted his headquarters from Berlin to Luxembourg, some 170 miles (274 km) to the north of Paris. On September 4, he was exultant. "It is the thirty-fifth day," he told a delegation of German politicians. By this he meant that the German armies were in the middle of the period when the Schlieffen Plan called for a decisive battle for Paris. Thirty-one days would see the armies nearing the French capital, and this in fact was happening. By forty days, according to Schlieffen, there would be a battle to control the city.

The kaiser and most officers in the German high command followed the invasion schedule of Count Albert Graf von Schlieffen almost as if it were the Bible. The former chief of staff of the German army, von Schlieffen had essentially finished his plan by 1905 but kept tinkering with it until his death in 1913. It called for a blocking force of two German armies to be arrayed on Germany's western border with France, to ward off any attack, while five other armies would swing down through Belgium and into France, destroying the French army and capturing Paris within six weeks.

This timetable was important because Schlieffen had figured it would take forty days before the Russian army would be able to mount an offensive from the east, at which point Germany would be fighting the two-front war it dreaded. So taking Paris within this forty-day period was essential. But despite the headlong rush of the German troops to Paris, there were certain problems. To begin with, the Allied troops, while retreating, were retreating toward their supply lines, while the German troops were moving away from theirs. Second, the German soldiers were exhausted. A French prisoner later wrote that he had seen the German troops of General Alexander von Kluck, head of the First Army, which was supposed to capture Paris, reach the end of their ropes after a long march on September 3. "They fell down exhausted, muttering in a dazed way, 'Forty kilometers! Forty kilometers!' That was all they could say."

But finally, and most important, at the penultimate moment, the Germans decided to change the plan.

Changing the Plan

German Chief of Staff Helmuth von Moltke—who was with the kaiser in Belgium, directing the operation, but who might have been better served being far closer to the action—had already changed the Schlieffen Plan once, by weakening his attacking forces to shore up Germany's border, which made progress through Belgium more slowly than von Schlieffen had intended. But now, almost miles away as the tactical situation was rapidly unfolding, von Moltke acquiesced to changing the plan again.

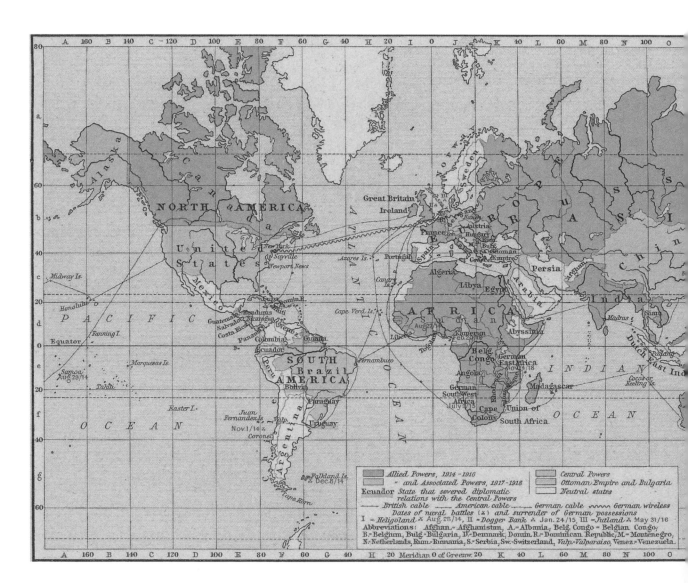

Kluck's First Army—exhausted but still moving with a will west of Paris—had seen the French Sixth Army under General Michel-Joseph Maunoury fall back to within 30 miles (48 km) of the capital. To the right of the French Sixth were the British Expeditionary Forces of General Sir John French, which had been defeated in several large battles and were falling back hastily. French, giving in to discouragement, thought the war lost. Three other French armies, badly beaten up but refusing to give in, were racing in from the east to help protect the capital city.

According to the Schlieffen Plan, the German army on the far west—Kluck's First Army— was to swing west of Paris before turning to take the city from the south. But

on August 31, seeing the disarray of the forces facing him, Kluck thought he had a better idea. He radioed von Moltke that instead of attacking Paris, he wanted to wheel north of the capital to roll up what remained of Maunoury and French's forces and cut them off from Paris, as well as stop those French forces now arriving from the east. After this was accomplished, he could join with the German Second Army, under General Karl von Bülow, and attack the French capital and end the war in the west.

"They Offer Us Their Flank!"

Von Moltke, who believed in giving his field commanders wide latitude, agreed to this plan, even though he and Kluck realized that it would leave the First Army's right flank exposed to the city. But, they decided, it didn't matter because the French were beaten anyway. What forces could possibly challenge the Germans?

Von Moltke and Kluck hadn't counted on General Joseph Gallieni, military governor of Paris in its present emergency. Gallieni, born in 1849, had a background in France's colonial wars, much like General Joseph Joffre. In fact the two men were rivals, with Joffre more than a little envious of Gallieni's influence and the respect with which he was held by most officers in the French army. Gallieni was offered the commander in chief job, but he turned it down, citing ill health, and retired from the army in April 1914. Joffre brought him back and made him military governor of Paris as German forces threatened, which meant that Gallieni was in charge of any French forces defending the city.

Gallieni immediately set about building barricades and rifle pits and repairing old fortifications. He reorganized Maunoury's Sixth Army, reinforcing it with whatever troops he could lay his hands on. Gallieni—one of the few in the French army who then understood how important airplanes were for reconnaissance—sent his small fleet of biplanes out from the city, probing for the German forces. And by September 3, Gallieni had realized that Kluck's army was no longer heading west of the city, but was now north of Paris, moving east.

When this news set in, Gallieni and his officers stared at the huge map on the wall of his headquarters, the German advance marked with colored pins. "They offer us their flank!" Gallieni's chief of staff, General Clergerie, exclaimed. The Germans had placed no blocking force between them and the capital. They could be hit, and hit hard, on their vulnerable rear and sides while their attention was elsewhere.

Gallieni leaped at once into action. On his own responsibility, he ordered General Maunoury to prepare to attack. He then called Joffre and tried to convince him over the telephone of the importance of Kluck's exposed flanks and how the French must take advantage of it. Slow to move—and distrustful of his rival—Joffre said he would have to think about it.

Seeking support for such an attack, Gallieni got into his car and headed for BEF headquarters to confer with Sir John French, but French wasn't there and Gallieni found the British officers he talked to dispirited and defeatist in manner. They were suspicious of this voluble little man with spectacles, a shaggy moustache, and a rather messy uniform. "No British soldier would be seen speaking to such a comedian," one present said.

But the comedian would not give up, even as the forces of French and Joffre were retreating. Gallieni relentlessly pushed forth his arguments until Joffre abandoned his initial reluctance. Joffre even went to BEF headquarters to try to convince Sir John French, at one point grasping the English commander's hands and begging him to have his troops join in the attack. French was so moved that tears rolled down his cheeks. He tried to speak in French, but failed. "Damn it, I can't explain," he told an interpreter. "Tell him that all man can do our fellows will do." Joffre—who would henceforth take credit for Gallieni's ideas—then sent a telegram to the ministry of war in Paris: "The struggle which is about to take place may have decisive results. It may also, in the case of a reverse, have the gravest consequences for the country."

The Taxis of Paris

The British had fallen too far back to immediately take part in the attack, so it was up to the French. Joffre sent Maunoury and his Sixth Army forward, and advance elements of it made contact with the German First late on September 5. But an alert German corps commander put up a fierce resistance when he sensed the French counterattack, and the French stalled.

Kluck and von Moltke now began concerned about that flank exposed to Paris and decided to withdraw the First Army farther north, but it was too late. On the morning of September 6, the French Sixth Army hit them hard while the Fifth Army attacked the German Second Army under von Bülow. The French threw everything they had into the attack. Gallieni had scoured Paris for every last French soldier home on leave, every last reservist, every last malingerer. He found that a train carrying the North African 45th Algerian Division, still in their far-too-colorful Zouave uniforms, was headed east, and he commandeered it and brought it to Paris.

But Gallieni had no way to get these and other extra troops to the front, some 40 miles (64 km) distant, because trucks were in short supply and railroads hard pressed. It was then that Gallieni hit upon using Paris' taxicabs and their famously irascible drivers to transport the troops to the fighting that was raging as the Germans began to slowly withdraw to the River Marne north and east of Paris. Gallieni sent troops out all over Paris to stop taxis, expel their protesting passengers, and tell them to gather at the Invalides Esplanade, the same place where the insolent biplane had dropped its insulting message.

WITH ALREADY TOO MUCH STRAIN ON PARIS' TRUCKING AND RAILROAD SYSTEM, GENERAL GALLIENI FOUND AN ALTERNATIVE WITH TAXIS. PILING FIVE SOLDIERS AT A TIME INTO EACH ONE, THEY BEGAN THE 40-MILE COMMUTE TO THE FRONT LINES.

Getty Images

Once there, Gallieni piled troops into them, five per cab, and sent them in a long procession to the front. When the drivers wanted to know who would pay them, Gallieni told them, "France will pay you!" and then jibed: "Are you afraid of gunfire?"

As the taxis left the square, hundreds of French civilians cheered. Only 6,000 French troops actually reached the battle in this way, not enough to materially affect its outcome, but the legend of the heroic taxis of Paris became a huge morale booster for France in the long war to come.

The Battle of the Marne

And the reason it was a long war to come—the reason why the war didn't end that hot early September—was because of the battle French and British troops fought for the next four days, one that Winston Churchill was to reference as one of the most important battles in the history of the world. The front line stretched 100 miles (161 km) from Verdun on the east to Paris on the west; most of the fighting raged around the River Marne and its tributaries. The area was a beautiful scene of streams, pastures, deep valleys, and wooded hills, although it was cut through east and north of Paris by the marshes of St. Gond, a wide swath of then nearly impassable swampland.

The Battle of the Marne was a series of fast, furious fights between forces that knew just how pivotal its outcome would be. The French knew that to lose the battle meant losing the war, while the Germans understood that any failure to take Paris would mean the failure of the Schlieffen Plan. As the Allied forces hit the German First and Second armies, a gap slowly widened between the German armies. The allies exploited that gap with attacks by French's BEF and General Ferdinand Foch's Ninth Army. Foch's army then withstood ferocious German counterattacks in the St. Gond marshes. The weather had turned from hot and sunny to cold and rainy, and the swamp became a horrible morass where wounded men drowned in shell holes while others fought hand to hand, knee deep in muck.

This was not the classic war of the trenches—that would soon start—but a more mobile war of attack and counterattack, of deadly skirmishes in woods and valleys, of bayonet attacks on farmhouse positions. Men on both sides were exhausted, using their last ounces of energy. A French officer described "men emaciated, in rags and tatters, most without haversacks, many without rifles, marching painfully, leaning on sticks...."

Yet the French held. Gradually realizing their position as untenable, the Germans withdrew to positions behind the River Aisne. They had sustained 250,000 casualties, the French about the same, while the BEF suffered about 12,000. But Paris was saved. Yet both Germans and Allies realized their northern flanks were not anchored. Now the race to the North Sea began, with the Germans seeking to turn the Allied flank and seize the channel ports and the allies fighting to keep them from doing so. Ten separate battles were fought throughout the fall of 1914, with neither side gaining the advantage, until a stalemate was reached, trenches were dug, and the war on the western front, as we know it, began.

Directly after the Battle of the Marne, General Helmuth von Moltke wrote his wife: "The appalling difficulties of our present situation hang before my eyes like a dark curtain through which I can see nothing." Within a few days, he had suffered a nervous breakdown, and he was relieved of command. On the face of it, the battle ended as a draw, but, in reality the failure of the German army to break through would set the stage for the long war of attrition that would eventually be won by the allies. In that sense, the Battle of the Marne was the battle that saved France, and the allies, from defeat.

THE SEA WAR: A FIERCE CLASH WITH STEEL BEHEMOTHS AND STEALTHY UNDEWATER HUNTERS

The Germans and British had been at pains to develop bigger and better battleships for some time. These were known as dreadnoughts, after the HMS Dreadnought, built in 1906, which outclassed every ship on the high seas at the time. This naval arms race contributed greatly to tensions between Great Britain and Germany,

BOTH BRITAIN AND GERMANY HAD FLEETS OF ARMORED BATTLE SHIPS OF THE SUPER-DREADNOUGHT CLASS, ONE SUCH IS SEEN HERE.

particularly because it was known that developing the finest naval fleet in the world was an obsession with Kaiser Wilhelm II. At the beginning of the war, both nations had fleets that contained heavily armored battleships—now in what was called the "super-dreadnought" class—which were studded with 12- or 15-inch (30 or 38 cm) guns that could fire heavy shells at a distance of 17,000 yards (16 km).

The question was what to do with them? The naval arms race had been predicated on the theory that the very heart of a modern nation's defense was a strong navy. But World War I, with its massive land battles, wasn't turning out quite that way. The German High Seas Fleet was from the first bottled up in the North Sea by Great Britain's Grand Fleet. The British had the greater number of dreadnoughts, which meant they would almost certainly win any large scale battle between the two fleets, so the Germans hoped to lure the English into minefields or actions in which the ships could be destroyed piecemeal.

The first two years of the war were a stalemate (helped in part because the British were reading the German naval code and hence knew their plans). But in 1916, the two mighty fleets finally clashed in the Battle of Jutland, which was the only battle ever fought between dreadnoughts in the First World War. On May 31, a British naval group made contact at about 3:30 in the afternoon with part of the German fleet and engaged in a running gun battle with it. The clash brought in the main German fleet, which chased the British ships, inflicting serious damage and sinking two ships. But now the main British fleet was brought into the battle. By 6 p.m., the first and only struggle between dreadnoughts occurred, with the British losing three battle cruisers, but with the Germans eventually withdrawing. It turned out to be a tactical draw, although the fact that the British fleet continued to control the North Sea gave it the ultimate victory.

To the surprise of both sides, the most influential naval weapon of the First World War turned out to be the submarine. Submarines had been around, in theory, for centuries, with crude ones in use as far back as the American Revolution, but the first fully functioning submarine, one that could dive, cruise on the surface with diesel engines, and fire torpedoes, was invented by an Irish-American named J.P. Holland in 1901. It was quickly seized upon by the navies of the world. At the beginning of World War I, the British and French had the largest fleets of submarines, totaling some 300 boats, while the Germans had only twenty-nine U-boats (Unterseeboots). But the Germans would build 390 U-boats during the course of the war, and they were by far the most effective practitioners of undersea warfare.

At the beginning of the war, German U-boat commanders would warn merchant ships before they sank them, allowing their crews to abandon ship, but as the war turned more deadly, this was abandoned. Not only that, but Germans, as they blockaded England, began to practice "unrestricted" submarine warfare, which meant they

torpedoed any ship, civilian or military, approaching British ports. This was highly effective for blockading purposes, but it had a highly negative impact on the German war effort, because it helped bring the United States.

THE AIR WAR: AN ARRAY OF FIRSTS—THE FIRST FIGHTERS, THE FIRST BOMBERS

The first military use of aviation came during the French Revolutionary Wars when the French used observation balloons to spy on the Austrians. The balloon had been used for observation in numerous wars since that time. But in 1900, Count Ferdinand von Zeppelin developed the "guided rigid airship"—in other words, a dirigible powered mechanically, which one could use for purposeful reconnaissance. After the Wright brothers developed the fixed-wing aircraft in 1903, the sky could bristle with weapons.

At the beginning of the war, the French, British, and Germans all had military air commands whose fixed bi-wing aircraft were used mainly for reconnaissance. Soon, however, the crews of these airplanes began to shoot at each other (in one case, throw bricks), and they were soon equipped with machine guns.

German aircraft designer Anthony Fokker developed "interrupter" gear, so that machine guns could fire through the plane's propeller. This gave the Germans, at first, a great advantage over British and French aircraft, whose guns were perched

IN THE PAST, WARFARE HAD SEEN ITS BATTLES ON LAND AND ON SEA, BUT NOW, WITH THE WRIGHT BROTHERS' INVENTION OF THE FIXED-WING AIRCRAFT IN 1903, THE BATTLES WOULD TAKE TO THE SKY.

Royal Aircraft Factory SE5, single seater with Vickers and Lewis gun, powered by Hispano-Suiza, 1914-18, Withams, B. (20th century) / Private Collection, / The Bridgeman Art Library atop their bi-wings or fired by gunners in rear seats. Soon however, planes such as the Sopwith Camel and Spad 13 evened the playing field, and the era of the great aces began. Flyers such as Manfred von Richthofen (the Red Baron), Ernst Udet, René Fonck, William Bishop, and Eddie Rickenbacker, captured the public imagination as they led squadrons into aerial battle over the western front.

Because fixed-wing aircraft at the time were relatively small, long-range German bombing raids at the beginning of the war were carried out by zeppelins, which had top speeds of more than 100 miles (161 km) an hour and could drop 4,000 pounds (1,814 kg) worth of bombs. The first zeppelin raid on London in May 1915 killed twenty-eight people. Subsequent attacks killed as many as 600 British, but the zeppelin proved too vulnerable to British fighters and anti-aircraft attack, and so the German High Command stopped such attacks in 1917, after losing seventy-seven zeppelins. King George V refused to evacuate during these raids, despite being urged to do so by advisors, setting an example that inspired the British people, who would in just over twenty years endure far worse bombings.

LIFE IN THE SUICIDE DITCH

The trench—the "suicide ditch" as frontline British soldiers called it—is the symbol of World War I on the western front, the place where soldiers on both sides lived in the mud, the holes in the ground from which they went "over the top," often to die.

Facing each other over a no-man's-land that averaged about 200 yards (183 m) across, but sometimes could be as small as 50 feet (15 m)—the trenches snaked across Europe from Switzerland to the North Sea.

Perhaps 12,000 miles (19,312 km) of trenches were dug in total on the western front. Some were elaborate affairs. The German trenches later in the war were deep, interlocking tunnels dotted with reinforced concrete pillboxes, but many were merely shallow depressions in the earth. However, most trenches were part of a system. The front line trench, with its wooden firing step built in, from which the troops could shoot their enemy, was backed up by supply trenches further in the rear, and they were all connected by communications trenches.

The purpose of all the trenches, of course, was to hide from the overwhelming artillery fire that rained down upon both sides. In between shellings and attacks, soldiers followed highly unpleasant daily routines, which included delousing each other with candles, treating their "trench" or immersion foot, which was a serious disease caused by prolonged exposure to the puddles that inevitably formed in the bottom of the trenches, and peering at the other side through periscopes—sticking one's head

up inevitably invited a sniper's bullet. At night, no-man's-land was alive with scouting parties, each out to seek information and capture prisoners.

Everywhere, the constant companion of the living was the dead. Left in no-man's-land, because to remove them was generally too dangerous, the dead became part of the landscape. British officer Edwin Vaughan wrote in his diaries about sitting in his trench staring at a corpse: "He had a diamond-shaped hole in his forehead through which a little pouch of brains was hanging, and his eyes were hanging down. He was very horrible, but I soon got used to him."

PICTURED HERE ARE BRITISH SOLDIERS IN THEIR TRENCHES. THE TRENCH WAS OFTEN CALLED THE "SUICIDE DITCH" AND IT BECAME A SYMBOL OF WORLD WAR I ON THE WESTERN FRONT.

Prints & Photographs Division, Library of Congress, LC-USZ62-75152

Getty Images

THE BATTLE OF TANNENBERG WOULD BE GERMANY'S RESOUNDING VICTORY ON THE EASTERN FRONT, PROVING ITS MILITARY EXPERTISE. IT WOULD BE QUITE THE OPPOSITE FOR THE RUSSIANS, WITH 50,000 WOUNDED OR KILLED AND 95,000 CAPTURED (PICTURED HERE).

THE BATTLE OF TANNENBERG: THE GERMANS DESTROY RUSSIA IN A GREAT BATTLE ON THE EASTERN FRONT

Tsar Nicholas II called it "a great calamity," and so it was—although for the Germans it was their most complete and decisive victory of the war, the victory that would elude them on the western front after the First Battle of the Marne. Yet, it almost certainly should have turned out the other way.

When the Germans committed most of their forces to attacking Belgium and France, they had only one army group, the Eighth Army, left behind to guard East Prussia. The Eighth Army was outnumbered by the two Russian army groups that faced it. Thus, as the Russians invaded Prussia in August 1914, it should have been easy for their First and Second armies to simply grab the German Eighth Army in a pincer movement and squeeze it to death. But the Russian commanders, General Rennenkampf of the First Army and General Samsonov of the Second, disliked each other powerfully, ever since Samsonov complained that Rennenkampf had not supported his division at the Battle of Mukden in 1905. In fact, the two men had come to blows over the incident.

This old grudge was to cost the Russians dearly, but at first didn't matter because the two armies advanced on separate wings, probing for the German flanks as the Germans retreated. But then the German Eighth Army commander was replaced by Field Marshall Pavel von Hindenburg, called out of retirement for the occasion, who brought along with him his chief of staff, General Erich Ludendorff.

These two men, particularly Lundendorff, changed the tide of history. Through superior intelligence the German generals realized that the two Russian armies, whose commanders were not communicating with each other, had drifted further apart than each apparently knew. Therefore Hindenburg and Ludendorff turned their forces on Samsonov's army alone, enveloped it, and destroyed it during two days at the end of August, while Rennenkampf, still nursing his old grudge, made no move to come to the Second Army's aid.

Ninety-five thousand Russians were captured, 50,000 were killed or wounded, and perhaps 10,000 escaped. Samsonov, unable to face the tsar, shot himself. Hindenburg and Ludendorff would then go on to push Rennenkampf's army back into Russia. The ultimate effect of the battle—what has been called the most complete German victory of the war—was to allow the Germans to concentrate on the western front, knowing that they faced no serious threat from the east. For the Russians, defeat at Tannenberg helped spell the demise of the tsarist government, which had pinned its hopes for survival on victory against Germany.

20

THE RUSSIAN CIVIL WAR

1918–1921

ONE OF THE MOST BITTER AND COSTLY CIVIL WARS OF THE TWENTIETH CENTURY DIRECTLY SHAPED THE FUTURE OF COMMUNISM AND THE SOVIET UNION FOR THE NEXT SEVENTY YEARS

A VICIOUS CIVIL WAR SET THE TONE FOR RUSSIA AND THE WORLD

IN 10/1917 LENIN + TROTSHY OUTSTEDED HERE

By the fall of 1917, the Russian Empire had lost millions of people in the horrible conflagration of World War I, not only soldiers—many of whom were sent into battle unarmed, to be turned into "gruel" by German cannon fire, as one commander wrote—but also civilians who had died of starvation and disease. The Romanov dynasty, as represented by Tsar Nicholas II, had been overthrown. The tsar and his family were now prisoners, and a provisional government under the relatively moderate Alexander Kerensky was put into place.

But in the famous October uprising of 1917, the far more radical Bolsheviks, led by Vladimir Lenin and Leon Trotsky, seized Petrograd (the former Saint Petersburg), ousted Kerensky from power, and, in March 1918, made a separate peace with Germany. The Bolsheviks, known as the Reds, were only in control of European Russia, and so began to fulfill their goal of consolidating their rule over all of what had formerly been the Russian Empire. Arrayed against them were the counterrevolutionary forces of the White army, consisting of former monarchists (many of them officers from the tsar's army), moderate socialists who wished to see a more democratic form of government; and a broad coalition of men and women dismayed by the iron hand the Bolsheviks had already begun to display.

Other forces fighting against the Reds were the Don Cossacks (Cossack horsemen from the Don River region in west Russia, who had long supported the tsar); armies from the Ukraine, Poland, Lithuania, Georgia, and other border states, who sought their independence; and the expeditionary forces of fourteen foreign countries, most notably Great Britain, France, the United States, and Japan, who were dismayed that the ideas of Bolshevism might spread to their own countries.

The war can be divided roughly into three phases. The first phase began in November 1917 when generals of the former Imperial Army, especially Mikhail Alekseev, Lavr Kornilov, Anton Denikin, and Alexey Kaledin, disguised themselves and found their way to south Russia, where, under Alekseev's direction, they formed the first White army, called the Volunteers. Kaledin was also the hetman, or leader, of the Don Cossacks in the area, and he organized them to fight against the Reds.

In response to this military threat, Vladimir Lenin, head of the Bolshevik government, proclaimed the establishment of the Red army in February 1918 and made Leon Trotsky the country's first commissar of war. The Treaty of Brest-Litovsk was negotiated with Germany in March, ending the war. Around the same time the Bolsheviks dissolved the Constituent Assembly (the country's first parliament-style stab at democracy), convincing even more moderate Russians to join the White army.

They also put into place a series of measures known as War Communism, which allowed the seizure of grain from Russian peasants—"those who have grain and fail to deliver it to properly designated rail stations ... are to be declared enemies of the people," Lenin declared in May. The initiatives may have been necessary to feed the Red army, but they caused famine, disease, and further unrest among the peasants of Russia.

In mid 1918, a group of 10,000 Czech soldiers, known as the Czechoslovakian Legion, who had fought on the side of the tsarist army during the war, embarked on a journey east along 5,400 miles (8,690 km) of the Trans-Siberian Railroad, where they planned to disembark at Vladivostok, ship to the western front, and join the Allied Powers fighting against the Germans.

When the Bolsheviks ordered them to give up their arms after the Treaty of Brest-Litovsk ended the Russian part in the war, the Czechs joined the White forces and in June set up anti-Bolshevik governments in Siberian towns. With their joint forces swelling to some 50,000, the Czech Legion and the White army, united under the command of former tsarist admiral Alexander Kolchak, eventually captured almost all of Siberia. In July 1918, as White forces and the Czech Legion neared the royal family's place of captivity in Yekaterinburg (modern-day Sverdlovsk), Tsar Nicholas II and his entire family were murdered on the orders of Lenin.

In August 1918, U.S., British, and Japanese forces landed at the Pacific Russian port of Vladivostok to support the Whites. U.S. and British troops also arrived at Archangel on the White Sea and helped establish a new White provisional government there. They also funneled supplies of munitions into the White effort, but without the full backing of their war-weary nations, the intervention of foreign countries had relatively little effect on the war. While this was happening, the Bolsheviks, inspired by Leon Trotsky stopped the advance of the White army at Sviyazhsk, changing the course of the war.

In September 1918, after Lenin was nearly assassinated, the Bolsheviks launched the Red Terror, which was aimed at eliminating political opponents inside the civilian population. The second stage of the Russian Civil War began after the Allied defeat of the Central Powers in November 1918. Kolchak, who had been named head of the White army in Siberia, planned a spring 1919 offensive to capture Moscow. He attacked east from Siberia, while General Denikin's armies headed north from southern Russia.

In the meantime, the army of General Nikolay Yudenivich attacked Petrograd from the Baltic region. Fighting raged all throughout Russia, with Denikin's forces coming within 200 miles (322 km) of Moscow while Yudenivich reached within 10 miles (16 km) of Petrograd, but by the end of the year, the better-supplied and more cohesive Red army had defeated the Whites in Siberia, the south of Russia, and the Baltic.

THE RUSSIAN CIVIL WAR RESULTED IN THE CREATION OF THE USSR. HOWEVER, IT ALSO CAUSED WIDESPREAD DESTRUCTION OF INFRASTRUCTURE, FAMINE, DISEASE, ECONOMIC DEVASTATION, THE EMIGRATION OF MILLIONS OF RUSSIANS, AND THE DEATHS OF MANY MILLIONS MORE.

In the third and final stage of the war, the White forces made a fighting retreat to the Crimean Peninsula under their capable commander Baron Peter Nikolaevich Wrangel. But decimated by casualties and disease, the White forces eventually had to be evacuated by the British and French navies in November 1920. Within the next year, the Kronstadt Uprising and the Green Rebellion, in which various peasant groups joined together to protest near-starvation conditions, would be bloodily put down.

Although the Bolsheviks had not been successful in reclaiming all of the Russian Empire (the Ukraine, Poland, and Finland became separate republics), they had fought a successful war that they had won mainly because of a unified purpose and command, and because they held the factories and manpower of the geographic center of the country. The disparate groups of Whites were never able to effectively find common cause, and they often lacked supplies and munitions.

The Russian Civil War resulted in the creation of the USSR. However, it also caused widespread destruction of infrastructure, famine, disease, economic devastation, the emigration of millions of Russians, and the deaths of many millions more. The emotional effects of such a savage war—what White Commander Anton Denikin later described as the "unbounded hatred everywhere"—lasted for a long time. The Bolsheviks had been arrayed against forces not only within their own country, but invading armies from without, and this militarized the Russian communist party.

After the death of Lenin and the ouster of Trotsky, Russia would be led by Joseph Stalin, whose dark paranoia resulted in the Great Terror of the 1930s, in which many of the methods put in service by the Bolsheviks in the Russian Civil War—including mass executions and a form of War Communism in which agriculture and industry were collectivized for the common good—were employed in the murder, by bullet or starvation, of millions of people.

NEAR AN OBSCURE TOWN, THE BOLSHEVIKS WIN A BATTLE THAT HALTS THE ADVANCE OF THE OLD ORDER
Trotsky at Sviyazhsk: September 1918

Sviyazhsk, some 250 miles (402 km) southwest of Moscow near the Volga River, is not a village advancing in the world. Its population is only about 300 or so, down from more than 1,000 a half century ago. This may be because Sviyazhsk is now located on a small island, in the middle of the deep, light-blue waters of the far-flung Kuybyshev Reservoir, created when a part of the Volga was dammed in the 1950s in a vast Soviet hydroelectric project.

Sviyazhsk's change of circumstance and dwindling size makes it one of the most obscure but important places in Russian and world history. It's not a place you read about in guide books. But in late August 1918, well before it became an island, the Russian Revolution was saved at Sviyazhsk because of the efforts of Leon Trotsky, an armored train, and a few thousand dedicated Bolsheviks. As W. Bruce Lincoln, one of the premiere historians of the Russian Civil War, wrote:

> "During August of 1918, Sviyazhsk became the Valmy of the Russian Revolution, the point where the Bolsheviks, like the armies of revolutionary France in 1792, first halted the advance of armies that marched to restore the old order."

The Hungry Spring

By the summer of 1918, the Russian Revolution had fallen on hard times. The initial euphoria of the great events at Petrograd in the fall of 1917, when the Bolsheviks had seized the Winter Palace and ousted Alexander Kerensky from power, had now broken against some very hard realities. The Russian people were starving. The masses in Russia at the time lived mainly on bread, but the harvest the previous fall had been poor, and the infrastructure of Russia's railways—falling apart as the old regime fell apart—proved inadequate to transport what grain supplies there were to the big population centers. Men and women in cities such as Petrograd, Moscow, and Novgorod ate what was called "famine bread," because the dough from which it was made was filled with water and vegetable shavings. And even then, they were on quarter rations.

The spring of 1918 later became known as "the Hunger Spring." Under orders of Vladimir Lenin, the Reds confiscated grain from peasants for the Red army. Starving crowds pleaded for bread; demonstrations turned hostile and had to be put down violently. Unemployment spread across the country, and soldiers newly released from the Russian army after the March peace treaty with Germany returned home to find no jobs and no food. Their response was to commit violent crimes against the citizenry. The Bolsheviks estimated that, during the early winter of 1918, 800 robberies were committed every single day in Petrograd.

Even worse, the military situation was becoming untenable. The successful spring and early summer offensive of the White army and Czech Legion robbed Russia of the vast grain stores of Siberia and pushed Red armies back toward the Volga River. The United Kingdom and France had already sent troops to Russia, supposedly to protect the massive piles of munitions they had sent to the tsar for use against Germany. But in reality, as everyone knew, they were hostile to the Bolshevik government. The Japanese, with designs on Siberia, had 70,000 troops there, and the Americans were soon to land 10,000.

"Everything Was Crumbling"

Everywhere, it seemed to a harried Leon Trotsky, Bolshevik war commissar, the revolution was coming apart at the seams. "A rumor began to spread," he later wrote, "that the Soviets were doomed … Everything was crumbling, there was nothing to hold to. The situation seemed hopeless."

As the White army, coupled with the units of the Czech Brigade, swept west, heading for the Volga, news came that an army under Alexey Kaledin, hetman of the Cossacks, and General Mikhail Alekseev, former supreme commander of Russian Imperial forces, had been formed south of the Don River, and was pushing back Red forces there.

It was what Trotsky called "the first wave of the counterrevolution," and it was graphically marked by the little blue flags he stuck in the map on the wall of his Moscow office, each flag marking another counterrevolutionary force taking another bit of Russia from the Bolsheviks. Educated socialist theorists like Trotsky and Lenin had expected the counterrevolution, but not such a rapid destruction of revolutionary forces. That summer of 1918, Trotsky received word that entire units and garrisons were deserting.

Despite the large amount of work Trotsky had put into constructing his Red army, it seemed like even he would be hard put to hold back the flood. He told a subordinate that "it is essential to start producing tanks in the Urals…using tractor parts, if necessary," despite the fact Whites, even as he spoke, threatened Red factories there. He desperately cabled Lenin: "We need to find a possible way of using asphyxiating gases." (This cable was ignored.)

By August 1918, White forces, along with units of the Czech Legion, had closed on the Volga and captured the town of Kazan, the easternmost terminus of the Moscow–Kazan railway line, which put them within striking distance of Moscow.

Trotsky in Sviyazhsk

Fifteen miles (24 km) west of Kazan was the small town of Sviyazhsk, which had been founded by Ivan the Terrible in the 1550s, but had no other claim to fame than this. Monitoring events at the front from Moscow, Trotsky learned that Sviyazhsk was where the Red soldiers fleeing the Whites around Kazan were gathering, pausing for breath before they con-

tinued their journey westward. With Trotsky's extraordinary energy, organizational skill, and ability to improvise, he decided at once to head to Sviyazhsk aboard a special train that contained a printing press, a telegraph, a radio station capable of receiving signals from Moscow, and a shipment of boots, medicine, food, watches, and arms.

Arriving at Sviyazhsk, Trotsky could hear the sound of heavy guns in the distance and found Red army soldiers wandering the streets, some in a state of panic. Just as Trotsky arrived, while he was still on his train, a White army brigade broke through to raid the rear of the Bolshevik lines and made an attack on Sviyazhsk. "This move caught us quite off our guard," Trotsky later wrote. As gunfire cracked against the armored sides of the train, he armed everyone he could, "even the cook." They moved about a mile from the train, and Trotsky himself set up a battle line. "We had a good stock of rifles, machine guns, and hand grenades," he said. "The train crew was made up of good fighters. The battle went on for eight hours …Finally, after they had spent themselves, the enemy withdrew."

After the fight, Trotsky learned that one cause of the breakthrough had been the desertion of an entire Red regiment from the front lines, including the regimental commander and political commissar who accompanied each regiment. Steeling himself, Trotsky had the commander and the commissar executed immediately. He then told his guards to pick out every tenth man in the ranks of the regiment—an old Roman method of discipline called decimation—and shoot them.

"A red-hot iron has been applied to a festering wound," Trotsky wrote Lenin. "[The Red soldier] must choose between the possibility that death lies ahead and the certainty that it lies behind."

"The Holy Demagoguery of Battle"

Trotsky's repressive discipline had its effect, but so did his supplies. Staying at Sviyazhsk for an entire month, he shuttled his and other trains from the front to the rear and back again "tens, even hundreds of times." He wrote that the resources brought by the train "served as that one shovelful of coal needed at a particular moment to keep the fire from dying out."

Apprised of the needs of the front line soldiers, Trotsky sent for 126 machine guns, three armored cars, sixteen aircraft (some carrying 1,000-pound bombs), and even gunboats, which arrived on the Volga to bombard Kazan. He sent an urgent plea to Moscow for any fighters willing to come and risk their lives on this front, and boys as young as fifteen responded, impressing even the hardened fighters at Sviyazhsk.

At last, Trotsky was ready to attempt to retake Kazan. He named as his commander General Ioakim Vatsetis, the squat, good-humored son of a Latvian peasant who had served in the tsarist army before joining the Bolsheviks the previous October. Vatsetis had been driven out of Kazan—in fact, he and his orderly had been the last to leave, under fire from the Whites—and now he was ready to battle his way back in. Before the attack Trotsky told Vatsetis and his fighters that "the taking of Kazan means merciless revenge against the enemies of the revolution." Then he shouted: "Do not allow the enemy to move a step further. Tear Kazan from his hands. Drown him in the Volga!"

Vatsetis and his men launched their attack at 3:30 in the morning on September 10, 1918, as gunboats boomed from the river. Kazan was an ancient fortress town with high walls, but they were no match for modern artillery, nor could they withstand the Red infantry pouring through the rubble-strewn breaches from three sides. Thousands of Whites fled to the east, hundreds died, and the city fell by the early afternoon.

At Sviyazhsk with Trotsky during those days was a twenty-two-year-old female soldier named Larissa Reisner, the wife of the commander of the Volga fleet of gunboats; Reisner headed the flotilla's intelligence-gathering section. Like so many Russians of her generation, she would not live long. (She died of typhus before she was thirty.) But watching Trotsky in action that month, she confided to her journal that she and her comrades "could die in battle with the last cartridge gone, oblivious to our wounds, for Trotsky incarnated the holy demagoguery of battle. This we used to whisper among ourselves on those nights of a quick-freezing autumn, lying jumbled in our heaps across the floor of [Sviyazhsk] station."

Although the next year, 1919, would bring extraordinary challenges to the Bolsheviks, Trotsky's intervention at Sviyazhsk had been decisive. To Bolshevik soldiers like Larissa Reisner and her comrades, he became a living symbol of what the Red cause had been missing—backbone and inspiration.

LEON TROTSKY: A MAN BEHIND THE SCENES WHO DID MUCH TO WIN THE RED VICTORY

Despite the fact that Leon Trotsky did not command a Red army in the field, his contributions to the building of the Red army did as much as any field commander to gain victory for the Bolsheviks.

Trotsky was born Lev Bronstein in southern Russia in 1879 to a small landowner who worked hard to provide for his wife and children. The handsome, blue-eyed Trotsky was a brilliant student whose intellect helped him overcome the stigma of being Jewish as he went through a state high school in Odessa. Radicalized early by harsh tsarist treatment of workers and peasants, he demonstrated against the imperial government, and he was arrested and placed in jail. When he got out, he went into exile, took on the pseudonym Leon Trotsky (an ironic tribute to one of his jailers of the same name), and began writing in support of the Marxist cause.

At the outbreak of the Russian Revolution, Trotsky was second only to Vladimir Lenin in power among the Bolsheviks, so it was no surprise when Lenin named him commissar of the new Red army in March of 1918. Trotsky set to his job with a will, proclaiming that "the Soviet Republic must have an army that can fight battles and win." A brilliant organizer, Trotsky knew that the raw recruits of the Red army must have experienced officers leading them, and so, against the advice of many of the Bolsheviks in power, insisted on allowing tsarist officers (eventually as many as 75,000) to serve.

"It is essential for us to have a real military force, one that is properly organized according to scientific military principles," he stated. He then convinced many of these tsarist officers (who, with good reason, feared for their lives) to serve with the Bolsheviks. Without this masterly task of persuasion, the Red army would have been stillborn. (Trotsky also made sure he used persuasion of a different sort. If a former tsarist officer seemed likely to desert, Trotsky would have him closely watched by loyal Bolsheviks with pistols drawn.)

Trotsky's actions at Sviyazhsk are a showcase for the ways in which a tough-minded, but compassionate and resourceful, commander could act to change the

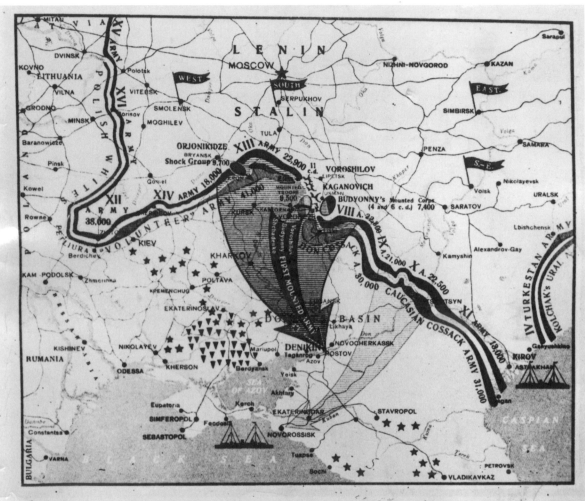

KEY

Fronts at time of maximum advance of White armies in direction of Denikin's main blow, October 1919

Areas of maximum concentration of troops

Headquarters of Red fronts

XIV   Numeration of Red armies

38,000 31,000   Number of men

A. A.   Army   c. d.   cavalry division

Entente fleet

Volga-Caspian Red flotilla

Stalin's plan for the main blow at Denikin

Trotsky's treacherous defeatist plan rejected at Stalin's instance by Party Central Committee

Lines of action of Shock Group and Budyonny's Mounted Corps

Offensive of First Mounted Army (began November 19, 1919)

Red Partizan detachments operating in Denikin's rear

Makhno bands

State boundaries in 1919

Railroads

SCALE
100   0   100   200   300   400 km

fortunes of his army. Yet Trotsky's service in the Civil War was to be the high-point of his career, mainly because of the machinations of his rival, Joseph Stalin. Stalin was a member of the Revolutionary Military Committee and a political commissar on several Civil War fronts who criticized Trotsky openly for his use of tsarist officers and set traps for him (demanding absurdly large amounts of supplies for a certain area, for instance, and then complaining to Lenin when Trotsky could not produce them). After Lenin's death, Stalin won the power struggle to become the new leader of Russia and forced Trotsky—far more talented, but less skilled in political infighting—out of the country. When Trotsky continued to write from exile in Mexico criticizing Stalin's regime, the latter had him murdered in 1940.

THE REDS: "A MODEL ARMY" ARISES OUT OF NOWHERE TO WIN A COUNTRY

The Red army was formed by decree of Vladimir Lenin in January 1918 and was known officially as the Workers and Peasants Red Army. It originally consisted of a core of Red Guards—the early military force of the Bolsheviks—as many as 75,000 former tsarist officers, and (although the force was officially supposed to be a volunteer one) hundreds of thousands of peasant conscripts.

Although the Reds outnumbered their White opponents—the army would grow to more than 5 million men (and women) by the end of the Civil War—it had numerous problems. Chief among them was desertion, which reached such endemic proportions that in 1919 alone, Bolshevik authorities re-captured some 1.7 million AWOL soldiers. Conditions were harsh, rations were short, and many members were "barefoot, naked, hungry, and lice-ridden," as Leon Trotsky, the army's commissar put it.

Although it may have been an exaggeration to say that Trotsky turned them into a "model army," as Lenin said, he was able to bring order and cohesiveness to large, untrained group. As the fighting intensified in all areas of the country, the Red army was divided up into numbered units (the 1st Red Army, the 12th Red Army, etc.) and sent wherever they were needed in the country. Each "army" consisted of perhaps 30,000 infantrymen supported by light artillery and cavalrymen. Although most of the country's Cossack horsemen had joined the Whites, the Reds had excellent cavalry units in the Konarmiia, or "horse army," an irregular but elite unit comprised of peasants who had learned to ride and who sometimes went into combat in civilian clothes.

Because the Reds operated from the center of the country, they were able to get resupplied from Russia's factories and also have use of its transportation system and

THIS 1919 MAP DEPICTS JOSEPH STALIN'S PLAN TO DESTROY GENERAL ANTON DENIKIN'S WHITE RUSSIAN ARMIES OF COSSACKS ON THE UKRAINIAN BORDER, CLOSE TO ROSTOV. THE BETTER SUPPLIED AND MORE COHESIVE RED ARMY WOULD DEFEAT THE WHITES AT THE END OF THE YEAR IN SIBERIA, THE SOUTH OF RUSSIA, AND THE BALTIC. DESERTIONS AND NATIONALIST UPRISINGS WOULD CONTRIBUTE TO THE DISSOLUTION OF THE WHITE CAUSE.

were thus shuttle from one area to another much faster than the Whites. And, deser-tions notwithstanding, those millions who remained in the army to fight had become indoctrinated with the Bolshevik spirit and became extremely difficult to beat.

THE HORRIFIC MASSACRE OF THE TSAR AND HIS FAMILY: AFTER THIS, THERE WAS NO GOING BACK

After Tsar Nicholas II had abdicated in March 1917, he, his wife, and five children became prisoners of Russia's first provisional government, headed by Alexander Kerensky. At first, with the British government offering asylum, it was assumed that the tsar and his family would soon be on their way to foreign land to live out their days as expatriates.

But the British withdrew their offer when it was thought that giving shelter to the tsar might stir social unrest in their own country at a time when Britons were already being bled dry by the war. As the Russian Revolution turned more to the left and the radical Bolsheviks gained power, Kerensky was afraid he might not be able to keep the Romanovs safe near Petrograd and thus had them transferred in August 1917 to the isolated town of Tobolsk, in western Siberia, some 1,500 miles (2,414 km) away. After Kerensky lost power in the fall of 1917, the Bolsheviks in turn sent the Romanovs to another isolated town, Yekaterinburg, in the Urals.

There the Romanovs lived in a large stone house with whitewashed windows (so they could not look out and no one else could look in), eating peasant rations of black bread and tea, playing card games, singing hymns, and praying for deliverance. They were surrounded by guards with machine guns. In the meantime, Russia's Bolshevik leaders debated what to do with them. Lenin wanted a show trial in which the tsar would be tried for his crimes, but it was now the summer of 1919 and White army forces were advancing on Yekaterinburg with the express purpose of rescuing Nicholas and his family. Deciding that the Bolsheviks would be foolish to "leave the Whites with a live banner to rally around," Lenin ordered the execution of the tsar and his entire family.

Early in the morning of July 17, 1919, with the sound of White artillery thundering in the distance, the Romanovs were awakened and told they were going to be moved to a different city because the Whites were about to attack. They were then taken to the cellar of their house —Nicholas and his wife, Alexandra; their hemophiliac son and heir to the throne, Alexei; and their daughters, Olga, Anastasia, Maria, and Tatiana. Several servants and the family doctor accompanied them.

Once there, their chief jailer, Yakov Yurovsky, read a statement condemning them to death. The tsar only had time to stand up and exclaim: "What!" when Yurovksy shot him twice in the head and then pumped two more bullets into Alexei. The rest of the guards opened fire on the other Romanovs as the room filled with screams, the echoing sound of gunfire, and the smell of cordite. When some semblance of silence returned, they heard groans from Anastasia, who had apparently only been wounded slightly. A guard pierced her abdomen with a bayonet several times, killing her. "Their blood flowed in streams," one witness later recalled.

No member of the royal family escaped, despite later persistent rumors that Anastasia had survived. The Whites arrived in Yekaterinburg less than a week later, to find no trace of the Romanovs' bodies. It wasn't until the late 1980s that it was finally discovered that Yurovksy had taken them to a nearby forest, had the corpses chopped apart and burned in gasoline fires, and then had pushed the bones into the bottom of the shaft of an abandoned mine and covered them with dirt. No trace of the Romanovs was to remain—not even a bone—for the Whites to use as an icon of a bygone age.

21

THE CHINESE CIVIL WAR

1927–1949

FOUGHT IN TWO LENGTHY PHASES OVER TWENTY YEARS, THIS STRUG-
GLE BETWEEN THE FORCES OF CHIANG KAI-SHEK AND MAO ZEDONG
RESULTED IN THE CREATION OF THE PEOPLE'S REPUBLIC OF CHINA.

THE VIOLENT TRANSFORMATION OF CHINA FROM IMPERIAL DYNASTY TO REVOLUTIONARY GOVERNMENT

In the late nineteenth and early twentieth centuries, when both Chiang Kai-shek and Mao Zedong were born and came of age, China was seeing the last days of the corrupt and enfeebled Qing Dynasty, which had ruled the country for 250 years. The Qings had been severely weakened by the Taiping Rebellion and were being eaten away by foreign powers. The Japanese held onto large portions of Manchuria after the First Sino-Japanese War of 1894 and annexed the island of Taiwan, while the British, French, and Germans expanded their influence over the rest of the country.

In 1911, the Qing Dynasty was finally toppled by reformer Sun Yat-sen, and China became a republic. The following year Sun Yat-sen formed the Nationalist Party, or Kuomintang (KMT), but he was pushed out of power by a former Qing general named Yuan Shikai, who proclaimed himself emperor. Sun Yat-sen, with his young follower and close advisor Chiang Kai-shek fought a series of battles against the forces of Yuan and were eventually able to defeat him, but the KMT was now too weak to consolidate its gains, and the country fell into warring factions as different warlords vied with each other for control.

In 1925, Sun Yat-sen died of cancer, and Chiang became the leader of KMT forces. At this time, Mao Zedong was a rising young member of the Communist Party who had organized labor strikes in major cities. Before his death, Sun Yat-sen had insisted on merging the KMT with the Communists, hoping the two groups would make a common cause in China. At first they did, forming the "United Front" in 1926 against the warlords who controlled the country, but then the alliance began to fall apart. The two had basically different goals. The KMT wanted to turn China into a republic and become a military and industrial power along western lines, while the Communists hoped for a mass peasant revolution along socialist lines.

Watching the growing power of the Communist Party—nearly 60,000 members strong—Chiang Kai-shek decided to strike first and attacked the Communists in Shanghai in the spring of 1927, rounding up and killing thousands. Mao Zedong barely escaped with his life. Fleeing to a provincial city, Mao famously proclaimed: "Political power is obtained from the barrel of a gun." He raised a guerilla army that battled Chiang Kai-shek's more numerous and better-equipped Nationalist army from 1929 to 1934.

Each time it seemed that the KMT had Mao and his forces encircled in the mountains of Jianxi Province in southern China, Mao would escape. But in 1933, a 700,000 strong Nationalist force, advised by German generals and with the aid of modern planes and artillery, cornered Mao. The latter responded by beginning, in March 1934, what would become known as the Long March a brutal, year-long trek to a remote base in northern China that cost the Communists nearly 150,000 casualties but saved Mao's army.

In December 1936, as Nationalist forces were closing on him once again, Mao audaciously kidnapped Chiang Kai-shek and held him hostage. In a stunning propaganda move, Mao announced he would release Chiang if the latter joined forces with him in fighting the Japanese, who were advancing through Manchuria. Chiang, under duress, agreed and the first portion of the Civil War ended as the Second Sino-Japanese War began, coinciding roughly with the outbreak of World War II. Here KMT forces in the south, armed and equipped by the Americans, fought pitched battles with the Japanese and suffered massive losses, while Mao's northern army took few casualties in its guerilla-style conflict in the north.

As World War II ended, the Chinese Civil War began again in earnest. With the Soviet Union's takeover of Manchuria, the Chinese Communists under Mao had a ready base (as well as significant amounts of captured Japanese arms) with which to attack Chiang's KMT army in the south. The Nationalists, while well-supplied with American equipment, were poorly led and motivated. Even so, the Nationalists slowly pushed the Communists and their newly renamed People's Liberation Army (PLA) back, until, at United States–brokered peace talks held in 1947, Chiang fatefully agreed to temporarily halt his advance. This gave the Communists breathing space, and in the summer of 1948, they began their final advance, destroying KMT forces at the pivotal Battle of Huai-Hai in November, taking, killing, or capturing 550,000 Nationalist prisoners.

In October 1949, Mao and his victorious army proclaimed the People's Republic of China, with their capital city of Beijing. In December, Chiang and his Nationalist government fled to the island of Taiwan. Perhaps 8 million people had died as a result of the Civil War since 1927; millions more faced starvation and runaway inflation, but Mao had won his war against overwhelming odds. Western observers expected China to takes it place with the Soviet Union on the world stage, but, torn apart by internal difficulties largely due to Mao's miscalculations, it would be decades before China would begin to come into its own.

THE BATTLE THAT WON CHINA FOR THE REDS AND CAUSED 500,000 CASUALTIES

The Battle of Huai-Hai: October–December, 1948

In the late summer of 1948, Communist forces under the overall command of Mao Zedong went on the attack in an offensive that would change the course of Chinese history. No longer were they guerilla warriors, hitting and then ducking for cover, the way they had been against the Japanese for the eight long years of the Second Sino-Japanese War. Nor were they the grim fighters on the run from overwhelming Nationalist forces, as they had been at the outset of the first phase of the Chinese Civil War, back in 1927–1934.

Instead, they were the People's Liberation Army (PLA), a modern army bearing modern arms, accompanied by tanks, airplanes, and heavy artillery, and they were intent on nothing less than the total destruction of the KMT forces that had plagued them for so long. The war had stretched for twenty years, involved millions of men and women, and was, in the way of civil wars, a highly personal conflict. The Communists knew that Nationalist leader Chiang Kai-shek hated them and had done—and was continuing to do—everything in his power to stamp them out as if they were cockroaches scuttling across his kitchen floor.

At the same time, the KMT troops knew that there was no place for them and their way of life in a China run by Mao. Across the wide plains and sere mountains of northern China and Manchuria, as the fall of 1948 began, there was finally a sense that endgame had been reached for both sides.

Peace treaty talks instituted by U.S. President Harry Truman immediately after World War II had failed to produce any results, despite the fact that both Mao and Chiang personally attended the conference in the then-capital city of Chongqing in August–September 1946. But as one English observer noted: "Neither Mao nor Chiang trusts one another. Each wants territorial, military, civil, political control. Yet each claps hands for democracy, union, freedom [and] nationalization."

When the Russians withdrew from the parts of Manchuria they had occupied after the Japanese defeat, they bequeathed to Mao's PLA a cornucopia of captured Japanese arms—700,000 rifles, 14,000 machine guns, and 700 military vehicles, including trucks, tanks, and armored cars. The PLA, husbanded as a guerilla force by Mao during the fighting against Japan, and never taking huge losses, had grown to nearly half-a-million-men strong, while the Nationalists had spent the war being bled dry by the Japanese in the south. It was apparent that final battle for the fate of China would take place in the north, and here the PLA had another advantage. Their political commissars had been careful to treat the local peasantry with respect, and now had a ready-made labor force to prepare for the immense battles ahead.

Intensive fighting broke out in the summer of 1946, fighting in which Chiang's forces, with the aid of hundreds of millions of U.S. dollars, made headway. With U.S. air power supporting them, they were able to airlift masses of troops to bases in Manchuria—Mao's territory—and bring the battle to him. The Nationalists were even able to take the Communist capital city of Yanan in March 1947. Chiang was now possibly close to winning the war. But, pressured by the Americans, he agreed to a truce with Mao while peace talks resumed.

That was all Mao needed. By the following year, he and the PLA were ready to launch their historic offensive.

Dividing by Three

During the summer of 1948, the PLA had engaged in a series of hard-fought battles with KMT forces that resulted in pushing the main Nationalist army into an area of central China bounded by Nanjing on the south, Tsinan on the north, Kaifeng to the west, and Soochow (known as Suzhou today) on the east. Following the tenets of The Art of War, by Sun-tzu, Mao decided these troops should be surrounded, separated, and destroyed one by one.

On October 11, Mao secretly issued the orders to attack the 500,000 KMT troops between the Huai River and the Lung Hai railway (the combination of locales giving the battle its name). The plan was carefully worked out ahead of time between Mao and his chief strategist Su Yu, who was the originator of the idea for the offensive. The PLA divided the KMT territory into three primary targets. Beginning in November, each segment would be attacked in turn. The PLA's half a million men matched those of the Nationalists; it was to be a set piece battle such as these two armies had never fought before. The Huai-Hai area where the battle would take place was enormous, about 7,600 square miles, and relatively flat. As November approached, the PLA commissars used hundreds of thousands of peasants to set up supply dumps and dig communications trenches as the PLA troops moved forward.

Then, at the end of October, the PLA attacked the Jinpu railway line, the crucial link to Nanjing and Nationalist headquarters there. This was to bait the trap; they knew that the attack would draw Nationalist forces to the railroad. On November 3,

Huang Baitao, the nervous commander of KMT 7th Army in nearby Xuzhou begged Chiang Kai-shek for permission to move his men toward the Jinpu railroad to fight off an entire PLA army (the so-called East Chinese Field Army, or ECFA) which was said to be moving in that direction. On November 5, Chiang approved this plan.

The Plan: Part One

On November 7, as the KMT 7th Army crossed a large canal on its way toward Jinpu, the ECFA opened fire on it with heavy artillery and then struck hard, with combined forces of tanks and infantry. Part of the 7th Army fled back to Xuzhou; the rest was trapped by the canal. The ECFA easily broke through and thus cut the 7th Army in half. It then turned in two massive flanking movements to destroy each half. Half of the fighting took place in Xuzhou; the other half on open ground around the city. The Nationalist defenders did not give in easily, and fierce fighting took place in the freezing cold. There was house-to-house combat in Xuzhou, with Communist forces having to burst through the doors of each building and home, throwing grenades and spraying rooms with their burp guns, whose barrels often became so hot that they melted.

Huang Baitao threw more and more reinforcements into the battle, only to see each unit chewed up by a PLA unit that had been waiting for just such an eventuality. Finally, by November 22, the 7th Army had ceased to exist, with more than 100,000 men killed, wounded, or captured. Huang Baitao committed suicide, and the PLA turned to Phase Two of its plan.

Part Two

The second phase called for the destruction of the Nationalist 12th Army, which Su and Mao had correctly assumed would come to the aid of the 7th Army. Led by one of Chiang's top commanders, General Huang Wei, the 12th attacked another PLA army, the Central Plains Field Army (CPFA), which retreated enough to lead the 12th Army into a trap sprung by ECFA, which surrounded and attacked Wei's forces. Encircled, the only way Wei could be supplied was by airdrop. Finally, at the end of November, the Nationalist general decided to try a breakout. But when the attempt was launched, the division leading the way—Chiang Kai-shek's elite 110th Division, which had fought bravely for the generalissimo during the war—unexpectedly defected to the Communists.

The destruction of the 12th Army now seemed inevitable. Chiang monitored the fighting from Nanjing with increasing concern. Part of his problem was his officer corps. Most of his senior officers were rivals with each other, men who were almost warlords in the old Chinese tradition, and in some cases they did not want to go to the aid of the

trapped troops of another general. Some of these officers considered that the war was lost already, and defected or deserted. And all of them, even the brave ones, offered only passive resistance, not striking out at the enemy but waiting to be attacked.

On December 12, a combined attack of the ECFA and CPFA spelled the end for Wei's entire army. Wei himself was captured.

Part Three

The end of the 12th Army left the PLA leaders with only one more goal to be obtained, the destruction of the KMT 13th Army (as well as parts of the 2nd Army— the rest of this unit was the only KMT unit to escape the trap in northern China.) Unexpectedly, Mao called a halt to the fighting for ten days. This was to allow the PLA, some of whose units were badly shot up, to regroup. But it was also a propaganda ploy. As December continued, heavy winter weather set in, including a severe snowstorm that made it impossible to supply the Nationalist 13th by airdrop. Su Yu then presented relatively lenient surrender terms to General Du Yuming, Chiang Kai-shek's personal protégé and representative in the field. Du rejected them, but the

SOLDIERS OF A CHINESE NATIONALIST MORTAR DETACHMENT WATCH HEAVY ARTILLERY SHELLS EXPLODE SHORT OF THE COMMUNIST LINES FROM THEIR POSITION, SOUTH OF SUCHOW, CHINA, NOV. 25, 1948.

Associated Press

PLA made sure that common Nationalist soldiers freezing and starving on the field knew about them. Units of the 13th Army began to desert en masse, to the point where Du had lost half his army by the end of December.

The only thing left for Du to do was order a breakout, which he planned for January 6th. Unfortunately from the Nationalist point of view, that day was the same day Su had decided that his combined PLA forces would attack. The collision of both armies created intense fighting, but two days later, the 13th Army had completely collapsed. Attempting to escape to the west, Du was himself captured on January 10, 1949, and the great Huai-Hai battle was at an end.

In total, the PLA killed, wounded, or captured 500,000 men in the two-month-long battle. Within weeks, major Chinese cities like Beijing fell to the Chinese as they swept south. On January 20, Chiang resigned his leadership of the Nationalists. By the following December, he had fled to Taiwan, leaving Mao in possession of China.

Today, the flat battlefields of Huai-Hai are visited often by tourists and students, who reverentially walk from monument to monument. The PLA Military Academy, and with good reason, calls the Battle of Huai-Hai "the campaign that won China."

MAO ZEDONG: "THE BARREL OF A GUN"

When most westerners think of Mao Zedong, they summon up an image from propaganda posters of the 1960s, which show a corpulent Mao, face beaming, pointing the way to victory for the Chinese masses. The Mao of the Chinese Civil War was tall and lanky, an awkward young man from the country, who loved spicy hot food and plump peasant girls.

But both Maos shared the same burning desire: to unite China, whatever the cost, under the banner of Communism. Or perhaps it would be more accurate to say the banner of Communism as held by Mao himself—because Mao's main goal, like his antagonist, Chiang Kai-shek, was to be in total and complete control of China.

Mao Zedong was born in 1893 in the rural province of Hunan. Although Mao had a later tendency to exaggerate the poverty of his upbringing, his parents, who owned a small farm, were considered prosperous by the standards of Chinese peasantry. At the age of thirteen, Mao—able to read and use an abacus—left school and went to work for his father to whom he was not close. (His father was "the first capitalist I struggled against," Mao told a journalist in 1936.) His mother arranged a marriage for him with a peasant girl who was, at age nineteen, five years older than Mao. The girl died of unknown causes two years later, and Mao later denied having been married at all, but it is possible that the trauma of her death forced him to look outward, to discover the world around him.

One thing Mao discovered was new books that urged readers to change China—saying that the old order of the Qing Dynasty was dead. Mao was not then a Communist—he was most impressed by a book about George Washington's role in winning the American Revolution—but was encouraged in the spring of 1911 when Sun Yat-sen's successful uprising was launched against the Qings.

By 1918, Mao had left Hunan Province to study at Beijing University, where he read Marxist theory and joined a group of students inspired by the Bolshevik uprising in Russia. By 1921, Mao had joined the Communist Party and had begun to work organizing unions in China. When Sun Yat-sen decreed that the Communist Party and the KMT would work together, Mao became head of the KMT Propaganda Department, where he met, for the first time, his future rival Chiang Kai-shek. After the United Front fell apart and Chiang attacked Communists power centers and party centers in Shanghai and other areas, Mao fled to the country (his second wife would be executed by KMT troops) and began the brilliant guerilla resistance for which he is known.

"We must know that political power is obtained from the barrel of a gun," Mao wrote at the time. If he was the gun, the masses of Chinese that he rallied to him were the bullets. Despite enormous hardships, despite being outnumbered and outgunned by

THE VICTORIOUS MAO ZEDONG PROCLAIMS CHINA THE NEWLY APPOINTED PEOPLE'S REPUBLIC OF CHINA.

Chairman Mao announces the birth of the People's Republic of China on top of Tiananmen in 1949, August 1959 (color litho), Chinese School, (20th century) / Private Collection, © The Chambers Gallery, London / The Bridgeman Art Library International

KMT forces, Mao and his men survived time and time again to fight again. The first phase of the civil war, culminating in the Long March and Mao's audacious kidnapping of Chiang, was a hard-won victory for Mao. The second phase, beginning at the end of World War II, had actually been won during the war, when Mao kept his forces in remote areas of China and harried the Japanese with guerilla actions, rather than fighting pitched battles, as did Chiang.

Mao's historic victory in 1949 came because he had outwitted and outfought Chiang Kai-shek almost every step of the way. When the two men met at the failed U.S. attempt to broker a peace treaty in 1945, Chiang pointed to Mao at a cocktail party and said sarcastically: "Look—isn't he a prize exhibit?" But the "prize exhibit" had won the greatest prize of all: the entire country of China.

CHIANG KAI-SHEK: THE RUTHLESS OPPORTUNIST WHOSE CORRUPTION CAUSED HIS OWN DOWNFALL

The figure that Chiang Kai-shek presented to the word was quite different than that presented by Mao Zedong. Chiang stood ramrod straight, wore a western-style military uniform, and appeared quite cultured and in control. During the first phase of the Chinese Civil War, before the shine wore off his reputation, he was a darling of the U.S. press and government, who saw him as best representing U.S. interests against the unruly Communism of Mao.

The press didn't report upon Chiang's volcanic temper or his bouts of debauchery with alcohol and Shanghai "sing-song girls," or the fact that he was so opportunistic that he proposed marriage to Sun Yat-sen's widow almost immediately after Sun Yat-sen died. When she turned him down, he married her younger sister, so he could be called Sun Yat-sen's brother-in-law.

This streak of ruthless opportunism would take Chiang Kai-shek far, although ultimately he overplayed his hand. He was born in 1887 in the eastern seaboard province of Zhejiang, to parents who owned a salt shop, but who claimed to be descended from nobility. Imperious, controlling, and reckless—on a dare, he once stuck his head in a large water jar and nearly drowned—Chiang always needed to be the center of attention.

At the age of sixteen, he left his village to attend school in the district capital, and there became inflamed with revolutionary ideas on liberating China from the Qing Dynasty. In 1905, Chiang cut off his queue, or long pigtail, which was worn as a sign of submission to the imperial dynasty, and sailed to Japan to attend military school.

Chiang returned in 1911 as commander of an artillery company that helped Sun Yat-sen destroy the Qings, and he became a key player in later fighting against those who sought to wrest the new republic from Sun. When Sun Yat-sen died, Chiang assumed the mantle of leadership, even thought it meant murdering several rivals (one of whom he personally shot while the man was in his hospital bed). After briefly forming a "United Front" with Communist forces, he became alarmed by their growing power and decided to make what he hoped would be a preemptive strike against them. Allying himself with Chinese underworld powers, Chiang rounded up and killed thousands of Chinese labor union members in Shanghai in 1927, thus setting off the Chinese Civil War.

In the years to follow, Chiang, who did not command his army in the field, saw his Nationalist forces come close numerous times to wiping out the Communists, only to have the Communists escape time and time again. Gradually, the sympathy of the people of China began to side with Mao. This was less because of Mao's Communist teachers and more because of the fact that Chiang's forces were notably corrupt and that Chiang himself was seen to be in the pocket of the Americans because of his reliance on them and their money. Ultimately, after World War II, even the Americans turned against Chiang, tired of the corruption of his government, his scheming, and the fact that his "democratic" National Party was merely a mechanism to give power to Chiang.

When Chiang was defeated, he and about 2 million of his followers proclaimed the Republic of China on the island of Taiwan. Chiang lived a long and inconvenient exile there, recognized as the real Chinese government by western powers only because of the exigencies of the Cold War. Dying in 1975 at the age of eighty-four, Chiang lived long enough to see Richard Nixon visit China and shake hands with Chiang's old nemesis, Chairman Mao, beginning the first step in formalizing relationships between the two countries.

SUN YAT-SEN, SITTING, WITH CLOSE ADVISOR CHIANG KAI-SHEK, WAS THE IMPETUS OF THE CIVIL WAR, LAUNCHING THE FIRST SUCCESSFUL UPRISING AGAINST THE QING DYNASTY. IT WAS THROUGH SUN YAT-SEN THAT CHIANG RECEIVED HIS MILITARY AND POLITICAL EXPERIENCE AND IT WAS THROUGH HIS DEATH THAT CHIANG ROSE TO POWER, GOING SO FAR AS TO MARRY THE YOUNGER SISTER OF SUN YAT-SEN'S WIDOW TO CLAIM TIES TO THE FORMER GREAT LEADER.

Sun Yat-Sen (1866-1925) and Chiang Kai-Shek (1887-1975) (b/w photo), Chinese Photographer / Private Collection, Archives Charmet / The Bridgeman Art Library International

THE LONG DESPERATE MARCH THAT SAVED THE COMMUNISTS— AND MADE A LEGEND OF MAO

It began with the sound of artillery roaring on a cloudy October day in 1934. After holding off KMT troops for almost a year, the sound of their guns were getting closer

and closer, and the Chinese Communist troops in their mountain base in the southern province of Jianxi knew that it was time to break out to bases an incredible 6,000
miles (9,656 km) to the north.

The men and women of the army left carrying typewriters, desks, printing presses,
bedrolls, everything they could get their hands on. Surrounding them was an army
of 500,000 Nationalist soldiers who, for once, were being skillfully led by a German
advisor, and so they were entrenched, with barbed wire and pillbox strongpoints that
the Chinese would have to battle through.

Mao was leading the Chinese 8th Army—his advisor Zhou at his side—but the
man who unofficially had the most power in the army was a Russian advisor named
Otto Braun. It was Braun who advised the Chinese to bring with them all they could
carry, and it was Braun who directed them in a frontal attack on Nationalist positions
at Xiang, which resulted in 45,000 Chinese casualties.

After Braun was suspended from command, Mao became the March's effective
leader. He immediately changed their Communist way of marching, taking a circu-
itous route and breaking up the army into smaller units. In a year's time, Mao and his

armies crossed eighteen mountain ranges—including the Snowy Mountains, which contain some of the highest mountains in the world—twenty-four rivers, and a vast swamp known as the Chinese Grasslands, which claimed hundreds of lives with men simply sinking in quicksand.

They fought off not only the KMT, but the armies of provincial warlords as well. When Mao arrived in Shaanxi Province in October 1935, only 50,000 of the original 200,000 men remained, but the Communist army had survived and the march itself became the stuff of legend, a huge propaganda coup: "The Long March is a manifesto," Mao wrote in December 1935. "It has proclaimed to the world that the Red army is an army of heroes…."

22

WORLD WAR II

1939–1945

THE DEADLIEST CONFLICT IN HUMAN HISTORY WAS FOUGHT BY
SOLDIERS FROM EVERY PART OF THE WORLD IN THE SERVICE OF THE
ALLIED OR AXIS POWERS AND ENDED WITH THE RISE OF TWO GREAT
POSTWAR SUPERPOWERS, THE UNITED STATES AND THE SOVIET UNION.

THE MOST EXPLOSIVE CONFLICT THE WORLD HAS EVER KNOWN TRANSFORMED THE GLOBE IN EVERY RESPECT

After the end of World War I, many millions of Germans were left in a state of smoldering resentment by the harsh terms of the Treaty of Versailles. The Great Depression of the 1930s was exacerbated in Germany by the billions of dollars of war reparations owed, as well as by the fact that large portions of its territory had been taken away. Germany, with a population of 65 million, was also forbidden to have a large standing army, but during the Weimar Republic that governed Germany immediately after the war, secret armed paramilitary groups had arisen. When Adolf Hitler took power in 1933, these powerful groups (the Sturmabetilung, or SA, and the Schutzstaffel, or SS) became the nucleus of the new German army.

Hitler led the German National Socialist, or Nazi, Party, which is to say he was a fascist. Essentially, he preached the message that Germany needed to push its boundaries outward to accommodate its expanding population, and thus wars for territory needed to be fought. Further, a demographic restructuring of Germany along racial lines was essential—all those races, in particular the Jews, which were deemed "impure" or "undesirable" would be (it was soon clear) liquidated, particularly if they lived in territory that Germans desired to possess.

To this end, Hitler stepped up German rearmament throughout the 1930s, ignoring the ineffectual protests of the governments of countries such as France and Great Britain, which were themselves mired in economic difficulties because of the Great Depression. These countries (and the equally ineffectual League of Nations, which was the precursor to the United Nations) did nothing when Hitler sent an army into the Rhineland (a zone along the French-German border demilitarized after World War I) in 1936, and in 1938 annexed Austria, and took control of the Sudetenland, a Czechoslovakian region of German-speaking people.

In the latter case, British Prime Minister Neville Chamberlain acquiesced to Hitler's demands, in return for an agreement that he would not move into the rest of Czechoslovakia. Chamberlain came back home to Great Britain announcing "peace in our time," but within six months Hitler had annexed the rest of Czechoslovakia. Within a year, on September 1, 1939, the date traditionally given as the beginning of World War II, Hitler had begun his invasion of Poland. (Hitler intended to invade the Soviet Union, but he had for the time being signed a nonaggression pact with Soviet leader Joseph Stalin, agreeing to divide up Poland.)

Hitler's rapid assault on Poland—with Stuka dive bombers, tanks, and infantry—was the very first blitzkrieg, or "lightning war." France and Germany were bound by treaty to help Poland and thus declared war against Germany on September 3, 1939. The following April, Hitler's mechanized legions invaded Norway, and in May they attacked Holland, Belgium, and France. The French army was utterly defeated, and a British expeditionary force sent to help was driven back to the English Channel coast, where it was evacuated at Dunkirk.

In the meantime, in the Far East, the Japanese were pursuing a policy of expansion as well. They had invaded and seized Manchuria from the Chinese in 1937, and they were engaged in a continuing war with China. Border skirmishes with the Red Army in western Manchuria proved the Russians a tougher nut to crack than they were during the Russo-Japanese War.

The Japanese turned their attentions south, planning an invasion of oil-rich Southeast Asia. The United States–owned Philippines stood in their way, and Japanese war planners knew that they would sooner or later have to attack the United States. Seeing the string of German victories, the Japanese reached a mutual defense agreement with Germany and Italy, which was ruled by Benito Mussolini. This Tripartite Pact established the Berlin–Rome–Tokyo Axis, and Germany, Italy, and Japan became known as the Axis Powers.

Beginning in August 1940, Hermann Göring, the head of Germany's powerful Luftwaffe, launched a massive bombing campaign against England, beginning with Royal Air Force bases (RAF), to soften up England prior to a German invasion. The RAF suffered horrendous losses, but it held out. (During one two-week period, one in four English pilots was killed.) The Germans then switched tactics, bombing British cities in terror bombings. but the British, led by their resolute prime minister, Winston Churchill, refused to give up. German victories in Greece and the Balkans made 1940 a victorious year for the Axis.

By the spring of 1941, however, as Great Britain suffered devastating bombing as well as a German submarine naval blockade, the country's situation was dire. But in March of that year, the United States, officially neutral, passed Lend-Lease legislation that allowed it to send war material to countries whose security affected its own. Massive supplies were sent in convoys to Great Britain through the perilous North Atlantic seas, which were infested with German U-Boats.

Great Britain's situation became somewhat better when Hitler made the huge blunder of attacking the Soviet Union in June 1941 with a force of a 1.5 million soldiers. Caught at first by surprise, the Soviets reeled back, losing some 3 million soldiers—dead, wounded, and captured—before the Soviet line stabilized and the Russian winter set the Germans back.

On December 7, 1941, Japan launched a surprise aerial attack on the U.S. naval base of Pearl Harbor, Hawaii. Devastating though it was, the attack—devised by Admiral Isoruku Yamamoto—missed the United States' aircraft carriers, which were out at sea, and thus was only a limited tactical success. The United States quickly declared war against the Axis Powers.

In the Far East, the Japanese attacked and captured the Philippines, Burma, Malaya, the Dutch East Indies, and Singapore by April 1942 and occupied numerous South Pacific islands. But an attempt to capture Port Moresby, New Guinea, and thus cut off communications between the United States and Australia failed when the Americans turned back and destroyed the Japanese invasion force at the Battle of the Coral Sea in May 1942. A month later, an attempt to destroy the U.S. fleet was thwarted at the Battle of Midway when the carrier-based airplanes of the U.S. Navy sank four Japanese aircraft carriers, and the Americans began to turn the tide against the Japanese in the Pacific.

In May 1942, an offensive by the famed German Afrika Korps, under General Erwin Rommel had driven the defending British forces in Libya nearly back to Cairo, but then British resistance stiffened and they stopped the Germans in two battles at El Alamein, in July and October 1942. A month later, British and U.S. troops (commanded by General Dwight D. Eisenhower) landed in Morocco at the rear of the Germans and caught them in a pincer. German troops in Africa were forced to surrender in May 1943. With their southern flanks secure, the allies invaded Sicily in July and Italy in September.

Another blow to the Germans came with their stalled attack on the Russian city of Stalingrad. The German offensive had picked up steam since the winter of 1941–42, and they attacked Stalingrad in August 1942. But unexpectedly tough resistance from the Russians turned the battle for the city into an epic bloodbath in which 400,000 Germans would lose their lives and an entire German army would surrender within four months' time, forever blunting Hitler's invasion.

In the meantime, in the Pacific, U.S. war planners had decided upon a two-prong offensive against the Japanese. One arm of the offensive, based in Australia, would attack up the New Guinea coast, through the Solomon Islands, and on to the Philippines and Tokyo, bypassing and cutting off numerous Japanese-held islands along the way. The other offensive arm would thrust along some of the smaller islands of the Central Pacific, to the Marianas, the Philippines, and the Chinese coast, and from there to the Japanese home islands. This latter strategy made it crucial to keep the Nationalist Chinese government in the war, to protect the United States' left flank. Masses of arms and material were sent to Chiang Kai-shek's armies, which even so barely held their own against the Japanese.

The U.S. "island-hopping" began with an attack on the Japanese-held Solomon Island of Guadalcanal in August 1942, where a hard-fought six-month battle ended in U.S. victory in February 1943. In the meantime, U.S. Marines fought battles at coral atolls such as Tarawa, Peleliu, and Bougainville, building bomber bases as they went. By November 1944, B-29 bombers operating out of airfields in the northern Marianas and China were able to reach targets in Japan.

After much debate, the allies finally decided to invade France along the Normandy coast on June 6, 1944. With an armada of 6,000 ships containing an attacking force of 175,000 British, Canadian, and U.S. troops, the allies won a hard-fought toe-hold in France. After bloody fighting during the summer months, the allies were able to drive the Germans into full blown retreat that August.

THE GERMAN OFFENSIVE ATTACKED STALINGRAD IN AUGUST 1942.
BUT UNEXPECTEDLY TOUGH RESISTANCE FROM THE RUSSIANS TURNED
THE BATTLE FOR THE CITY INTO AN EPIC BLOODBATH IN WHICH
400,000 GERMANS WOULD LOSE THEIR LIVES.

However, the Germans were far from down yet. In December 1944, secretly assembling some 250,000 troops and 1,000 tanks, they launched the Battle of the Bulge in the Ardennes Forest in Belgium, very nearly breaking through U.S. and British lines. Despite a fierce struggle, they were thrown back, and the allies continued their march toward Berlin, using powerful bombers to destroy German cities, factories, and troops. All the while, the victorious Soviet Army pushed the Germans back from the east. After Hitler committed suicide in his Berlin bunker, Germany surrendered on May 7, 1945.

This left the allies free to concentrate all their might on the Japanese. U.S. air raids over Japan increased in intensity, targeting civilian populations. U.S. Marines island-hopped right to Japan's Bonin (Iwo Jima) and Ryukyus (Okinawa) islands by April 1945, but Japanese resistance had become even more ferocious as their homeland was invaded, especially with the introduction of the kamikaze, or suicide, pilot.

Fearful of the casualties that would ensue if the Americans and British invaded Japan as planned that November, the new U.S. President Harry S. Truman opted to drop the newly developed atomic bomb on Japan. The first bomb was dropped on Hiroshima on August 6, 1945. Three days later, another bomb was dropped on Nagasaki. With 200,000 dead from these two bombs alone, the Japanese capitulated. On September 2, 1945, aboard the U.S. battleship USS Missouri, the Japanese signed the surrender agreement that ended World War II.

After the war, the United Nations was formed in the hopes of keeping peace, but no one was able to say with equanimity that the war to end all wars had been fought. World War II, with its millions of dead, had simply been too awful. The immediate result of the war was the elevation of the United States and the Soviet Union to superpower status, where they almost immediately squared off in the Cold War, each threatening the other with potential nuclear annihilation.

The colonial world order was now gone forever, with countries vying for self-determination. The discovery that Hitler had perpetuated the Holocaust in which more than 6 million Jews were killed in concentration camps changed how people everywhere viewed the notion of evil. It also helped hurry the state of Israel into existence.

THE BATTLE THAT SPELLED THE BEGINNING OF THE END FOR THE AXIS
D-Day: June 6, 1944

As the huge flotilla crossed the dark, choppy waters of the English Channel, the roar of protecting planes overhead, reporters in the holds of ships with the troops of the different Allied countries—the Americans, British, and Canadians—noticed an interesting phenomenon take shape. Most of the U.S. soldiers were green recruits who had never seen combat before. Normally one might expect these to be the most nervous, but in fact these young GIs appeared to be the coolest, almost glad to be taking part in history. They were, after all, about to make the first assault on Fortress Europa, Hitler's territory since 1940, and strike right at the heart of the German empire.

The GIs laughed, cleaned their rifles, and sharpened their bayonets. They knew there was a tough task ahead and that some of them would die, but they all thought that someone would be someone else.

It was a different picture with the British and Canadian battalions that had seen three years or more of warfare. In their case, as one observer wrote, "Everybody who was any good had been promoted or become a casualty." These men had faced Hitler's Wehrmacht, his proud and combative infantry, and they knew how fiercely they could fight, especially now, defending their own territory. As the sky lightened—but did not clear—on this overcast early morning of June 6, 1944, these men knew just what was in store for them. They did not kid themselves that they, personally, would be the targets of a hailstorm of death and destruction.

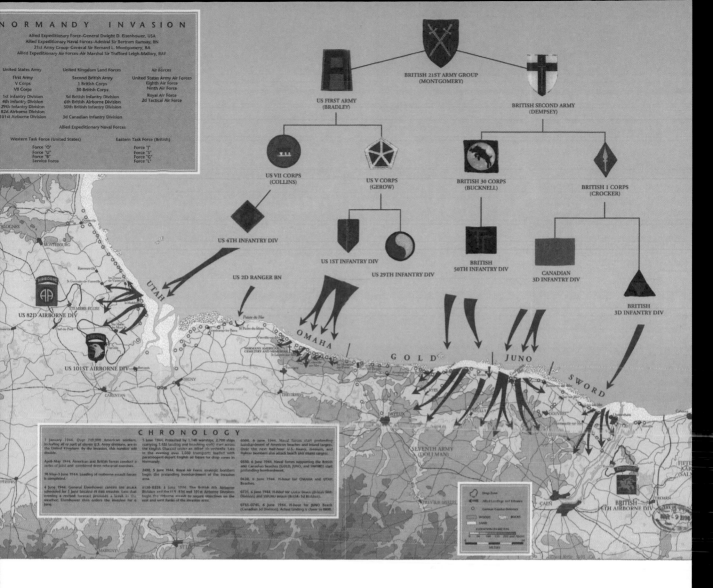

Green recruit or veteran, the hopes of the allies rested on these 150,000 men who were approaching 60 miles (97 km) of French coastline in some 6,500 ships. Despite the fact that the might of the world was stacked against Hitler, he was proving remarkably difficult to finally beat. In Italy, Allied forces were pushing up through the peninsula, but at a glacial pace over rugged terrain. Meanwhile, in Russia, the Soviets were also winning victories, but the German troops were giving way slowly. Nightly, Allied forces pounded German cities and industry, and yet the Germans kept on fighting.

Everyone, Germans or allies, knew that there would be a major invasion somewhere along the channel coast. The Germans defenses stretched all the way from Scandinavia to Spain, but they could not possibly fortify all areas equally. Their war planners had come to the conclusion that the Allies would attack across the Straits of Dover, heading

THE JUNE 6, 1944, LANDING OF THE ALLIES ON THE BEACHES OF NORMANDY IS SHOWN IN THIS U.S. ARMY CENTER OF MILITARY HISTORY MAP. THE BEACHES INVADED WERE SWORD, JUNO, GOLD, OMAHA, AND UTAH, WITH THE FIRST THREE ATTACKED BY CANADIAN AND BRITISH FORCES AND THE LAST TWO BY THE AMERICANS. ALL TOTAL, ABOUT 10,000 MEN OUT OF 155,000 WERE KILLED OR WOUNDED DURING THE INVASION.

for the Pas de Calais, the area of France closest to England. Calais had a natural harbor that the Allies could use. It made so much sense to the Germans that they stationed their main reserve—the Fifteenth Army, containing about 100,000 men—there.

It was not that the rest of the Atlantic Wall, as the Germans called it, was poorly fortified. Field Marshal Erwin Rommel—the famed Desert Fox—had been given charge of building up the defenses and was determined not to let the Allies get a foothold in France. He was certain that they would exploit any foothold with their massive advantage in armor and bombers.

Allied war planners—knowing from their top secret Ultra intercepts that the Germans were massing around Pas de Calais—had no intention of attacking there. The allies did stage a massive and elaborate deception to make the Germans think that an attack on Calais was imminent. However, the real target of Allied leaders, such as General Dwight D. Eisenhower, commander of Supreme Headquarters Allied Expeditionary Force, and General Bernard Law Montgomery, head of Allied ground forces, was Normandy, France. Here, specifically at the Cotentin Peninsula, on five beaches designed Juno, Gold, Sword, Utah, and Omaha, the beginning of the end of World War II would begin in an attack aptly named Operation Overlord.

The Largest Flotilla

As the Allied troops fought off seasickness and climbed down into their landing boats, bobbing up and down in the heavy chop of the English Channel, they watched a preparatory bombardment of the enemy positions. It was an awesome sight. Thousands of planes flew overhead, dropping bombs that turned the coastline into a curtain of smoke. Heavy booming thuds echoed back across the water, the footsteps of a thousand giants. The Allied air force had full ownership of the sky, with barely 200 Luftwaffe planes to oppose them.

Unbeknownst to those soldiers on the boats, the land battle for Normandy had begun the night before, when 20,000 men of the U.S. 82nd and 101st Airborne Divisions and the British Sixth Airborne had been dropped by parachute behind enemy lines. Their goal was to block off approaches to the Normandy beaches to keep the Germans from reinforcing them. But most of the jumpers went astray in the inevitable confusion of a combat parachute drop in darkness, and only one in twenty-five paratroopers landed in his assigned drop zone. Nevertheless, the chaos served its purpose, keeping the Germans guessing about what was coming. Many German commanders dismissed the disorganized paratrooper attacks as just another commando raid, even after one German general was ambushed and killed by 101st Airborne troopers who happened upon his staff car.

But there was a moment, as the sky brightened but just before the Allied bombers swept in, that the German gunners in their pillboxes on the shore could see exactly what was happening. Spread out on the waters before them was the largest flotilla the world had ever known. Then the bombers came, and the gunners put their heads down.

When the gunners manned their machine guns again, troops in landing craft were nearing the shore.

The beaches being invaded were, from east to west, Sword, Juno, Gold, Omaha, and Utah. The first three were attacked by Canadian and British forces, and the last two were attacked by Americans. On Sword Beach, the British, although confronted with minefields and beach obstacles, managed to land 28,000 troops with only 600 casualties and push to within a few miles of their objective, the town of Caen.

What happened on Juno Beach depended on what part of the beach you landed on and when you landed on it. In the first wave on Juno, Canadian casualties were nearly 50 percent, but in other areas of the beach where resistance was not so stiff, the allies made it ashore almost unopposed.

On Gold Beach, however, the British took extremely heavy casualties. Their landing craft lowered their ramps in 6 feet (1.8 m) of water, and numerous soldiers, weighed down by heavy equipment, drowned. Other soldiers got to the beach, only to face withering fire and an unreal scene of chaos. As one soldier remembered: "The beach was strewn with wreckage, a blazing tank, bundles of blanket and kit, bodies and bits of bodies. One bloke near me was blown in half by a shell, and his lower half collapsed in a bloody heap on the sand."

On Utah Beach, mass confusion reigned. Stiff currents had carried the U.S. Fourth Division almost 2 miles (3 km) from where it was supposed to be, and the troops had no idea where they were. However, this turned out to be a stroke of luck, because they had landed in an area that was not quite so heavily defended. They managed to quickly break through the seawall and link up with paratroopers from the 101st Airborne.

Bloody Omaha

It was on Omaha Beach that the slaughter truly reached epic proportions. Because the beach there was the only stretch of open sand in either direction for some miles, the German planners knew that the Allies would have to make use of it.

Omaha Beach is only 6 miles (9 km) long and about 400 yards (365 m) deep at low tide, which it was when the invasion was taking place. Much of the beach was shingle or shale, and there were high bluffs facing it in the front and on either side, making it a kind of natural amphitheater. German defenses here were formidable. Every inch of the beach was pre-sighted by machine guns, mortars, artillery, and underground ammunition chambers and pillboxes at the top of the cliffs, which were connected by a series of well-dug trenches. Five small ravines led up the cliffs, but at the top of each was an 88, the ubiquitous, and deadly, German light artillery gun of choice.

The minute U.S. soldiers landed here at about 6:40 a.m., the German defenders opened fire. The Germans were amazed at the Americans' audacity. "They must be crazy," one of them said to one of his comrades. "Are they going to swim ashore right under our muzzles?" The first landing craft on the beach simply disappeared in a hail of fire. Other GIs crawled up the beach, hiding in long snaking lines behind beach obstacles, while the machine guns raked up and down, like deadly garden hoses. (One German gunner would fire 12,000 rounds that day.) Finally, the Americans, urged on by brave noncoms and officers, realized that if they stayed where they were, they would die. And so they began to move forward, singly, in ones and twos, until they reached the comparative shelter of a seawall near the base of the cliff. By afternoon, a few men had made it up the draws, and more followed.

Ultimately, 40,000 men would land at Omaha Beach during the course of the day and spread out for about a mile from the top of the cliffs, where they dug in—as forces were digging in all up and down the 60-mile (97-km) stretch of Normandy beaches—waiting for the inevitable German counterattack.

The Beginning of the End

The counterattack might have been inevitable, but it never came. German commanders thought that the real objective of the Allied attack was still the Pas de Calais, and that Normandy was just a diversion. It would take German commanders weeks to figure out otherwise, and by that time the allies had secured a firm beachhead 120 miles (193 km) long and 10 miles (16 km) deep, while more men and material poured into the man-made harbors that the Allies created in Normandy.

All told, about 10,000 men were killed or wounded out of a total of about 155,000 on D-Day, but this high price meant the final destruction of Hitler's Germany. A lot of hard fighting still lay ahead, but the first major step had been taken.

THE MEN OF YALTA

The three men were in all their power and glory—Winston Churchill, cigar in hand, Franklin Delano Roosevelt, cape thrown over his shoulders, and Joseph Stalin, in military uniform—when they met in February 1945, at Yalta, in the Crimea to decide the fate of the postwar world.

Each had been instrumental in helping bring the defeat of the Axis Powers closer and closer to reality. Churchill was prime minister of Great Britain, replacing Neville Chamberlain, who had appeased Hitler and his Nazis and thus lost all credibility with the people of Great Britain. Churchill knew that he needed to provide inspiration for Great Britain to continue against the odds. His speeches during the dark days of the summer and fall of 1940 resounded with powerful inspiring language, as in his "finest hour" speech to the British parliament, where he declared that the Battle for Britain had begun. He said: "If the British Empire and its Commonwealth last for a thousand years, men will say, 'This was their finest hour.'"

President Franklin Delano Roosevelt, who had ably led his country through the Great Depression, also began to subtly steer the United States toward war, despite numerous isolationists who thought that the United States should not interfere in what was going on in Europe. But Roosevelt, through Lend-Lease legislation, was able to provide aid to Great Britain. Then, when the Japanese attacked Pearl Harbor, Roosevelt declared war with the ringing words: "December 7, 1941…was a day which will live in infamy." He, like Churchill, presided over a country that saw defeats in the

PICTURED: THE BIG THREE AT THE YALTA CONFERENCE IN THE CRIMEA REPRESENTED THE THREE MAJOR WORLD POWERS AT THE WAR'S CONCLUSION.

Getty Images

early days of the war but that found its war footing very quickly and accepted ration-ing and other forms of privation on the civilian front so that the military might make greater strides against Germany, Italy, and Japan.

Premier Joseph Stalin was a different case. He was the totalitarian dictator of a country whose citizens he had ruthlessly purged (or starved because of his agricultural collectivization) by the millions. And he had been fooled into thinking that Hitler was his ally early in the war. Nevertheless, as Russians reeled back under the initial onslaught of Operation Barbarossa, Hitler's massive attack on Russia, Stalin, too, provided the backbone that kept his country from capitulating.

At Yalta, these three leaders came together to decide what would happen after Germany and Japan had been defeated. It had already been decided that Germany would be divided into zones overseen by Russia, Great Britain, and the United States. But at Yalta, Stalin agreed to allow France to rule a zone—as along as it came from English or U.S. territory.

Foremost on Stalin's agenda was Poland. He wanted the country in the Soviet Union, claiming that it had traditionally been "the corridor through which the enemy passed into Russia." Roosevelt agreed to this, although it constituted selling out Poland to Russia. This was much to Churchill's dismay, because Great Britain had already recognized that Poland should become a free state after the war. But Roosevelt wanted something in return—Stalin's promise to attack Japan, with which it had a nonaggression pact, within ninety days after Germany's defeat.

Roosevelt has been heavily criticized for this decision, but at the time he did not know whether the atomic bomb would be developed in time to use against Japan, and he knew that any invasion of the Japanese home islands would be a bloodbath. He hoped that the creation of the United Nations—which Stalin agreed to join at Yalta—would help ameliorate Poland's plight. Roosevelt would die of a cerebral hemorrhage in just over two months after Yalta. At the war's end, Stalin did attack Japan, but mainly as a power grab in Manchuria. And Poland was unfortunately sucked back behind what Churchill would later name the "Iron Curtain."

WEAPONS OF WAR
The Land War: Panzer Attack—The Mechanized Cavalry That Changed the Land War

While tanks and armored vehicles were just being introduced in the First World War, they were to become a decisive factor in the Second World War. In between the wars, military planners at first thought that tanks should merely be used as support tools for infantry.

However, numerous forward-thinking war planners—including Englishmen J.F.C. Fuller and Basil H. Liddell Hart and German general Heinz Guderian—believed in the use of all-mechanized armored divisions. The Germans in particular pioneered the idea of panzer (armored) divisions, creating the first ones in the mid-1930s. Infantry accompanied these divisions, in armored half-tracks, and there was mobile artillery as well, but the real killing force was two regiments of tanks that could be used to punch holes through enemy lines in advance of regular infantry. The Germans put this to good effect in Poland and France and during the initial stages of their rapid advance into Russia.

The primary German tank of the war was the Tiger I, which was put into battle in early 1941. It was heavily armored, so much so that it had a problem crossing most bridges. It carried (along with two machine guns) the powerful German 88 gun, along with an extremely effective Zeiss optical aiming sight, so that the Tiger could knock out enemy tanks at a range of 1,600 yards (1.5 km).

This spelled trouble for U.S. Shermans and Russian T-34s, which had to close to 500 yards (457 m) or so before they could hope to penetrate the Tiger's armor. But a major drawback of the Tiger was how long it took to produce. In the same amount of time that German factories could turn out 1,300 Tigers, 40,000 Shermans and 60,000 T-34s could be built. Ultimately, even with its overwhelming firepower, this doomed the Tiger.

The Sea War: The Aircraft Carrier Made the Air War Mobile

Just as the tank was the symbol of land warfare in World War II, the aircraft carrier represented the sea. After World War I, many naval commanders continued to pin their strategic dreams on the huge dreadnought-class battleships, and these certainly played a crucial part in the naval war.

But aircraft carriers were pivotal. At the end of World War I, certain ships in the U.S. and British navies had been converted so that biplanes might take off from their decks, but the first purpose-built aircraft carrier was the HMS Hermes, built in 1918. This and other carriers built by the British, Japanese, and Americans in the interwar years carried ever larger planes whose function changed from mere scouting ahead of a task force of ships to bombing and torpedoing enemy vessels.

The first real blow from aircraft carriers came when British carrier ships destroyed half the Italian fleet at anchor at Taranto, Italy. The Japanese planes that devastated Pearl Harbor came from aircraft carriers. In return, aviator Billy Mitchell shocked the Japanese by bombing Tokyo only a few months after Pearl Harbor with sixteen B-25s secretly launched from a U.S. aircraft carrier.

In the most famous naval battle of the war, the Battle of Midway, fought mainly with naval aircraft, the Americans destroyed four carriers belonging to the Japanese and changed the course of the war in the Pacific.

The Air War: The Heavy Bomber Sewed Destruction On Military and Civilian Targets

World War II's most destructive power, bar none, came from the sky, with the advent of the heavy bomber and its ability to drop tons of high explosive and incendiary bombs on both military and civilian targets. While the iconic image of World War I is long trenches snaking off through a barren wasteland, the one that most fully symbolizes World War II are the haunting ruins of a city, piles of rubble with a few scattered walls standing upright.

The British used the Wellington or the Lancaster; the Americans flew the B-25, B-17 Fortress, or B-29 Super Fortress; and the Germans employed the Junkel 88 or the Heinkel III, or even a jet bomber developed in late 1944, which was almost impossible to intercept because of its speed but came too late to affect the course of the war. The Japanese bomber was the fast but thinly armored Betty.

All of these airplanes were used against military targets, and all were used against civilian ones, as well. Deliberate terror bombing of civilian targets in an attempt to break enemy morale was a chief weapon of World War II, used most extensively after 1943 by the allies. In total, the United States and Great Britain dropped 2 million tons (1.8 billion kg) of bombs on Europe, killing 600,000 German civilians, 60 percent of them women and children. (About 60,000 British civilians died from German bombing.)

In the war in the Pacific, Americans wreaked havoc on the Japanese civilian population. In the low-level night bombing perfected by U.S. General Curtis LeMay, U.S. Superfortresses dropped incendiary bombs of jellied gasoline on the enemy, burning the wooden cities to the ground and creating huge firestorms. (Japan no longer had the air defenses to fight off the bombers, thus it could fly closer to its targets.) Two hundred thousand Japanese were killed, and another 13 million were made homeless. However, until the atomic bomb was dropped on Hiroshima, killing 80,000 people within a few hours, Japan refused to surrender.

In general, since the war's end, it has been recognized that strategic bombing of military targets is highly effective in helping defeat an enemy. However, bombing population centers, far from bringing about a loss of morale, actually stiffens one's opponents' resistance.

IN A STILL-CONTROVERSIAL DECISION, PRESIDENT HARRY TRUMAN DROPPED THE ATOMIC BOMB ON JAPAN; THE MUSHROOM CLOUD OVER NAGASAKI IS SEEN HERE. IT TOOK THE TWO ATOMIC BOMBS AND THEIR COMBINED KILLING OF 200,000 BEFORE THE JAPANESE SURRENDERED.

Prints & Photographs Division, Library of Congress, LC-USZ62-39852

The Atomic Bomb: "An Extremely Powerful Bomb of a New Type"

In August 1939, Albert Einstein wrote several letters to President Franklin Delano Roosevelt, informing him that nuclear fission—fragmenting a uranium atom's nucleus by bombarding it with neutrons—might result in "an extremely powerful bomb of a new type." Einstein also told Roosevelt something even more alarming: The Germans had forbidden the export of uranium and were already working on this experimental weapon. He urged Roosevelt to help set up a program to develop an atomic bomb ahead of the Germans.

At Roosevelt's request, scientists who had already been working on nuclear fission—including Enrico Fermi, Edward Teller, and J. Robert Oppenheimer—came together with numerous others in the early 1940s. Fermi, at the University of Chicago, built the first successful nuclear reactor, which showed that controlled nuclear fission could work. This was a huge step in the development of the atomic bomb, whose complex mystery was solved step by step by the top secret Manhattan Project, headed by Oppenheimer, with locations in New York and all over the country, including the Los Alamos Laboratories in New Mexico.

On July 16, 1945, the first atomic bomb, its core the more stable and powerful plutonium rather than uranium, was exploded atop a tower near Alamogordo, New Mexico. Fermi wrote that the explosion resulted in "a huge pillar of smoke with an expanded head like a gigantic mushroom." The blast, more powerful than even the scientists thought, brought on temperatures so hot (7,000°F [3,871°C]) that the nearby sand was fused together.

President Roosevelt had died earlier that year, but President Harry S. Truman made the decision to drop the atom bomb on Japan only a month after this first test. It was a decision that ended World War II, and helped begin the Cold War.

THE HOLOCAUST: THE MASSACRE THAT EMBODIED MAN'S INHUMANITY TO MAN

As historian John Keegan has pointed out, one of the things that makes Hitler's killing of more than 6 million Jews (as well as other "undesirables," such as Gypsies, the mentally challenged, Polish and French resistance fighters, and clergy) even more shocking is that, while hundreds of thousands, even millions, were killed in campaigns by the likes of the Romans, Mongols, and Spanish, "massacre had effectively been outlawed from warfare in Europe since the seventeenth century." With Hitler, massacre on an unimaginable scale was back.

After the Nazis took power in the 1930s, Jews in Germany suffered under a series of restrictive legal measures that culminated in the Nuremberg Laws of 1935, in which Jews were deprived of German citizenship. There were about a half a million Jews in Germany at the time and while a fifth of this population attempted to migrate,

many of them went to nearby countries that were soon subsumed in the Nazi onslaught. Heinrich Himmler, head of the German SS, devised four task groups divided into Sonderkommandos, or Special Commandos, which killed roughly 1,000,000 Jews in the newly conquered areas of Poland and Russia. But these deaths were mainly by shooting, which Himmler considered unproductive and slow.

In 1942, he proposed what he called the Endlosung, or Final Solution, at the behest of Hitler. The Endlosung took Jews from the ghettos in major cities to where they had been confined and brought them to concentration camps. Some of these were work camps, where inmates were literally worked to death. Others, like Treblinka and Sobidor, were simply extermination camps where Jews were herded into gas chambers as soon as they arrived.

By the spring of 1944, there were twenty concentration camps and some 160 smaller labor camps, and some 6 million Jews—40 percent of the world's Jewish population—had been killed. The fact that a supposedly civilized people in the middle of the twentieth century could massacre so many is one the world has struggled with ever since. However, the wave of sympathy for the plight of the Jews immediately after World War II was in part what helped them gain their own homeland and statehood.

SEEN HERE ARE TWO INMATES OF THE AMPHING CONCENTRATION CAMP IN GERMANY JUST AFTER BEING LIBERATED BY U.S. TROOPS.

23

THE ARAB-ISRAELI WAR

1948–1949

THIS WAR SAVED THE EXISTENCE OF THE FLEDGLING STATE OF ISRAEL,
BUT IT CREATED CIRCUMSTANCES THAT WOULD CAUSE ALMOST UNCEASING
CONFLICT BETWEEN JEWS AND ARABS FOR THE NEXT HALF A CENTURY.

THE BEGINNING OF THE ISRAELI STATE WAS THE START OF ENDLESS CONFLICT

It was all about a narrow strip of land between the Mediterranean Sea and the Jordan River that has been inhabited almost continuously since Paleolithic times. The land goes by many names—Canaan, Israel, the Holy Land, and Palestine (derived from the Latin name for some of the land's early inhabitants, the Philistinus, or Philistines). The Old Testament called it "the land of milk and honey." The Jewish people had their origins in Palestine, in the land they called Israel, and which they ruled from the twelfth century BCE to the second century CE. But the conquering Romans drove them from Palestine after successive Jewish revolts, and the country was eventually ruled by numerous occupiers—Byzantines, Arabs, Seljuk Turks, Crusaders, and Mamluk and Ottoman Turks.

All of these, with the exception of the Byzantines and Crusaders, were Muslims, and the law of Mohammed was the law of the Palestine—which for centuries had become a quiet backwater, considered of little use to anyone. By the 1880s, some 25,000 Jews lived there, well outnumbered by the Arabs who surrounded them. But then Jewish emigrants from Eastern Europe began arriving, swept along by the Zionist movement, which called for a return to the Jewish homeland. (Zion was the name for one of the hills of Jerusalem and became the name for Israel itself.) By 1914, there were almost 100,000 Jews in Palestine, in a community known as Yishuv, 15 percent of the total population. The Jews, like their Arab-speaking neighbors, were subjects of the Ottoman Empire. Palestine was not viewed as a separate state, merely an area between Jerusalem and Beirut.

After World War I these former Ottoman territories became a British protectorate. The British, in return for their help in defeating the Ottomans, had promised self-determination to both the Zionists and Arabs of Palestine. In 1922, the British divided Palestine into two different territories. The land east of the Jordan

River became Transjordan (today's Jordan) while the land to the west, from Egypt in the south to Lebanon and Syria in the north, remained Palestine. Jews and Arabs then began terrorist attacks against each other, and the British tried to keep the lid on the growing violence. However, the Zionists slowly acquired more and more territory because they were more organized, because of steady immigration to Israel, and because they had more money to make land purchases.

After World War II ended and the world became aware of the Holocaust, sympathy turned to the Zionist cause. A clamor grew to allow a Jewish homeland in Palestine. The British government, which would soon leave Palestine to self-determination, and whose enthusiasm about a Jewish state had waned, decided to turn the matter over to the United Nations (UN).

IN NOVEMBER OF 1947, JEWS CELEBRATED UN RESOLUTION 181, WHICH PARTITIONED PALESTINE INTO BOTH JEWISH AND PALESTINIAN ARAB HOMELANDS.

Associated Press

In November 1947, against British wishes, the UN passed Resolution 181, which called for the partition of Palestine into both a Jewish and an Arab Palestinian homeland. The Jews accepted this proposal, but the Arabs rejected it, and the first of two distinct stages of the Arab-Israeli War began. While the differing sides obviously worshipped different religions, the Arab-Israeli War was not a religious war, per se, because for centuries, with some exceptions, Muslims had allowed Jews freedom of religion in Muslim-controlled lands. Instead, it was a war over precious territory, with each side considering that its survival as a people was at stake.

The first stage, from November 1947 to May 1948, saw a ragtag Jewish army known as the Haganah (meaning "defense")—aided by its more radical terrorist arms, the LHI and the IZL—fighting against Arab guerilla fighters who coalesced into a group called the Arab Liberation Army (ALA). There were 650,000 Jews in Palestine, compared to twice that many Palestinian Arabs and 40 million Arabs in surrounding states. But the Jews, led by David Ben-Gurion had organized themselves for war, while the Arabs, among whom there was a great deal of factional infighting, had not. Still, the civil war from November to May was a vicious one, with terror groups on both sides setting off car bombs among civilian populations.

Jerusalem, sacred to both Arabs and Jews, was to be at the center of the fighting. The Jews held most of the so-called New City of Jerusalem, while the Arabs surrounded much of the Old City. Haganah and the ALA clashed over supply roads

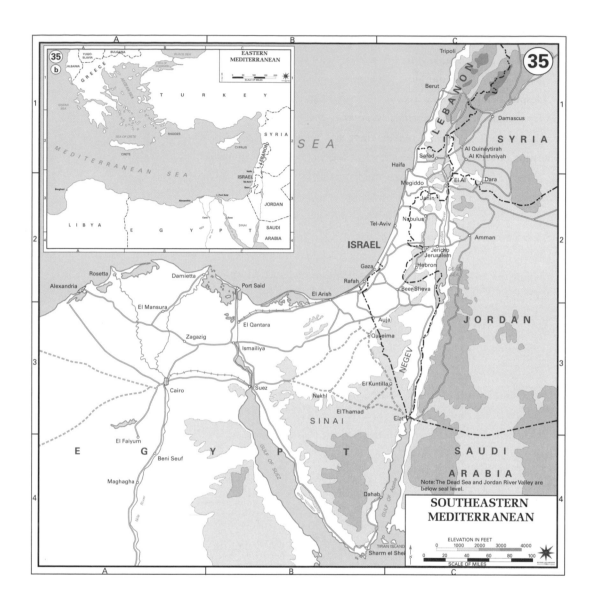

going into the city, while Arab snipers infiltrated Jewish areas and shot civilians. Arabs also attacked outlying Jewish settlements, or kibbutzim, like those at Kfar-Szold and Etzion Bloc, where outnumbered settlers held out against the odds, buying precious time for Israel.

By April, although the Jews had not yet lost a single settlement to the Arabs, they were reeling under heavy losses and suffering a shortage of men and materials. But then David Ben-Gurion mounted Operation Nachshon, the largest Jewish operation of the war to date, which opened up a corridor out of besieged Jerusalem and also killed the Arab militia commander Abd al-Qadir al-Husseini, which was a grievous blow to Arab morale.

Despite being outnumbered, the Jews held their own in this first part of the war and even expanded their territory. But when the British mandate ended and Israel proclaimed itself a sovereign state, there was a Pan-Arab attack on the new state, consisting of an invasion by the armies of Egypt, Syria, Transjordan, Iraq, and (on a smaller scale) Lebanon. Jordanian troops took control of the Old City of Jerusalem, while Egyptians attacked and overran Jewish settlements in the Negev Desert in the south. But by July, the consolidated army of the Israelis—now called the Israeli Defense Force (IDF)—had taken central Galilee and pushed the Arabs back.

In July, the UN brokered a four-week truce, but when the Egyptians began fighting again, the Israelis pushed back the Arab countries on all fronts, gaining possession of all of the Negev Desert in the south (with the exception of the Gaza Strip). After another truce, broken by the Egyptians who refused to allow the IDF to supply Jewish settlements in the Negev, Israel pushed the Egyptians back into the Sinai Peninsula and forced the other Arab countries to withdraw as well.

Between February and May 1949, Israel signed separate peace agreements with all the combatants except Iraq, which withdrew its forces but would not agree to a treaty. In a stunning victory, Israel had taken more than 400 Arab villages and towns, had increased its original land allotment under Partition by one-half, and had swelled its armed forces to more than 200,000 strong.

But in the process, 700,000 Palestinian refugees had been created, expelled to other Arab states, and a smoldering resentment would grow against Israel. In a sense, the Arab-Israeli War of 1948 never really ended. There were further wars—in 1956, 1967, and 1973—as well as Palestinian uprisings as the descendants of those original refugees sought their homeland, as the Zionists once so fervently sought theirs.

THE BATTLE THAT ALLOWED JERUSALEM TO SURVIVE
Operation Nachshon: April 1948

On March 28, 1948, Jewish leader David Ben-Gurion cabled a political ally in New York from his headquarters in Tel Aviv: "This is the most terrible day since the beginning of the war."

It was an uncharacteristic note of despair from the resilient leader, but, indeed everything seemed to be going wrong for the Jews. Although the civil war was barely four months old, they had already lost 1,000 men. Jerusalem was surrounded by ALA forces and, as one Haganah captain reported, "there is starvation in the city." On March 27, a Haganah convoy filled with food and ammunition had tried to force its way into the city to relieve the population, only to be ambushed by the ALA and nearly destroyed. (During this last week of March, 136 supply trucks were sent through to Jerusalem, but only 41 made it.)

On March 28, the day Ben-Gurion sent his cable, another Jewish convoy had been attacked while trying to reach isolated Jewish settlements in western Galilee. In bitter fighting that lasted into the night, forty-seven Haganah soldiers were killed, and their bodies were mutilated by the Arabs. That fate awaited any convoy soldier caught by the ALA, which is why many of the men in the Galilee convoy committed suicide rather than risk capture.

IN THE ATTACK WOULD BEGIN ON APRIL 5, AND IT WOULD BE CALLED OPERATION NACHSHON AFTER THE BIBLICAL FIGURE OF NACHSHON BEN AMINADAV, WHO WAS THE FIRST TO STRIDE INTO THE PARTED RED SEA.

There was even worse news on the political front. The Americans, who had supported the partition of Palestine and the creation of a Jewish state, now seemed to be wavering in their support as the bloody civil war continued. The United States' ambassador to the United Nations, Warren Austin, told the UN Security Council in mid-March that "there seems to be general agreement that the [partition] plan cannot now be implemented by peaceful means …. we believe that a temporary trusteeship for Palestine should be established."

President Harry Truman tried to reassure Zionist leaders in the United States that Austin had spoken without his permission. (In his diary, Truman complained the State Department "pulled the rug out from under me today.") But Ben-Gurion knew that any delay in the creation of Israel might cause the shaky political coalitions within the Yishuv to collapse. With the British ready to pull out of Palestine in May, and with the armies of neighboring Arab countries massing to invade, something needed to be done, and quickly.

"If Jerusalem Falls…"

On March 31, Ben-Gurion called a meeting of the political and military wings of the Haganah. He told them that it was necessary to loosen the Arab death grip on Jerusalem by any means possible. "If Jerusalem falls, the whole country might fall," he told Yigael Yadin, chief of staff of the Haganah. He wanted a huge Haganah force to clear the road from Tel Aviv to Jerusalem.

Yadin pointed out the difficulty of this. The Haganah forces were hard-pressed everywhere in the country, he said. Not enough could be spared for such an effort. There weren't even enough weapons to arm them all.

Ben-Gurion retorted: "We'll take men, arms, and mortars from the settlements."

Yadin replied that this would leave these communities unprotected, but Ben-Gurion was insistent. "The fall of Jewish Jerusalem could be a deathblow to the Yishuv," he said. "The risk is worth everything." Finally, he won the day. It was decided to create a Haganah brigade of 1,500 men, organized into three battalions, by thinning ranks of Jewish troops all over the country. This was to be the first time that the Haganah had operated on such a large scale. Its goal would be to secure the Tel Aviv–Jerusalem road by creating a corridor 2 to 6 miles (3 to 9.5 km) wide. They would do this by clearing all Arab forces away from the road and by considering all Arab-held villages along the route as possible bases of ALA operations.

The attack would begin on April 5, and it would be called Operation Nachshon after the Biblical figure of Nachshon Ben Aminadav, who was the first to stride into the parted Red Sea when the Jews escaped ancient Egypt. The operation was part of a larger strategic calculation by Ben-Gurion and his military planners, one that they called Plan D. They knew the British would be withdrawing from Palestine in six weeks' time and that Arab countries would almost certainly invade shortly thereafter. Plan D called for destroying or severely weakening the capabilities of the Palestinian Arabs and the ALA before such an invasion began. The Jews must regain control internally before facing a foe from the outside, or they were doomed.

Arms from the Sky

On the very night that Ben-Gurion was meeting with his advisors, a chartered U.S. Skymaster cargo plane landed secretly in a remote airfield near the Arab village of Beit Daras, north of the Gaza Strip. It held 200 rifles, 40 machine guns, and 160,000 bullets—a shipment of Czech arms that the Haganah had long been trying to arrange. Two days later, another plane landed, carrying 200 machine guns, 450 rifles, and 5 million bullets, its crates of arms covered with potatoes and onions. The arms were taken by sea to Tel Aviv, where they were handed out to the gathering Haganah fighters. The soldiers were so joyful that they kissed the guns, "which were still coated in grease," as one soldier later noted.

With this relatively huge stockpile of weapons, Operation Nachshon was ready to begin. The official kick-off date for clearing the Jerusalem road was April 6, but two important small operations began earlier. On the night of April 2–3, a Haganah company attacked and captured the small but strategic village of al-Qastal, some 5 miles (8 km) west of Jerusalem, which overlooked the road into the city.

And on the night of April 4–5, a group of Israeli commandos snuck through an orange grove west of Jerusalem, near the village of Ramla, and attacked the four-story building that was the headquarters of Hassan Salame. Salame was a dreaded, Nazi-trained

Palestinian militia leader, whose men had been responsible for numerous attacks on Jewish convoys into Jerusalem. The Haganah commandos blew up the headquarters and killed two dozen Arabs. Although Salame himself escaped (he was to be killed in action against the Israelis the following June), his prestige was dealt a serious blow by this incident. Many of his militia deserted him, which kept his forces from any real role in the fighting to come.

The Road to Jerusalem

Operation Nachshon launched in the early morning of April 6, and for the most part it took ALA forces and Arab militia completely by surprise. In the past, the Jews had played a mainly defensive role and operated on a company-strength level, but now they came down the Jerusalem road 1,500 strong, well armed, and on the offensive. Two Arab villages along the road, Khulda and Deir Muheizin, fell almost immediately. With al-Qastal in the hands of the Jews, the Haganah quickly launched a sixty-truck convoy, which made it to Jerusalem and was met by cheering crowds.

But the battle was far from over. Abd al-Qadir al-Husseini, commander of the army of the Holy War, understood the strategic significance of the village of al-Qastal, which the Jews now held and which commanded the main road that ran into Jerusalem from the west. If the Arabs could recapture it, they might stop the Jewish convoys once again. After being denied arms and reinforcements by Arab High Command, al-Husseini decided to attack the village anyway. Because of a shortage of men, Haganah leaders had garrisoned it with raw recruits. They then compounded this mistake by arguing over who was responsible for its command.

In the meantime, al-Husseini's men gathered by the hundreds and began laying down mortar and sniper fire on al-Qastal. On the night of April 7–8, al-Husseini launched his attack, sending hundreds of men at the perimeter of the village. The Haganah held on, but barely, as streams of machine gun tracers lit up the air and grenade and mortar explosions rocked the town.

Early on the foggy morning of April 8, a Jewish sentry heard a noise and fired at it. There were cries and the sound of a body thudding to the ground. It turned out that he had killed al-Husseini, who had gotten lost on a reconnaissance mission with two aides. The Jews at al-Qastal knew they had killed someone big when they examined his body, but they could not figure out who it was. But then they heard the radio waves filled with Arabs frantically wondering where their commander was. As the day wore on, more and more Arabs showed up at the foot of the hill below al-Qastal. "I saw thousands of Arabs," one Jewish survivor wrote. "Buses, trucks, and donkeys brought them from Suba." Determined to find al-Husseini, or at least his body, they attacked that afternoon "like madmen," said the same Jewish survivor.

With their ammunition depleted, the Jews defending al-Qastal could no longer hold on and tried to retreat eastward down the slope, with the Arabs now filling the village. While their officers heroically covered their retreat from an orchard, dozens of Haganah were able to escape, but anyone left behind was killed and mutilated by the Arabs. By nightfall, al-Qastal belonged to the Arabs, and they had also found the body of Abd al-Qader al-Husseini.

Parting the Red Sea....

Early on the morning of April 9, the Haganah counterattacked al-Qastal, only to find it empty except for dozens of Jewish bodies. The Arabs had simply left the strategic village, abandoning it to go to the funeral of al-Husseini, which was held in the Arab-controlled Old City of Jerusalem. The Haganah immediately razed the village and then built a defensive perimeter around it. From up on the hill, they could watch another convoy snaking its way safely into Jerusalem.

The battle for Jerusalem would continue for the rest of the war. In just a month's time, the British would leave, David Ben-Gurion would proclaim Israel's statehood, and the Pan Arab invasion would begin. But for now, Operation Nachshon had parted the Red Sea just enough to allow the Jews to survive another few weeks.

DAVID BEN-GURION: FOUNDER OF A NATION

Any number of brilliant leaders helped Israel rise to nationhood, but the one indispensable person was David Ben-Gurion, who would go on to become the nation's first prime minister. Ben-Gurion was born in small-town Poland in 1886, the son of a lawyer who believed deeply in the Zionist movement. Ben-Gurion acquired this belief, further strengthened by the pogroms that occurred in Poland while he was there, the almost casual attacks that seemed to come in historic waves.

In 1906, Ben-Gurion, like so many Zionists, immigrated to Palestine, which was then a part of the Ottoman Empire. He became a farmhand and was also a socialist, but his main ambition in life was the creation of a Jewish state in Palestine. Although small of stature, Ben-Gurion was fiery and charismatic, yet somewhat authoritative and didactic.

He was expelled from Palestine in 1915 for his political activism and went to the United States, where he became involved with Zionist groups in New York. His experiences in the United States left him less enchanted with the byzantine, ever-changing socialist groups, as well as more democratic in inclination. After World War I, he returned to Palestine, which was then governed by the British, and rose to become a prominent leader in the Yishuv, or Jewish community, there. In the

1930s, as reports reached the Jews in Palestine of the atrocities being perpetuated on Jews in Nazi Germany, Ben-Gurion became even more dedicated to creating a homeland for persecuted Jews.

With World War II in the offing, Ben-Gurion crafted a brilliant strategy. The British (and other countries in the world) refused admission of Jewish refugees, so Ben-Gurion set up an underground rescue system that brought them from Europe to Palestine, where the British authorities promptly locked them up in camps, thus creating world sympathy for the Zionist plight.

At the same time, Ben-Gurion encouraged thousands of young Jews to enlist in the British army to fight the Nazis and gain valuable combat experience. Although Ben-Gurion did not hate the Arabs, he knew that any Jewish state would have to be forged in the crucible of war, and so during the years leading up to 1948 created a shadow army, the Haganah, which was ready to fight when the time came.

In the end, Ben-Gurion's planning was the key to the Israeli triumph in the war. He became prime minister in 1948 and would hold that position until 1963 (with the exception of a two-year period in the middle 1950s), guiding the state of Israel through its crucial formative period.

AN ICONIC PICTURE OF DAVID BEN-GURION, THE FOUNDER AND GUIDING LIGHT OF THE EARLY ISRAELI NATION.
Getty Images

THE PALESTINIAN REFUGEES: A PROBLEM THAT REFUSES TO GO AWAY

One of the most enduring problems created by the 1948 Arab-Israeli War was the Palestinian Arab refugee. By April 1948, a month before Israel declared itself a state, 100,000 Arabs, mainly from the more heavily populated centers of Jaffe, Haifa, and Jerusalem, had already left the country. By June, 400,000 had left and by war's end, in early 1949, about 700,000 refugees had left their homes.

Why did the Arab Palestinians flee, but not the Jews? In one sense, this was because the Jews had nowhere to flee to, surrounded by hostile Arab countries. But much more important, the Jews had faith in their leadership and a strong central political organization. The Palestinians had none of this. In fact, ordinary Palestinians became disillusioned with their leaders, many of whom were fleeing the country as fast as they could. The flight of the Arab elite—intellectuals, politicians, community leaders—was one part of the exodus that was disheartening.

Even more problematic was the fact that the ALA and other Arab military organizations had decided to force Palestinian women and children out of their homes and into exile.

The professed reason was so that they would not become targets for Jewish attacks. Another underlying reason was that the Arab military did not want these people to become citizens of a new Jewish state. But the ALA failed to bargain on the fact that many Palestinian men did not want to leave their families and thus went with them into exile.

While some historians, both Arab and Israeli, have written that the Israelis had a plan to evict Arabs from Palestine, this was probably not the case. In fact, the chief of staff of the Haganah, in preparing for the Pan-Arab invasion that did in fact take place, called on his officers to ensure "the full rights, needs, and freedom of Arabs in the Hebrew state."

The Palestinian refugees were in fact treated far more cruelly by Arabs in countries such as Egypt, Syria, and Jordan, which refused to take responsibility for them, or even allow them self-determination in the parts of Palestine (the Gaza and the West Bank) that the Arabs retained after the war. As one Egyptian diplomat said to a British journalist, "We don't care if all the refugees will die. There are enough Arabs around."

THE SPRAWLING DHEISHEH REFUGEE CAMP, FOUNDED IN 1949, HOUSED REFUGEES FROM 45 ARAB VILLAGES WEST OF JERUSALEM. TODAY, IT HAS 12,000 INHABITANTS.

Associated Press

TWO MASSACRES...

Both sides in the Arab-Israeli War of 1948 accused each other of indiscriminately killing civilians, charges that would be debated for years to come. In fact, as in any civil war, both sides were guilty of atrocities.

Death at Deir Yasin

During the same Operation Nachshon that saw the death of Abd al-Qadir al-Husseini and the fighting around al-Qastal, Israeli forces attacked and captured the small Arab village of Deir Yasin, which lay on the road between Jerusalem and al-Qastal. Deir Yasin had little military significance, but the aftermath of the battle, as historian Benny Morris has written, "proved to be one of the key events of the war."

There had long been a history of hostility between the Arabs of Deir Yasin and the Jewish inhabitants of the nearby Jerusalem suburb of Giv'at Shaul, which had been attacked more than once by gunmen from Deir Yasin in the years preceding the war. Since the 1948 war started, the two villages had signed a nonaggression pact, but Arab snipers in Deir Yasin still fired occasionally on Jews in Giv'at Shaul, although it is not known whether the Arab villagers supported them.

In any event, on April 9, as the battle for al-Qastal raged, Jewish forces advanced on Deir Yasin. These were mainly irregular troops of the LHI and the IZL. The LHI (the initials come from the Yiddish initials that stand for Freedom Fighters of Israel) was a radical Jewish militia also known as "the Stern gang" after one of its initial leaders. The IZL (its initials stood for National Military Organization) was also known as the Irgun; one of its leaders, Menachem Begin, would become a future prime minister of Israel. Regular Haganah forces also assisted, but they were in the minority.

The attack on the village began with IZL and LHI forces using bullhorns to urge the villagers to surrender. But when fire from the village was unexpectedly heavy, Jewish forces moved in and indiscriminately began tossing grenades in homes, blowing up some entirely, and shooting women and children as they tried to flee. Some male villagers were taken to an LHI base in western Jerusalem and executed. Altogether about 120 villagers were killed that day, both combatants and noncombatants.

The Palestinian Arabs made effective propaganda use of this massacre in radio broadcasts that fired up the sentiments of Arabs in neighboring states. King Abdullah of Jordan, who had earlier promised the Jews and Golda Meir he would not invade, pointed to the massacre as the reason why he had changed his mind.

Death at Etzion Bloc

In the weeks before the Pan-Arab invasion of the newly declared state of Israel in May 1948, both sides within Palestine fought with renewed vigor, the Israelis to prepare defenses against the oncoming invasion, the Arabs to clear a path for the invading armies of Syria, Jordan, Egypt, and Lebanon.

The so-called Etzion Bloc lay on an important road between Bethlehem and Hebron and consisted of four kibbutzim that had been established there in the early 1940s. Relations between the kibbutzim and their Arab neighbors were never good, and as the war began, the Arab mayor of Hebron warned the Jews to leave their land or "you will be removed by force." This the Jews refused to do, and the Etzion Bloc kibbutzim became a major staging ground for Jewish forces attacking Arab or British convoys along the road.

MANY OF THE VICTIMS OF THE MASSACRE ARE BURIED IN DEIR YASIN CEMETERY, WHICH IS PICTURED HERE.

Popperfoto/Getty Images

The British wanted these attacks to stop and allowed the Jordan Legion, which at this time was still officially a part of the British army, to capture the kibbutzim, which contained about 500 Haganah fighters and armed kibbutz members. On May 12, the legion attacked in the early dawn hours, accompanied by artillery, armored cars, and a large force of Arab militia. During fighting that lasted all day, the legionnaires overran Jewish positions at the Kfar Etzion, and the next day the one hundred Jewish defenders who were left surrendered. A Jewish eyewitness reported that a photographer came up and took pictures of the prisoners. After the photographer left, the Arabs, yelling "Deir Yassin!" opened fire with machine guns and threw hand grenades into the mass of prisoners.

Almost all of these one hundred prisoners were murdered; some of the women fighters were raped and afterward killed, despite the efforts of a few Jordanian officers to stem the bloodshed. The other three Jewish settlements, subjected to continuous attack, were too terrified to surrender until the Red Cross arranged for their safe transport. Even then many were killed by legionnaires and militia. In the end, 350 prisoners were taken to Transjordan and held there safely until the war was over. Still, the Etzion Bloc massacre enraged Jewish forces and apparently figured in a number of smaller killings of Arab prisoners as the war progressed.

24

THE VIETNAM WAR

1955–1975

NORTH VIETNAM INFLICTED A DEVASTATING AND HISTORIC DEFEAT
ON A UNITED STATES SEEKING TO STOP COMMUNISM IN SOUTHEAST
ASIA, BUT UNABLE TO COME UP WITH A COHERENT STRATEGY TO FIGHT
WHAT WAS AT THE TIME THE LONGEST WAR IN U.S. HISTORY.

THE DIVISIVE WAR THAT CHANGED THE COURSE OF U.S. AND VIETNAMESE HISTORY

The country of Vietnam had been divided at the 17th parallel in 1954 after the forces of Ho Chi Minh defeated the French in 1954 at the battle of Dien Bien Phu. North of the demarcation line was the Democratic Republic of North Vietnam, and south lay the Republic of South Vietnam.

Elections were mandated to be held in 1956, but then civil war broke out between the communist government of the north and the corrupt, but nominally democratic government of the south, backed by the United States, which was afraid that a communist victory in Vietnam would lead to a communist takeover in all of Southeast Asia.

At first U.S. aid to South Vietnam and its series of presidents was confined to military advisors and financial assistance. But soon it became clear to U.S. President Lyndon Johnson that the Army of the Republic of Vietnam (ARVN) was losing the war against the Viet Cong guerillas operating in the south and supplied by North Vietnam. After North Vietnamese patrol boats clashed with a U.S. intelligence-gathering destroyer in the Gulf of Tonkin in August 1964, Johnson secured the approval of Congress to send U.S. combat troops to South Vietnam and begin bombing North Vietnam.

The war then escalated as North Vietnam sent regular army (NVA) troops to infiltrate the south. The first major clashes between these two forces took place in the Ia Drang Valley in South Vietnam in November 1965 and underscored the differences in their approaches to the war. The Americans favored the new tactic of air mobility—moving large bodies of men quickly from battlefield to battlefield via the helicopter—as well as using close support of artillery and fighter strikes. Without this technology, the North Vietnamese pursued a strategy of getting as close as possible to their enemy, rendering bombs and artillery useless.

The war raged through 1968, with Americans under General William Westmoreland seeking to deny Viet Cong guerillas the help of the populace by moving thousands of

Vietnamese to so-called "strategic hamlets" built for them and guarded by ARVN troops, while at the same time attacking the NVA from firebases built around the country. The massive bombing of North Vietnam continued unabated until 1968. But the strategic hamlet program was a failure because it alienated the peasant population by taking them away from their homes. Plus the Americans were never able to trap the NVA into a large enough set-piece battle to inflict irreparable harm on them.

In January 1968, the Viet Cong and North Vietnamese launched the Tet Offensive, a major, concerted attack against thirty-six cities in South Vietnam. They caused widespread destruction there, but they were defeated on the battlefield with heavy losses. Despite this, the attack shook the U.S. public. Calls for ending United States' involvement in Vietnam, which had been growing, now reached fever pitch.

PICTURED: VIET CONG TROOPS SHOOTING AT THE ENEMY AIRCRAFT

President Johnson stopped the bombing of North Vietnam and began negotiating with the North Vietnamese in Paris, while announcing that he would not run for a second term. In March 1969, U.S. strategy switched to that of "Vietnamization," which meant gradually allowing the South Vietnamese to do all the fighting themselves. The next year, under President Richard Nixon, the United States gradually withdrew its 500,000 troops, as civilian protestors in the United States grew steadily more vocal, especially after news of the My Lai Massacre was revealed.

After the killing of students at Kent State University by the Ohio National Guard in May 1970, most of the country wanted war to end. At last, Nixon's negotiator Henry Kissinger and North Vietnam diplomat Le Duc Tho reached a peace agreement in Paris in October 1972. The last U.S. combat troops were withdrawn from the country in March 1973, although the South Vietnamese would continue to fight on, supplied with U.S. weapons, until they were overwhelmed by the North Vietnamese army in April 1975.

The war in Vietnam—the second-longest war in U.S. history, after the current war in Afghanistan—was also the first war ever lost by the United States and is probably the most traumatic event in its twentieth-century history. U.S. citizens were divided against each other during the war and developed a powerful distrust of their government, while the United States also lost face around the world. However, a triumphant North Vietnam had united the country at last, despite severe losses, and it would gradually became apparent after a period of postwar adjustment that it would not march in lockstep with Soviet Russia or communist China.

THE NORTH VIETNAMESE LOST THE BATTLE—BUT WON THE WAR
The Tet Offensive: 1968

It seemed to a lot of people, many of them in the U.S. intelligence community, that something was simmering that January of 1968. In the fall, North Vietnamese Army (NVA) regular troops had launched strong attacks against U.S bases at Khe Sanh and Con Thien along the 17th parallel, attacks that would retrospectively be seen as successful attempts to draw U.S. reinforcements north, away from Saigon.

Early in January, a document found on the body of a dead Viet Cong officer talked about a "concerted offensive" to be held very soon. And as Tet—the annual Vietnamese celebration of the lunar New Year—approached on January 31, it appeared to many Americans that there were more and more Vietnamese men in major cities such as Saigon and Hue who appeared strong and whippet-thin, yet pale, as if they had been spending a good deal of time trekking through shady jungles.

In fact, they had. In the month before January 31, 1968, thousands of Viet Cong and NVA troops had shed their uniforms and blended into the civilian population, prepared for the mightiest offensive the North had ever launched against the south and the Americans. It would involve attacks on thirty-six provincial capitals, more than one hundred towns and cities, with almost 200 Viet Cong and NVA battalions—70,000 would take part in the initial attack.

And it would all occur to the sound of fireworks, horns, and drums.

"An Allied Intelligence Failure"

On the night of January 30–31, most Americans in South Vietnam were listening to and taking part in Tet celebrations. In fact, in Saigon, more than 200 colonels assigned to the U.S. embassy went to a boisterous drinking bash at the home of a fellow officer, leaving only one extra guard on the embassy, despite the high level of alert.

Later, one U.S. officer would call the fact that so many warnings had been ignored "an allied intelligence failure ranking with Pearl Harbor." But most U.S. troops in Vietnam were on high levels of alert at least half the time, and no one had passed on any sense of urgency to those around Saigon. After all, wasn't there a truce in place for the Tet celebrations?

Certainly, the North Vietnamese had agreed to one, and in response the South Vietnamese gave half its troops home leave. And while everyone was celebrating, the

North Vietnamese and Viet Cong infiltrators picked up their guns and hand grenades and left their hiding places. Through the haze of gunpowder from fireworks
and the shrieks of laughter, they headed for their assigned targets as part of a plan
that had been designed mainly by General Vo Nguyen Giap. He had decided that the
south was ready for a general uprising, that people there would oust the Americans
and corrupt South Vietnamese governments. In fact, this was not true, but it turned
out to be the best miscalculation Giap ever made.

In the early morning darkness in Saigon—the most important target of the infiltrators—nearly 4,000 Viet Cong gathered in small teams and headed to their targets.
Nineteen highly trained Viet Cong commandos piled into a truck and a taxi cab,
arrived outside the U.S. embassy at about three o'clock in the morning, and blasted a
hole in its wall with plastic explosives. Then they charged in, firing.

All across the country, other actions were taking place almost simultaneously.
The Viet Cong attacked twenty-five military bases, putting frantic Americans under
siege as the realization dawned that what they thought were Tet firecrackers were
in fact actual bullets and explosives. Outside Saigon, the Viet Cong blew up the
Long Binh ammunition dump, causing a spectacular explosion that could be seen
for miles. The Saigon suburb of Cholon was turned into a staging ground for Viet
Cong and NVA attacks that briefly were able to take over the national radio station,
assault the presidential palace, and keep General William Westmoreland prisoner in
his U.S. Military Assistance Command, Vietnam,
headquarters.

PRESIDENT LYNDON JOHNSON
PREPARES TO ADDRESS
AMERICANS AND ANNOUNCE
HIS DECISION TO HALT
BOMBING OF NORTH VIETNAM
IN MARCH 1968.

Time & Life Pictures/ Getty Images

But it was the assault on the U.S. embassy
that gained the most notoriety in the first night
and day of the attack. Despite the fact that one
U.S. officer derisively referred to it as a "pid-
dling platoon action," despite the fact that U.S.
Ambassador Ellsworth Bunker was hustled off to
safety, the Viet Cong sappers and guerillas had
actually penetrated U.S. territory and killed GIs
there. Because this was Saigon, U.S. reporters
and camera crews were present, and they filmed
the chaos. Instead of the images the U.S. public had been seeing—images of smoke pluming
from the jungle as jets launched air strikes at Viet
Cong and NVA positions, or of GIs firing their
M-16s from the relative safety of trees and bushes,

CIVILIAN DEAD IN HUE DURING
THE 1968 TET OFFENSIVE. TENS OF
THOUSANDS OF NONCOMBATANTS
DIED BEFORE THE AMERICANS
DROVE THE NORTH VIETNAMESE
FROM THE CITY.

the U.S. public suddenly saw rubble within Saigon and dead bodies. They heard the firing coming from infiltrators and the panicked voices of the television reporters.

It was pure chaos to a U.S. public that had been told, by none other than General Westmoreland, that they were winning the war. Trusted television announcer Walter Cronkite put it for most Americans when he asked, "What the hell is going on? I thought we were winning the war."

Hue City

Actually, within weeks, the Viet Cong and North Vietnamese were being pushed back with heavy losses, but this mattered little to a public with these images emblazoned on its mind. And there was worse to come. The iconic battle of the Tet Offensive would take place at Hue City, in central Vietnam. A beautiful place situated on the Perfume River, Hue is the ancient "imperial city" of the Nguyen Dynasty, a place that was filled with museums, lovely parks, and about 140,000 people, including many foreigners (mainly French) and a large number of Catholics. As the Tet Offensive began, a division of NVA seized much of the city and then raised its flag over the Citadel, the fortified inner city of the ancient kings.

The soldiers then embarked on a preassigned massacre: to cleanse the city of all those who had spoken out against North Vietnam. NVA commanders had lists of people—including government officials, students, and priests—and rounded them up by the thousands. Many were shot. A favorite fate for the clergy was burying them alive.

But in early February, three battalions of U.S. Marines came to take the city back, attacking from the north in assault boats that crossed the Perfume River with NVA bullets pinging off their sides. In cold, foggy weather that often restricted the Marine's ability to call in air strikes, the Americans dug the NVA out of their spider holes and sniper's nests, fighting their way through streets littered with military and civilian dead. An estimated 5,000 NVA soldiers met their deaths in Hue, as well as tens of thousands of civilians, including 3,000 executed by the Communists.

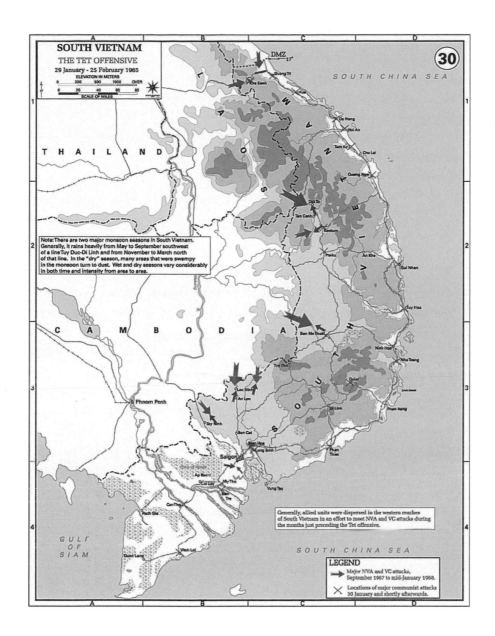

The stink of death was in the air; one officer commented that "the horrible smell was everywhere. You tasted it as you ate your rations, as if you were eating death." Marines blasted their way into the Citadel and at last removed the NVA flags.

But U.S. firepower destroyed the once beautiful city of Hue, leaving 116,000 citizens homeless. As one U.S. major commented, describing another fight for a nearby town: "We had to destroy the town in order to save it." Hue was saved, but devastated.

THIS MAP SHOWS THE INFILTRATION POINTS OF THE NORTH VIETNAMESE AND VIET CONG (MARKED BY RED ARROWS) AS THEY PREPARED TO MAKE THEIR ATTACKS DURING THE TET OFFENSIVE.
United States Military Academy

In the end, the Tet Offensive appeared to be a costly failure for Giap. After fighting that lasted into April, the NVA and Viet Cong had lost a staggering 50,000 men dead and had been pushed back from every position they had taken. In fact, the Viet Cong had ceased to exist as an effective fighting force.

But though they had lost in battle, it turned out that Giap and the North Vietnamese had won the propaganda war. Americans did not like what they were seeing on their television sets, in a war they were supposedly winning. When General Westmoreland, who could rightly proclaim an allied victory, asked for an additional 200,000 men, Lyndon Johnson turned him down, kicked him upstairs to chief of staff, and decided to ask for peace talks with Vietnam. The beginning of the end was at hand for the North Vietnamese—who had, after all been fighting since 1945. A poem written by the then-ailing Ho Chi Minh—he would die the following September—and broadcast on Hanoi Radio sums up the feelings of the North Vietnamese that pivotal early part of 1968:

This spring far outshines previous springs.

Of triumphs throughout the land come happy tidings.

Forward!

Total victory shall be ours!

GENERAL VO NGUYEN GIAP: THE "TOUGH AS NAILS" LEADER WHO OVERCAME EVERYTHING THE UNITED STATES COULD THROW AT HIM

General Vo Nguyen Giap—still alive as of this writing—is one of the fiercest patriots Vietnam has ever known, perhaps even fiercer than the legendary Ho Chi Minh. He was born into a moderately well-to-do family in Quang Binh province in what would later become North Vietnam, to parents who were also proud patriots who wanted to drive the French colonial forces out of Vietnam.

Giap went to an elite school in the ancient imperial capital city of Hue, and he turned more and more radical after reading Ho Chi Minh's Marxist-inspired writings. In the early 1940s, Giap left Vietnam for China, where Ho Chi Minh was in exile. French authorities threw his wife, a fellow Marxist, in prison, where she died.

In 1942, Giap returned to Vietnam to join a guerilla group that waged jungle warfare against both the Japanese and French. After 1945, when the Japanese were defeated and the French failed to recognize an independent Vietnam, Giap rose to become Ho Chi Minh's chief strategist in the Viet Minh war against the French, sculpting the tactics that defeated the French at the decisive battle of Dien Bien Phu, in 1954.

When the war against the Americans reached a fever pitch in the 1960s, Giap was carving out strategy there, too. As commander of the People's Army of North

Vietnam, which came to be called the NVA, he sought successfully to neutralize the superior firepower of the Americans by "grabbing the enemy by the belt" and fighting a war of small unit actions.

GENERAL VO NGUYEN GIAP IS ONE OF THE FIERCEST PATRIOTS VIETNAM HAS EVER KNOWN, PERHAPS EVEN FIERCER THAN THE LEGENDARY HO CHI MINH.

Giap was mainly responsible for the Tet Offensive of 1968—an offensive that failed militarily, with great loss of life. But in adversity, Giap was, as one U.S. historian later put it, "tough as nails." He saw that Americans were unwilling to continue the war politically and thus continued to fight, even though severely weakened.

By war's end, Giap had been mainly replaced as active commander by General Van Tien Dung, after which he became defense minister. While there is currently some reevaluation of his reputation occurring among historians—Giap lost at least 500,000 NVA troops in battle, a startling number—there is little doubt that his contribution to the North Vietnamese victory was crucial.

THE MY LAI MASSACRE: A SLAUGHTER OF INNOCENTS CHANGED THE AMERICAN MIND ABOUT THE WAR

A famous antiwar poster of the 1960s showed the bloodied bodies of Vietnam peasants, old women, and infants, lying in a ditch. The type on the poster posed this question: "Women and children, too?" And the answer was obvious: "Women and children, too."

Numerous atrocities were committed by both sides during the war in Vietnam— the North Vietnamese execution of civilians at Hue being just one of them. But the massacre of more than 300 unarmed civilians by U.S. troops, and the pictures the U.S. public saw on television, brought home the war home as never before.

On March 16, 1968, Charlie Company of the 111th Brigade, Americal Division, entered the village of My Lai in the South Vietnamese district of Son My. Viet Cong guerillas had a major presence in the district, and Charlie Company had fought a frustrating war against these shadowy figures in black pajamas who used hidden mines and booby traps as their main way of combating the far superior U.S. forces. Numerous members of Charlie Company had been killed or maimed by such devices in the weeks leading up to March 16. The men who entered the village on a typical search and destroy mission (searching for the enemy, destroying any of his munitions or supplies) were angry and frightened.

They were led by Captain Ernest Medina, who had previously told the troops that the only people left in the village would be Viet Cong. Some of his soldiers later claimed that he had ordered them to shoot women and children, but he denied this. In any event, one officer, Lieutenant William Calley, told his men to enter the village firing, even though there were no reports of enemy fire. A BBC reporter as well as a U.S. Army photographer were present and saw Americans round up men, women, and children, aged from one year to eighty-one years, and kill them with machine gun fire, bayonets, and hand grenades. Calley ordered a group of villagers into a ditch and mowed them down with his M-16.

Despite the efforts of a few heroic individuals who attempted to stop the killing, including a U.S. helicopter pilot who rescued a dozen villagers from certain death, Charlie Company killed more than 300 civilians that day. The massacre was covered up for more than a year. When news leaked out, the story angered the antiwar movement, and it caused the general public, which had not previously questioned the rightness of the war, to wonder about the morality of U.S involvement. Only one person present at the massacre, Lieutenant Calley, was ever convicted of murder. He was sentenced to life in prison after a court martial, but upon orders from President Richard Nixon, he served only a four-and-a-half-month sentence.

THE GULF OF TONKIN INCIDENT: THE CONTROVERSIAL CONFLICT CREATED A REASON TO ESCALATE THE WAR

If there was a casus belli for the stepped-up U.S. involvement in Vietnam, it came from what is now generally known as the Gulf of Tonkin incident. On August 2, 1964, the destroyer USS Maddox fought a brief battle with three North Vietnamese assault boats in the Gulf of Tonkin, off North Vietnam's east coast. Beyond that, much is in dispute. How close the Maddox was to the coast depends on who is telling the story. The Maddox reported that it was about 30 miles (48 km) away, in other words, well into international waters. The North Vietnam claimed it was within 5 miles (8 km) of the coastline, which they claimed as their territory.

It must be said that the Maddox was not on a pleasure cruise. It was crammed full of electronic eavesdropping equipment designed to listen in on North Vietnam communications. This was particularly sensitive for the North Vietnamese because on November 1, there had been numerous covert action incursions over its border by United States–sponsored South Vietnamese intelligence teams, which were trying to infiltrate the country. The North Vietnam boats that sortied out may have thought the Maddox was a part of these efforts.

In any event, the Maddox claimed that the assault boats fired torpedoes at the destroyer and returned fire, damaging one assault boat and destroying another. The North Vietnamese claimed that there were no torpedoes fired, but they admitted an exchange of surface fire initiated by the Maddox and that no North Vietnamese assault boat was damaged or destroyed.

On the night of August 4, the Maddox, joined by another destroyer, the C. Turner Joy, returned to the same area where they had been previously attacked and claimed that they were assaulted once again. Historians universally believe that this attack did not occur and was probably caused by a misreading of radar blips by edgy U.S. sailors.

These incidents were seemingly trivial, but they led to U.S. escalation of the war. Prodded by Lyndon Johnson, the U.S. Congress, on August 7, passed the Gulf of Tonkin Resolution, which allowed the president "to take all necessary measures to repel any armed attack against forces of the United States and to prevent further aggression." It was basically a blank check, signed and made out to Lyndon Johnson, to wage all-out war against North Vietnam without a formal declaration of war from Congress.

25

THE SOVIET-AFGHAN WAR

1979–1989

THE SOVIET UNION'S ENTRY INTO AFGHANISTAN AND SUBSEQUENT
DEFEAT BY AFGHAN MUJAHIDEEN FIGHTERS HELPED BRING ABOUT THE
DISSOLUTION OF THE USSR AND THE RISE OF ISLAMIC FUNDAMENTALISM.

A WAR THAT BECAME THE SOVIET UNION'S VIETNAM

The remote and mountainous country of Afghanistan has been a battleground for
great powers ever since the nineteenth century, when Great Britain and Russia, which
had clashed in the Crimean War, fought over which country would control western Asia. The British waged two wars in Afghanistan (1839–1842 and 1879–1880)
that were in large part provoked by Russia's attempt to dominate the country, which
would threaten the British presence in India.

In both cases, Britain was able to pacify Afghanistan, but only at great cost and with
the realization that Afghan's legendary Muslim tribal fighters were never completely
quelled. Eventually, through an Anglo-Russian agreement in 1905, Afghanistan
became a buffer state between Russia and Great Britain's India, with Great Britain
controlling its affairs. Finally, in 1919, Afghanistan won its full independence.

However, it is perhaps only natural, as Afghani historian M. Hassan Kakar wrote,
that "seeing their country… sandwiched between two 'infidel' giants, the Afghans
became xenophobic, inward-looking, and jealously guarded their independence."

A century after the last Anglo-Afghan War, Afghan suspicions of foreigners continued to be borne out. In the 1970s, the Soviet Union, which had aided
Afghanistan financially and with military training during the 1950s, became concerned about the growing United States' influence in Pakistan, Afghanistan's
neighbor to the southeast, with whom it shared many ethnic and tribal similarities.
The Russian government was concerned that its access to the Persian Gulf—and
the world's oil—might be impeded by an Afghanistan too overtly friendly to the
United States, as Pakistan had become.

The Soviet Union therefore sought an opportunity to exert greater control over
Afghanistan and found it in a civil war that had begun within the ranks of the People's
Democratic Party of Afghanistan (PDPA). In September 1979, the hard-liners of the
party led by Deputy Prime Minister Hafizullah Amin seized power and killed President

Nur Muhammad Taraki. The Russians didn't trust Amin. Some of them even thought he was a Central Intelligence Agency (CIA) agent, although no proof exists of this.

By mid-December, the Soviet Union had decided to invade Afghanistan to protect its interests there. Soviet units had been infiltrating the country for some time, many in civilian clothes or wearing the uniform of the Afghan army. On the evening of Thursday, December 27, 1979, the USSR attacked Kabul. Seven-hundred KGB agents dressed in Afghan army uniforms seized the presidential palace and assassinated Amin. The Russians then installed former Deputy Prime Minister Barbrak Kamal as Afghan president.

Soviet troops of the 40th Army then spread out and took control of major population centers and supply routes in the country, intending to leave the fighting against the mujahideen guerillas to the Soviet-trained Afghan army. But the mujahideens didn't make it easy. Due in large part to decisions made by the administrations of U.S. presidents Jimmy Carter and Ronald Reagan to stem the Russian tide in Afghanistan, the CIA began to aid the mujahideen, eventually spending more than $10 billion to equip and train them to fight the Russians. The result was a powerful and intractable insurgency that harried the Russians with hit-and-run attacks. Mujahideen fighters quickly became expert at firing the shoulder-held Stinger anti-aircraft missiles provided to them by the United States, knocking out hundreds of Soviet helicopters.

MUJAHIDEEN FIGHTERS QUICKLY BECAME EXPERT AT FIRING THE SHOULDER-HELD STINGER ANTI-AIRCRAFT MISSILES PROVIDED TO THEM BY THE UNITED STATES, KNOCKING OUT HUNDREDS OF SOVIET HELICOPTERS.

By 1985, U.S. aid had reached its peak, and the war had turned even more brutal. Russian tactics changed, with their special forces (spetsnaz) attacking villages that had first been bombarded by plane or artillery. Most Afghan men of fighting age had fled to the mountains, and the Soviet goal was to destroy the homes of the Afghan people and create refugees. A third of the 15 million people who lived in Afghanistan at the time were forced to flee to Pakistan and Iran, creating a huge refugee population.

As the war continued, Islamic fighters from Arab countries began to join the mujahideen. These included Osama bin Laden, a Saudi millionaire who, along with other militant Islamists, would form the terrorist group al-Qaeda in Afghanistan in 1988.

In 1986, the Soviets realized that they had placed themselves in a quagmire. Soviet Premier Mikhail Gorbachev called Afghanistan "a bleeding wound" and needed to find a way to exit the country. Under the auspices of the United Nations, Russia signed the Geneva Accords in the spring of 1988, effectively ending Russian participation in the war. The last Soviet soldier left the country in February 1989.

However, a civil war continued within Afghanistan between competing moderate and fundamentalist Muslim groups. The war was ultimately won by the fundamentalist Taliban, which was supported by Osama bin Laden. Bin Laden's assassination of the United States–backed moderate Afghan military leader Ahmad Shah Massoud came two days before his attacks on the United States on September 11, 2001, which precipitated the U.S. invasion of Afghanistan in November of that year.

THE BATTLE IN THE CAVES PROVED THE POWERLESSNESS OF THE RUSSIANS
The Caves of Zhawar

Mikhail Gorbachev was elected general secretary of the Communist Party on March 11, 1985, shortly after the death of Konstantin Chernenko. One of his first orders of business that spring was the Afghanistan war—specifically, the fact that the Soviets had suffered thousands of casualties and were being outfought by the mujahideen fighters whom many Soviet officials called "bandits," albeit bandits well-armed by the U.S. Central Intelligence Agency (CIA).

After studying the matter, Gorbachev reached a conclusion. The Soviet army and its Afghan allies, the solders of the Democratic Republic of Afghanistan (DRA), had exactly one year to destroy the resistance of the Muslim tribespeople. If they were not successful, Gorbachev would try to bring about an end to the war through diplomatic channels, in which case the Soviet army would be handed the worst defeat of its history. In June, the Soviets launched a major new offensive against the forces of Ahmad Shah Massoud in the Panjshir Valley. That August, another massive offensive, the largest of the war to date and led by new 40th Army commander Boris Gromov attacked and temporarily relieved the besieged Soviet and DRA garrison at Khost, near the border with Pakistan.

But neither of these offensives was successful enough to satisfy Mikhail Gorbachev. The Soviets decided that the next and last target for a major offensive, because Gorbachev's deadline was running out, would be the extraordinary mujahideen cave complex at Zhawar.

After initial losses to the guerillas when the war began, the Soviets had learned a much better, albeit cruel and inhumane, way of fighting them. Attacking villages after the Islamic fighters had left, the Soviets targeted civilian populations and turned the rural towns and farms into wastelands, forcing the population to flee into refugee camps in Pakistan. That way, they would no longer be there to supply the mujahideen.

As a result of this, the mujahideen were forced to establish a series of supply depots and transfer bases within Afghanistan, much as a conventional army would. From these bases, supplies and rested fighters would make their way through the country to engage the Soviets. The new Soviet strategy then became one of attacking these bases, which were fortified and defended, in hopes of destroying the vital communications and supply links of the rebels.

One of the most important, and extraordinary, of these bases lay at Zhawar, in the rugged eastern Afghanistan province of Paktia, just 4,000 yards (3.6 km) from the Pakistan border. Zhawar lay in a remote canyon squeezed between two mountain peaks, the entrance to which faced southeast, toward Pakistan. It had originally been a mujahideen training base, but it had expanded into a supply and troop transfer base.

The mujahideen had used bulldozers and explosives to carve eleven huge tunnels deep into the side of the canyon, some of them reaching back almost a quarter of a mile (400 m) into the rock. The tunnels actually contained a hotel (with overstuffed furniture), a mosque with brick facing, a hospital, a garage, an arms depot, a communications center, and a huge kitchen. It was all guarded by the 500-man-strong mujahideen "Zhawar Regiment," which had two tanks, several howitzers, and anti-aircraft defenses.

All in all, it was a formidable target, but an important one. If the Soviets and DRA could destroy Zhawar, their victory might be enough to forestall Gorbachev's peace overtures.

The First Attack

In September 1985, the DRA, backed by Soviet airpower, launched its first attack. Its intelligence units had told it that most of the mujahideen commanders, including Jalaluddin Haqqani, who was the highest ranking mujahideen commander, were away on a pilgrimage to the holy city of Mecca. It was a perfect time for an assault. The DRA, supported by air strikes and artillery bombardments, were able to take the mujahideen stronghold of Bori, a few miles from Zhawar, and then attack west toward the stronghold itself. But the mujahideen reacted swiftly after their initial disarray, sending in a blocking force of eighty fighters. In a furious night battle, the DRA lost two armored personnel carriers and four trucks and retreated.

However, the next day, prodded on by their Soviet advisors, the DRA returned, fighting their way across the mountains toward Zhawar until they were stalled by a twenty-man mujahideen blocking force in a pass called Manay Kandow. The mujahideen, though few in number, were in a virtually unassailable position, firing machine guns and AK-47s from a cave beneath a huge slab of rock high on the side of a mountain. Every time the DRA would call in artillery, the mujahideen would simply retreat farther into the cave until the bombardment was over, then leap to their firing positions to beat back the advancing DRA infantry.

For ten days, the DRA tried to breech the pass, and for ten days the small force of mujahideen held them off. Finally, the Soviets called in heavy airstrikes that repeatedly battered the slab of rock that protected the mujahideen cave. Finally, the

AFGHANISTAN

Total Area : 647 500 sq. km
(250 000 sq. miles)

LAND HEIGHT		POPULATION	
3000m/9843ft		over 1 000 000	▣
2000m/6562ft		over 100 000	◎
1000m/3281ft		over 50 000	○
500m/1640ft		over 10 000	●
200m/656ft		under 10 000	·

0   100 km

0   100 miles

N

THIS MAP OF AFGHANISTAN SHOWS THE ELEVATION OF THE COUNTRY, WHERE RUGGED MOUNTAIN HEIGHT MADE FIGHTING AGAINST THE MUJAHIDEEN SO MUCH MORE DIFFICULT.

Dorling Kindersley

rock began to shift and shake over the heads of the Islamic fighters. Fearful that it had become unstable under the relentless pounding, the mujahideen retreated. The DRA took the high ground, advancing to within a mile (1.6 km) of the cave complexes at Zhawar. But now, in a last-ditch effort, mujahideen fighters brought up their two T-55 tanks and opened up on the DRA, who did not realize that the enemy had heavy weapons. Caught in the open, they were forced to retreat, hearing the victory shouts of the mujahideen ringing in their ears.

The Last Attack

What was to be the second and last attack on the fierce caves of Zhawar began in late February 1986. It involved a much larger force—12,000 DRA troops, with 2,000 Soviet advisors. By this time, Gorbachev had already announced that he was about to perform a phased withdrawal of half of the Soviet troops from Afghanistan, but the Russian commanders in the field still hoped that a successful attack on Zhawar, performed mainly by the DRA, would change Gorbachev's attitude toward the army's plans in Afghanistan.

The chief element of this new attack on the mujahideen stronghold was an airborne assault by DRA commandos to be made on Dawri Gar mountain, which rose high above the eastern side of the Zhawar canyon. In the meantime, other DRA elements would attack through the passes. But the air assault was made at night and in the darkness confusion reigned. The commandos actually landed 5 miles (8 km) inside Pakistan, where they were surrounded by Pakistani troops and, after a firefight, taken prisoner.

Despite this, the rest of the DRA forces attacked in helicopter assault groups and were met at their landing zones by mujahideen fighters, who shot them as they piled out of their helicopters. At the same time, however, Soviet fighter-bombers made runs at the Zhawar caves, first flying southeast into Pakistan and then turning to make their attacks at the southern-facing entrances to the tunnels. Laser-guided precision bombs exploded into the caves, killing dozens of mujahideen or sealing them up inside the rubble. At one point, mujahideen commander Jalaluddin Haqqani was trapped in a cave with his fighters, but he managed to dig his way out.

A Hollow Victory

A major battle was now raging, with firestorms seen over the mountains and explosions echoing down the mountain passes. The mujahideen held steady, even as the Soviet artillery began to bombard their positions inside Zhawar twenty-four hours a day. Airplanes dropped illumination flares at night, and the eerie light they cast threw long shadows over the mountain walls as Soviet bombers arrived to drop their payloads on the cave complex.

The DRA commanders, having failed in their assault, left for Kabul on April 17 as the Russians in charge stepped in and ordered an all-out assault. The Islamic fighters, weakened by days of bombardment, their morale suffering because of a persistent, though untrue, rumor that Jalaluddin Haqqani was dead, finally evacuated Zhawar and fled to the nearby mountains.

When DRA and Soviet army units arrived in the cave complex, they were astounded. They discovered forty-one separate man-made caves, walls faced with brick, and entrances protected by iron doors. The hospital had ultrasound equipment manufactured in the United States. There was a library filled with books, in numerous languages. And none of it had been disturbed by the near continuous bombing. Ironically enough, after fighting so hard to get into Zhawar, the Soviets and DRA stayed for only five hours. They were cut off from their supply lines, and they knew that, even then, the mujahideen would be mounting a counterattack. Quickly booby--trapping and mining the cave complexes, the Soviet commander gave the order to retreat. The troops moved west with the sound of explosions ringing in their ears.

These explosions, however, had not come close to destroying Zhawar. The mujahideen arrived shortly after the Soviets left and immediately began restoring the place. It was up and running within four months. The battle to prove that the Soviets could be victorious in Afghanistan represented the final nail on their coffin. Gorbachev now had firsthand proof that the ineptitude of the DRA could simply not be overcome. After the war, Zhawar would continue to be used by Islamic fighters. Osama bin Laden's presence there in 1998 would cause U.S. President Bill Clinton to launch cruise missiles at the cave complex in an attempt to kill him and al-Qaeda members training there.

Clinton was unsuccessful, of course. Zhawar is far too tough a nut for a few cruise missiles to crack. And to this day, Osama bin Laden is thought to be hiding out in a similar complex, probably not far away from the caves of Zhawar.

AHMAD SHAH MASSOUD WAS ONE OF THE PREMIER FIGHTERS OF THE SOVIET-AFGHAN WAR AND LED THE RESISTANCE AGAINST THE TALIBAN UNTIL HE WAS MURDERED BY AL-QAEDA ASSASSINS TWO DAYS BEFORE THE SEPTEMBER 11, 2001, ATTACKS ON THE UNITED STATES.

AHMAD SHAH MASSOUD: "THE LION OF PANJSHIR" WAS A FIERCE AFGHAN LEADER

Ahmad Shah Massoud was born in Afghanistan's Panjshir Valley in 1953—fittingly so, because it was in the Panjshir that he became famous fighting the Soviet invaders of his beloved country. Massoud was the son of a police commander and was rela-

tively well-to-do and well-educated. He spoke several languages. He went to Kabul University in the early 1970s. There, like any number of young Muslims of the time, he became enamored of traditional Islamic tenets and joined a group of Islamic students that opposed the increasing Russian presence in Afghanistan.

In 1975, Massoud took part in a revolt against Mohammed Daoud Khan, a communist-backed politician who had taken over the country in a coup in 1972. The revolt failed, but Massoud gained valuable experience, especially in organizing guerilla cells in his home province of Panjshir. After this period, Massoud allied himself with the less radical Islamic groups that would battle the communist PDPA party in a civil war in the late 1970s. When the Russians invaded, Massoud already commanded a small army.

As the war progressed, Massoud was the commander favored more and more by the Americans. While he was a devout Muslim, he was more tolerant of other beliefs than other, more radical jihadists. Massoud began to score important victories against the Russians fighting in the Panjshir against repeated offensives and bombing so heavy that, at one point, Massoud evacuated all 30,000 inhabitants of the valley.

Even though Massoud was nicknamed the "Lion of Panjshir" and became a national hero, he was controversial among other mujahideen leaders. In 1983, after fighting the Russians for three years, he arranged a cease-fire with them. While this was temporary, other Afghan rebel leaders saw it as Massoud caving in to Soviet pressure. But by the end of the war, Massoud led an army some 13,000 strong. After the Soviet withdrawal, he continued a civil war against other Islamic groups fighting for control of Afghanistan. But, without U.S. aid, which had been withdrawn at the end of the Soviet-Afghan War, Massoud lost to the Taliban fighters who by the early 1990s controlled 90 percent of the country.

Massoud then became leader of a group called the Northern Alliance, a loose confederation of fighters that continued to oppose the Taliban regime and radical Islamic terrorists like Osama bin Laden. On September 9, 2001, two days before the 9/11 attacks on the United States, Massoud allowed himself to be interviewed by two journalists who were almost certainly al-Qaeda agents. One of them detonated a bomb in a video camera, killing the assassin and Massoud.

Most intelligence agencies believe that Osama bin Laden had Massoud killed to curry favor with the Taliban, who would soon need to protect bin Laden from the wrath of the Americans.

SHOULDER-HELD ROCKETS SPELLED DOOM FOR RUSSIAN HELICOPTERS

If there is an iconic image from the Soviet-Afghan War, it is that of a mujahideen fighter standing on a rocky landscape with a Stinger missile launcher balanced on his shoulder, ready to take aim at a Soviet attack helicopter. The image is striking because of its combination of elements that personify the war itself—the traditional dress of the tribesman and the sleek modernity of the Stinger.

The Stinger, developed in the United States in the early 1980s, is a shoulder-held, battery-powered, surface-to-air missile that is light, relatively easy to use, and, most important, heat-seeking. It hones in on the heat signatures given off by helicopter and airplane exhaust. Therefore, one only has to aim it in the general direction of the target, and it will generally find it and kill it. Because the Soviet Army in Afghanistan relied heavily on helicopters for troop transport, supporting fire, and evacuation of wounded, the Stinger was the perfect weapon for the mujahideen to employ.

William Casey, director of the CIA, gave the word in the mid-1980s that hundreds of Stingers should be sent to Afghanistan. CIA operatives trained Muslim fighters in the use of the weapon, which proved enormously effective. The Stinger could knock helicopters out of the air at 12,000 feet (3.6 km), which kept the Soviets from flying the low-level attack missions they had become accustomed to. The mujahideen were so successful in their attacks that Soviet field commanders became reluctant to call in medevac helicopters for the wounded, which further demoralized Soviet troops.

After the war, as documented in Steve Coll's book Ghost Wars, the CIA became concerned that Stingers in the hands of terrorists could be used to shoot down passenger liners. They then put in place what Coll calls "a kind of post-Cold War cash rebate system," buying back missiles from Afghan warlords to the tune of $80,000 to $150,000 apiece.

A MUJAHIDEEN FIGHTER WITH A SHOULDER-HELD STINGER MISSILE, ONE OF HUNDREDS PROVIDED BY THE CIA.
Getty Images

OSAMA IN AFGHANISTAN: THE MAKING OF A TERRORIST

It is an irony not lost on the U.S. government that the man who was the driving force behind the worst attack on United States soil since Pearl Harbor was trained and funded by the CIA.

However, Osama bin Laden, privately wealthy, would have targeted the United States anyway. Born in 1957 in Saudi Arabia to a wealthy and fecund construction business owner (bin Laden's father would ultimately sire fifty children), bin Laden grew up with close ties to the powerful Saudi royal family. Like many young men of his social milieu, bin Laden was well educated at a prestigious college, although in Jedda. He did not attend the private British boarding schools many of his brothers and sisters were enrolled at.

In 1979, when the Soviet-Afghan War began, bin Laden was a college sophomore with a $1 million annual allowance and a teacher named Abdullah Azzam, a radical Palestinian who would later go on to found the terrorist organization Hamas. Through Azzam and other radicalized Islamic teachers, bin Laden learned about jihad—a holy war to restore Islam to its original purity and drive the West out of Islamic holy places.

Bin Laden probably first went to Pakistan in 1980, where he met with members of the mujahideen fighting the Soviets, a group that were at the time supported strongly by the Saudi government. Bin Laden's efforts to aid the mujahideen included providing money to build roads through the rugged countryside, roads that would be used to deliver weapons to the Islamic fighters.

By 1984, bin Laden—by all accounts a highly intelligent and personable young man—had founded an organization called Maktab al-Khadamat (MAK), which means "Office of Services." MAK was a conduit through which bin Laden funneled the increasing number of radical Islamic fighters who sought to battle the Soviets in Afghanistan. However, this was not enough for bin Laden. Soon he joined Arab forces fighting the Russians in eastern Afghanistan, just across the border from Pakistan. In April 1987, bin Laden and fifty Arab volunteer fighters held off 200 Soviet attackers for four or five days in a mountain stronghold. Osama bin Laden, despite the need for insulin shots to treat diabetes, fought bravely. His exploits were reported to the public by two Arab journalists who were present.

Bin Laden was now seen in the eyes of the Arab world as a jihadist of the first order. He split with MAK, whose service and supply role he considered too tame, and he helped found al-Qaeda. After clashing with Saudi authorities over the increased presence of Americans in the country, bin Laden had his citizenship revoked by Saudis and was expelled from the country. He returned to Kabul, from where he and al-Qaeda launched numerous terrorist attacks against the United States, culminating in the attacks of September 11, 2001.

BIBLIOGRAPHY

CHAPTER 1: THE GRECO-PERSIAN WARS

Bradford, Ernle. *Thermopylae: The Battle for the West.* New York: Da Capo Press, 1980.

Creasy, Sir Edward and Joseph B. Mitchell. *Twenty Decisive Battles of the World.* New York: MacMillan & Co., 1964.

Green, Peter. *The Greco-Persian Wars.* Berkeley: University of California Press, 1996.

Strauss, Peter. *The Battle of Salamis: The Naval Encounter that Saved Greece—and Western Civilization.* New York: Simon & Schuster, 2004.

CHAPTER 2: THE WARS OF ALEXANDER THE GREAT

Green, Peter. *Alexander of Macedon, 356–323 BC. A Historical Biography.* Berkeley: University of California Press, 1991.

CHAPTER 3: THE PUNIC WARS

Dando-Collins, Stephen. *Caesar's Legion: The Epic Saga of Julius Caesar's Tenth Legion and the Armies of Rome.* Hoboken, New Jersey: John Wiley & Sons, 2002.

Goldsworthy, Adrian. *The Punic Wars.* London: Cassell & Co., 2000.

Prevas, John. *Hannibal Crosses the Alps: The Invasion of Italy and the Punic Wars.* New York: Da Capo Press, 1998.

CHAPTER 4: THE BARBARIAN INVASIONS

Bury, J. B. *The Invasion of Europe by the Barbarians.* New York: W.W. Norton & Co., 2000.

Chambers, James. *The Devil's Horsemen: The Mongol Invasion of Europe.* New York: Atheneum, 1979.

Klingaman, William K. *The First Century: Emperors, Gods, and Everyman.* New York: HarperCollins, 1990.

Reston, James. *The Last Apocalypse: Europe at the Year 1000 AD.* New York: Doubleday & Co, 1998.

Ward-Perkins, Bryan. *The Fall of Rome and the End of Civilization.* Oxford: Oxford University Press, 2005.

CHAPTER 5: THE MUSLIM CONQUESTS

Klingaman, William K. *The First Century: Emperors, Gods, and Everyman*. New York: HarperCollins, 1990.

O'Shea, Stephen. *Sea of Faith: Islam and Christianity in the Medieval Mediterranean World*. New York: Walker & Co, 2006.

CHAPTER 6: THE RECONQUISTA

Creasy, Sir Edward and Joseph B. Mitchell. *Twenty Decisive Battles of the World*. New York: MacMillan & Co., 1964.

Davies, Norman. *Europe: A History*. Oxford, New York: Oxford University Press, 1996.

O'Shea, Stephen. *Sea of Faith: Islam and Christianity in the Medieval Mediterranean World*. New York: Walker & Co, 2006.

CHAPTER 7: THE NORMAN CONQUEST

Creasy, Sir Edward and Joseph B. Mitchell. *Twenty Decisive Battles of the World*. New York: MacMillan & Co., 1964.

Howarth, David. *1066: The Year of the Conquered*. London: Penguin Books, 1981.

Reston, James. *The Last Apocalypse: Europe at the Year 1000 AD*. New York: Doubleday & Co, 1998.

CHAPTER 8: THE CRUSADES

Madden, Thomas F. *Crusades: The Illustrated History*. Ann Arbor: University of Michigan Press, 2004.

O'Shea, Stephen. *Sea of Faith: Islam and Christianity in the Medieval Mediterranean World*. New York: Walker & Co, 2006.

CHAPTER 9: THE MONGOL CONQUESTS

Chambers, James. *The Devil's Horsemen: The Mongol Invasion of Europe*. New York: Atheneum, 1979.

Weatherford, Jack. *Genghis Khan and the Making of the Modern World*. New York: Three Rivers Press, 2004.

CHAPTER 10: HUNDRED YEARS WAR

Davies, Norman. *Europe: A History*. Oxford, New York: Oxford University Press, 1996.

Seward, Desmond. *The Hundred Years War: The English in France, 1337–1453*. New York: Atheneum, 1978.

CHAPTER 11: THE SPANISH CONQUEST OF MEXICO

Leon-Portilla, Miguel. *The Broken Spears: The Aztec Accounting of the Conquest of Mexico*. Boston: Beacon Press, 1962.

Thomas, Hugh. *Conquest: Montezuma, Cortés, and the Fall of Old Mexico*. New York, Simon & Schuster, 1995.

CHAPTER 12: THE THIRTY YEARS WAR

Davies, Norman. *Europe: A History*. Oxford, New York: Oxford University Press, 1996.

Wedgwood, C. V. *The Thirty Years War*. New York: New York Review of Books, 2005.

CHAPTER 13: THE SEVEN YEARS WAR

Anderson, Fred. *Crucible of War: The Seven Years' War and the Fate of Empire in British North America, 1745–1766*. New York: Knopf, 2000.

McLynn, Frank. 1759: *The Year Britain Became Master of the World*. New York: Grove Press, 2004.

CHAPTER 14: THE AMERICAN REVOLUTION

Bobrick, Benson. *Angel in the Whirlwind: Triumph of the American Revolution*. New York: Simon & Schuster, 1997.

Creasy, Sir Edward and Joseph B. Mitchell. *Twenty Decisive Battles of the World*. New York: MacMillan & Co., 1964.

CHAPTER 15: THE FRENCH REVOLUTIONARY WARS

Furet, Francois & Richet, Denis. *The French Revolution*. New York: The MacMillan Company, 1965.

Hibbert, Christopher. *The Days of the French Revolution*. New York: William Morrow & Co., 1980.

Schama, Simon. *Citizens: A Chronicle of the French Revolution*. New York: Alfred A. Knopf, 1989.

CHAPTER 16: THE NAPOLEONIC WARS

Rothenberg, Gunther E. *The Napoleonic Wars*. New York: Smithsonian Books, 1999.

Schom, Alan. *Napoleon Bonaparte*. New York: HarperCollins, 1997

Schom, Alan. *One Hundred Days: Napoleon's Road to Waterloo*. New York: Atheneum, 1992.

CHAPTER 17: THE TAIPING REBELLION

Pelissier, Roger. *The Awakening of China, 1793–1949*. New York: G.P. Putnan's
   Sons, 1963

Spence, Jonathan D. *God's Chinese Son: The Taiping Heavenly Kingdom of Hong
   Xiuquan*. New York: W.W. Norton & Co., 1996.

CHAPTER 18: THE U.S. CIVIL WAR

Linderman, Gerald F. *Embattled Courage: The Experience of Combat in the American
   Civil War*. New York: The Free Press, 1988

McPherson, James M. *Battle Cry of Freedom: The Civil War Era*. New York: Oxford
   University Press, 1988.

Mitchell, Lt. Col. Joseph B. *Decisive Battles of the Civil War*. New York: Fawcett
   Books, 1955.

CHAPTER 19: WORLD WAR I

Fussell, Paul. *The Great War and Modern Memory*. New York: Oxford University
   Press, 1975

Hart, B.H. Liddell. *The Real War: 1914–1918*. Boston: Little, Brown and
   Company, 1930.

Keegan, John. *The First World War*. New York: Alfred A. Knopf, 1999.

Kiester, Edwin, Jr. *An Incomplete History of World War I*. Sydney, Australia:
   Murdoch Books, 2007

Vaughn, Edwin Campion. *Some Desperate Glory: The World War I Diary of a British
   Officer, 1917*. New York: Henry Holt & Co., 1981.

CHAPTER 20: THE RUSSIAN CIVIL WAR

Crankshaw, Edward. *The Shadow of the Winter Palace: Russia's Drift to Revolution
   1825–1917*. New York: Viking Press, 1976

Lincoln, W. Bruce. *Red Victory: A History of the Russian Civil War*. New York:
   Simon & Schuster, 1989

Trotsky, Leon. *Stalin*. New York: Stein & Day, 1967.

Volkogonov, Dmitri. *Trotsky: The Eternal Revolutionary*. New York: The Free
   Press, 1996.

CHAPTER 21: THE CHINESE CIVIL WAR

Pelissier, Roger. *The Awakening of China, 1793–1949*. New York: G.P. Putnan's Sons, 1963

Spence, Jonathan D. *The Gate of Heavenly Peace: The Chinese and Their Revolution, 1895–1980*. New York: The Viking Press, 1981

CHAPTER 22: WORLD WAR II

Ambrose, Stephen E. *D-Day: June 6, 1944: The Climactic Battle of World War II*. New York: Simon & Schuster, 1994

Keegan, John. *The Second World War*. New York: Penguin Book, 1989.

Toland, John. *Infamy: Pearl Harbor and Its Aftermath*. New York: Doubleday & Co., 1982.

CHAPTER 23: THE ARAB-ISRAELI WAR

Karsh, Efraim. *The Arab-Israeli Conflict: The Palestine War, 1948*. London: Osprey Publishing, 2002.

Morris, Benny. 1948: The First Arab-Israeli War. New Haven: Yale University Press, 2008.

CHAPTER 24: THE VIETNAM WAR

Karnow, Stanley. Vietnam: A History. New York: The Viking Press, 1983.

Langguth, A.G. Our Vietnam: The War 1954–1975. New York: Simon & Schuster, 2000.

CHAPTER 25: THE SOVIET-AFGHAN WAR

Kakar, M. Hassan. Afghanistan: The Soviet Invasion and the Afghan Response, 1979–1982. Berkeley, California: University of California Press, 1995.

GENERAL REFERENCE

Black, Jeremy. *The Seventy Great Battles in History*. London: Thames & Hudson. Ltd., 2005.

Cowley, Robert, and Geoffrey Parker. *The Reader's Companion to Military History*. Boston: Houghton, Mifflin & Co., 1995

Cummins, Joseph. *Great Rivals in History*. Sydney: Pier 9, 2008.

Cummins, Joseph. *History's Greatest Hits*. Sydney: Murdoch Books, 2007.

Cummins, Joseph. *Turn Around and Run like Hell*. Sydney: Murdoch Books, 2007.

Daniels, Patricia S., and Stephen G. Hyslop. *The National Geographic Almanac of World History*. Washington, D.C., 2003.

Kohn, George Childs. *Dictionary of Wars, Third Edition*. New York: Checkmark Books, 2007.

ABOUT THE AUTHOR

Joseph Cummins is the author of *The World's Bloodiest History*, *Why Some Wars Never End*, *History's Greatest Untold Stories*, *Anything for a Vote: Dirty Tricks, Cheap Shots, and October Surprises in U.S. Presidential Campaigns*, *Great Rivals in History: When Politics Gets Persona*l, and *President Obama and a New Birth of Freedom*. He has also written a novel, The Snow Train. He lives in Maplewood, New Jersey.

INDEX